S0-CFS-520

LONDON TRANSPORT

Capital ⊖ Guide

p228 London Gardens pamphlet

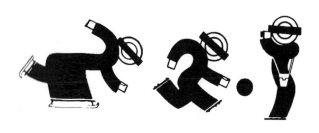

For Quentin, a true celebrator of London living

First published in Great Britain in 1995 by Boxtree Limited

Concept and additional text © Biddy Hayward 1995
Text © Boxtree Limited
Written by Elaine Gallagher
Published in association with the London Transport Museum

London Transport owns the complete copyright in and trademark
of the logo of London Transport.

1 2 3 4 5 6 7 8 9 10

All rights reserved. Except for use in a review, no part of this book
may be reproduced, stored in a retrieval system or transmitted in
any form or by any means, electronic, mechanical, photocopying,
recording or otherwise, without prior permission of Boxtree
Limited.

Designed by Design 23

Printed and bound in Great Britain by
Butler & Tanner Ltd, Frome and London, for

Boxtree Limited
Broadwall House
21 Broadwall
London SE1 9PL

A CIP catalogue entry for this book is available from the
British Library.

ISBN 1 85283 920 1

LONDON TRANSPORT

Capital Guide

LONDON FOR LONDONERS

B🌳XTREE

Published in association with the
London Transport Museum

CONTENTS

INTRODUCTION

LIVING IN THE CITY

MIND, BODY AND SPIRIT

LONDON CALM

CAPITAL MAPS

London Underground and
British Rail Routes

Bus Routes and Tourist
Attractions

Where to Catch your Bus

Night Bus Routes in
Central London

Postal Code zones

LONDON CALENDAR

HELP LINES

INTRODUCTION

It is all too easy to live and work in London and completely forget all that this great city has to offer 24 hours a day, 365 days of the year. People who have lived in London all their lives will freely admit that they have never researched or discovered anything that is unique to the city and yet so much is available if only you look.

The sole objective of this book is to centralize a huge range of information which will enable you to use your time living and/or working in London more effectively and enjoyably. The guide cannot pretend to give total or complete information on any of the subjects covered in the sections listed but it will give you an initial point of contact. And once you have that point of contact you will find that further information is freely given.

We continue to research and collect information to ensure that the London Transport Capital Guide provides the very best information currently available. If you want to make a special recommendation, register an unhappy experience, or share one of the City's secrets please write in to: The Editor, Capital Guide, Boxtree Limited, Broadwall House, 21 Broadwall, London SE1 9PL.

Celebrate city living and make London work for you!

LIVING IN THE CITY

GETTING AROUND

Each day Londoners make 26.4 million journeys in the capital, whether on foot, by car, tube, bus, train, bicycle or taxi. Cars are the most popular means of transport, but with the horrors of parking and clamping in central London the other options are probably the better ones.

TRAVEL INFORMATION

For the full range of services including maps, timetables, phone cards, souvenirs and tourist information visit a London Transport Travel Information Centre (TIC).

British Rail (Railtrack) Stations: Euston and Victoria

Underground Stations:	Heathrow 1, 2, 3 Kings Cross Liverpool Street Oxford Circus Piccadilly Circus St James Park
Bus Stations:	West Croydon Hammersmith
Heathrow Airport:	Terminals 1, 2 and 4.

• For the latest travel news London Transport run a 24-hour recorded phone service 0171 222 1200 or 0171 222 1234. Whichever number you dial you will have a choice of a) recorded latest travel news or b) an operator. Alternatively you can use BBC Ceefax (p. 521) and ITV Teletext (p.194).

• The map section at the back of this guide includes maps of London's bus routes, Underground and British Rail network

UNDERGROUND

London's Underground system is made up of 273 stations (46 of them are listed buildings) and 254 miles of track, along which we make 2.5 million journeys every day. The Metropolitan line line was the first to be built, opening in 1863, and the Jubilee Line, in 1979, the last.

Underground trains start running at 5.30am Monday to Saturday inclusive and 7am on Sundays. Last trains vary depending on the line but Monday to Saturday none are before 11.30pm and some are as late as 1am. On Sundays the Underground closes down at about 11.30pm. The service runs every day except Christmas Day.

Fares operate on a zonal system with charges being based on the different combinations of the 6 zones.

Tickets can be purchased in 3 different ways:

- On an ad hoc basis from ticket machines;

- Travelcards: probably the most cost effective but bear in mind that the One Day Travelcard is subject to early morning 'rush hour' travel restrictions. Travelcards are also accepted on most buses contracted on behalf of London Transport, Docklands Light Railway and most British Rail trains within the paid-for zones. Daily and weekly tickets are available from booking offices and ticket machines.

- Travel Passes/Season Tickets: Various combinations of zones with no rush hour restrictions. Available weekly, monthly and yearly from booking offices. A passport-sized photograph is needed when ordering a travel pass.

For further details, and to establish the best fares for your specific travel requirements, enquire at your local ticket office.

Most central London stations now have automatic ticket gates on entry and exit. Don't forget to pick up your ticket once the gates have opened. Should you have completed your journey the machine will keep your ticket, but valid season tickets or One Day Travelcards will be returned.

- Tickets have to be purchased for your entire journey before you travel or you are liable to a penalty fare of £10.

- Journey Planners to enable you to use the Underground as efficiently as possible are available free from ticket offices and Travel Information Centres (TICs).

- Smoking is illegal anywhere on the Underground and eating is not encouraged.

- As on crowded shopping streets, beware of pickpockets at the height of the rush hour crush.

- All complaints, queries and requests for refunds are dealt with by the London Underground Customer Service Centre, 55 Broadway, SW1. (0171 918 4040).

- London Transport publish a booklet called *Access to the Underground*, which gives details of lifts and ramps at individual Underground stations for disabled passengers. Available at Travel Information Centres (listed below) or London Transport, Unit for Disabled Passengers, 55 Broadway, SWIH 0BD (0171 918 3312).

- If you lose property on the Underground or buses, write or visit the London Transport Lost Property Office, 200 Baker Street, W1. 9.30am – 2pm.

BUSES

Buses are by far the best way to see and get to know London but they, like cars and taxis, can be slow-moving when traffic is heavy.

Red routes have been declared a big success in helping traffic, especially buses, to move more freely and it is planned that another 315 miles of them will be in place by the end of 1997.

Buses stop automatically at the compulsory stops (white background) unless they are full but don't stop at request stops (red background) unless you ring the stop bell on the bus, or put out your arm on the street. All bus stops become request stops at night.

All Night Buses (except N31) pass through Trafalgar Square.

National Gallery - Stop C - North and East
Cockspur Street - Stop T - West
Canada House   - Stop V - South

The number on the bus is prefixed by the letter N. Many of these follow daytime routes but there are some special night routes. Maps and timetables are available from London Transport Travel Information Centres.

One Day Travelcards are not accepted on Night buses and fares are higher but they are a good speedy way to travel home.

• Travelcards are accepted on non-red buses – look for the London Transport Service sign on the front or side of the bus, which signifies that Travelcards are accepted.

• Complaints about London buses or requests for refunds should be made to London Transport Customer Relations on 0171 918 3291.

BRITISH RAIL

British Rail (Railtrack) provides additional railway services to the London transport system (see map A in the map section) and carries a similar zonal fare structure as the Underground in the London area. Don't forget that you can now catch trains from Waterloo to Paris!

Telephone enquiries for services to and from London are now handled by the following 4 lines or you can ring 0171 222 1234 for timetable information on central London British Rail Services:

PADDINGTON   **0171 262 6767**
South Midlands, West of England, West London and South Wales, Republic of Ireland via Fishguard.

KING'S CROSS   **0171 278 2477**
East and North East England, North London, Scotland via East Coast.

EUSTON/MARYLEBONE/ST PANCRAS   0171 387 7070
East and West Midlands, North Wales, North West England, Scotland via West Coast, North West London, Northern Ireland and Republic of Ireland via Holyhead.

CHARING CROSS/LIVERPOOL STREET/VICTORIA
WATERLOO/FENCHURCH STREET   **0171 928 5100**
East Anglia, Essex, Southern England, North East, East and South
London.

EUROPEAN RAIL TRAVEL CENTRE   **0171 834 2345**

EUROSTAR   **0233 617575**

• Since privatization was agreed on 1 April 1994, every sector of the
rail network will have a different Customer Relations department.
Contact the relevant department for the British Rail Operating Unit in
which you travelled and follow up your complaint in writing.

TAXIS

London's 'black cabs', 25,000 in total, are one of the most famous
sights in the world but regulations governing black cabs and minicabs
are in a mess. The London Transport Minister agrees that the current
system needs a complete overhaul and new legislation is currently
underway.

At present only black cabs are licensed and are far more tightly
controlled than minicabs. Black-cab drivers have their fares set by law,
they must conform to levels of safety and have insurance which covers
the passenger as well as the driver.

By contrast, anyone with a driving licence and a car can claim to be
a minicab operator, and there are no compulsory checks on either the
driver or vehicle. The police in particular want to see some sort of
controls and licensing system introduced for London's 40,000
minicabs.

Only black cabs are currently allowed to ply for hire on the street;
any minicab doing so is behaving illegally. Whereas in the past this
has been dealt with by civil law, in November last year it became a
criminal offence punishable by a fine of up to £2,500.

There are several big cab firms which supply a 24-hour service
but remember the meter starts ticking once the cab is on its way for a
pick-up, so the total fare will be higher than hailing on the street.

• 24-hour cab firms:

Computer Cabs	**0171 286 0286**
Data Cab	**0171 727 7200**
Dial-a-Cab	**0171 253 5000**
Radio Taxi Cabs	**0171 272 0272**

If it's late at night trying to find a cab in the heart of the West End can
prove difficult and it would probably save a lot of time to head either
straight for the nearest black cab rank or one of the main line stations
– Charing Cross is good for the West End.

• West End ranks include:

The Hippodrome, Charing Cross Road, WC1
Corner of Russell Street/Bow Street, WC2
Dover Street, W1.
The London Private Hire Car Association, which represents 80 of the

2000 minicab firms in the capital, has imposed a set of its own standards for inspection and grading and can supply details of a member firm in your area.

London Private Car Hire Association, 213 Kenton Road, Harrow HA3. (0181 863 4148).

• The Suzy Lamplugh Trust publishes various leaflets on safety for women, including one on travelling by minicab. Send an A5 self-addressed envelope with 36p stamp to: The Suzy Lamplugh Trust, 14 East Sheen Avenue, SW14. (0181 392 1839).

For women travelling alone who would prefer to be driven by another woman, the following minicab companies only recruit women drivers. Pick-up is normally within a certain radius of the office, but the journey can be anywhere in London.

LADYCABS	Camden	0171 272 3019
	Hackney	0171 923 2266
	Islington	0181 383 3113
	Muswell Hill	0181 272 3019
MY FARE LADY	Muswell Hill and West Hampstead	
		0181 458 9200
LADYDRIVE	Leyton area	0181 558 9696
LADY CARS	Brixton	0181 655 3959
	Camden	0171 916 4400

LADY'S WEST CARS
(mostly women drivers, specify when you call)

Kensington	0171 602 5511

Complaints:
BLACK CABS
If you are unhappy about the service you have received take down the cab's number (on the plate in the back of the cab) and contact The Public Carriage Office as soon as you can. Their powers extend to being able to suspend or even revoke a cabby's licence, depending on the offence.

The Public Carriage Office.   0171 230 1624

MINICABS
There is no set complaints procedure for minicabs. Initially you should complain to the minicab company, but if that doesn't produce a result, then your only alternative may be to go to the police. If you are involved in an accident and the driver is not insured for carrying passengers, you can take him to court. The Motor Insurance Bureau is an industry body which acts as a last resort fund to deal with claims from those involved in accidents with uninsured drivers. They can be contacted on 01908 830001.

COACHES

All coaches operate either from within or in the vicinity of Victoria Coach Station. Different companies operate different services but all the contact numbers are listed under Coach Station (Victoria) in the phone book or there is a recorded guide: 0171 823 6567.

AIRPORTS

GATWICK AIRPORT – 30 miles south of London – is best reached by Gatwick Express, which runs a 24-hour service. The journey takes about half an hour and from 5.30am till 8pm trains run every 15 minutes. Outside that time it is usually every half hour, and between 1am and 4am, every hour. There is also a Flightline 777 bus which leaves Victoria Bus Station, but allow for 2 hours travelling time and 3 if it's rush hour.

HEATHROW AIRPORT – 15 miles west of London – is best reached by the Piccadily line (approximately 1 hour from Piccadilly Circus). Alternative means of travel are the Airbus A1 (Grosvenor Gardens, SW1) and Airbus A2 (Woburn Place, WC1) bus routes but allow for a minimum of $1^{1}/_{2}$ hours and $2^{1}/_{2}$ if travelling during rush hour.

- 24-hour Airbus Travel Information   0171 222 1234

- Heathrow Airport   0181 759 4321

- All Flight Information (Heathrow and Gatwick) – Arrivals and Departures – 4.30am –10pm   01891 757757

LONDON CITY AIRPORT – 8 miles east of the West End of London – is best reached by BR Network SouthEast's North London Line. The West Ham and Stratford stations link it to the Central and District lines. Allow half an hour from the West End. There are also 2 Shuttlebus services; the Red Shuttlebus service operates between the Airport and Liverpool Street and takes approximately half an hour and the Yellow runs between the Airport and Canary Wharf (Docklands Light Railway) and takes approximately 10 minutes.
  As a new airport, it is still expanding its routes but internally it has flights to Liverpool and Edinburgh and European cities including Antwerp, Berlin, Brussels, Dublin, Frankfurt, Lugano, Paris and Zurich. It also does a series of weekend breaks to European capitals. First flights are currently after 8am.

- General Airport and Flight Enquiries: 0171 474 5555.

STANSTED AIRPORT – 35 miles north-east of London – is best reached by the Stansted Express train service at Liverpool Street. Trains run between 5.30am and 11pm Monday to Friday and from 6.30am at weekends. Journey time is approximately 45 minutes.

- General Airport and Flight Enquiries: 01279 680500

CYCLING

Around 250,000 Londoners cycle to work each day and a further 400,000 get on their bikes at least occasionally. However, with only 2.3 per cent of total journeys made by bike, the capital falls far behind other European cities such as Munich, where the figure is 9.8 per cent, and cycling king-pin Amsterdam, where it is 27.3 per cent.

The London Cycling campaign was set up to offer practical advice to cyclists and would-be cyclists in the capital. They also work to make London more cycle friendly, lobbying for more cycle routes, better road surfaces and improved traffic management. The Government is becoming more receptive to the push-bike brigade, with the result, it is to be hoped, that cycling will become safer. At present our accident rate per kilometre cycled is 5 times that of Holland.

The cycling campaign also produces a guide to cycling in London and a route map which shows both official cycling lanes and its own advisory routes.

The London Cycling Campaign, 3 Stamford Street, SE1. 0171 928 7220

• Herne Hill Velodrome holds family days to encourage all and sundry to go and ride on its banked circuit. Russell Williams, Herne Hill Velodrome, Burbage Road, SE24. 0171 737 4647

• Britain's first Bike Park opened in Covent Garden last year. It provides safe parking for 150 cycles for a small charge as well as a bike hire service and a workshop for repairs and maintenance. Open from 7.30am to 8.30pm (10pm in the summer) during the week and 8.30am to 6.30pm on Saturdays, the Bike Park also offers changing and drying facilities. The Bike Park, Stuckley Street, WC2. 0171 430 0083

Hiring bikes by the day or week:

• On Your Bike, 52-54 Tooley Street, SE1. 0171 378 6669 Also branches in W1 and WC2.

• The Mountain Bike and Ski Company, 18 Gillingham Street, SW1. 0171 834 8933

• Paolo Garbini offers the best range of cycling gear and accessories in the heart of London as well as a same day repair service.

Paolo Garbini, 36 Great Pulteney Street, W1. 0171 734 9912

WHERE TO LIVE

The property boom of the Eighties is now history. These days, with nearly 10,000 out of London's 2.5 million home owners believing that their property is worth less than their mortgage, the market moves much more cautiously and the whole ethos of buying property has changed.

We are now more likely to stay in a property for longer, and renting, still the most popular option on the Continent, has become fashionable again.

The role of the house has changed too. More and more of us are working from home, and it is estimated that in 1995, 15 per cent of all the capital's workers will be tapping computers and word processors from home.

Of course, places like Chelsea and Belgravia are as popular as ever if money is no object, but there are many other choices available to fit different budgets and objectives so it is well worth doing a little research into what each borough has to offer. The truth is that most people tend to stay in the area of London into which they first moved, or were brought up. If you are about to move, important things to consider are transport and shopping facilities and local parks. It's a good idea to spend some time wandering around your intended spot to get a feel of the atmosphere and whether it will suit you.

BUYING

At the end of 1993 the average price for homes sold in London was £82,500, with first-time buyers paying an average £63,500 to get onto the property ladder (figures from the London Research Centre). By the close of 1994 prices had started to rise, albeit slowly, and the property market was starting to emerge once again.

Once you start to look at a particular area it is well worth talking to several estate agents. The very big agencies such as Barnard Marcus will carry a larger range of property at the cheaper end of the market, whereas the more specialist agents tend to limit their choice of property to a certain size and standard, which really means above a certain figure!

Aside from doing the rounds of the local estate agents, most boroughs have local papers, which can be a good source of information. Wednesday's editions of the *Times* and *Evening Standard* specialize in property sales.

• The regulatory body for all British estate agents is the Estate Agents' Ombudsman (01722 333306).

A wise purchaser who has already arranged his funding might well find a bargain through the auction houses.

• The following auctioneers regularly hold auction sales for residential property in London:

Allsop	0171 437 6977
Barnard Marcus	0181 741 9990
Conrad Ritblat Sinclair Goldsmith	0171 935 4499
Erdman Lewis	0171 629 8191
Hambro Countrywide	01245 344133
The London Auction	01272 237237
Stickley and Kent	0171 284 0181

• The London Repossessions List (0181 209 0200), compiled from data supplied by banks, building societies and auctioneers, details around 2,500 properties in London and the Home Counties. It can be mailed to you for 3 consecutive months for a £50 subscription.

RENTING

In the current economic climate, and with a house or flat worth £49,500 requiring an income of at least £16,500 for a mortgage, renting is now popular once again. The 1988 Housing Act has helped by de-regularizing rents for new lets, making it easier for landlords to regain possession and reducing the minimum term for assured shortholds from 1 year to 6 months.

The result has been an increase in the number of flat-letting agencies, and with it plenty of incidences of unscrupulous practice. It's worth knowing that it is illegal for any agency to charge for putting your name on their books. Other scams include showing people around properties not actually available for rent, withholding deposits and charging for drawing up standard tenancy agreements which actually require no legal work.

Forewarned is fore-armed, but there are many reputable agencies around, and the best way to find one is by recommendation or through a professional body.

The Association of Residential Letting Agents (0171 734 0655) has over 700 bonded members and can give you the names of member agents in your area.

LEASEHOLD

There are up to 1.5 million leasehold properties in Britain, the majority in Greater London.

Since the change in the law in late 1993, which gave certain leaseholders the right to buy their freeholds, the minefield surrounding the subject has become even more complicated.

The Government has set up the Leasehold Enfranchisement Advisory Service to advise leaseholders who are confused about the legislation.

The Leasehold Enfranchisement Advisory Service (LEAS), Maddox Street, W1.
0171 493 3116

NOISE

One of the worst problems of urban living can be the nightmare of noisy neighbours. Recently there have been several memorable noise prosecution cases, including that of the group of builders in EC1 whose frequent renditions of the Banana Boat song resulted in a £9,000 fine for their employers.

For noise problems your first stop should be the environmental health department at your local borough. All London boroughs have an environmental health officer responsible for dealing with noise pollution, and 13 boroughs have 'party patrols', but these usually only operate at weekends. Westminster has a 24-hour a day noise patrol.

Other boroughs are pioneering schemes such as Hammersmith and Fulham's MEND, an arbitration service that works between warring neighbours to try to find a workable solution. Out of every 4 disputes bought to the service, 3 are settled.

One increasing problem seems to be noise from air traffic. The Department of Transport has a complaints line (0171 276 5323/5325) or you can contact the complaints line for aircraft noise from Heathrow airport (0181 745 7677).

BURGLARY AND INSURANCE

The good news is that last year burglaries were down 15 per cent and clear-up rates had risen to 16 per cent, but against an estimated 200,000 burglaries London still has some way to go before the burglars give up!

The 10 London boroughs with the highest level of burglaries per head of the population are:

1. Lambeth
2. Kensington and Chelsea
3. Hackney
4. Westminster
5. Lewisham
6. Camden
7. Southwark
8. Haringey
9. Brent
10. Newham

Your local police station can arrange a visit from the Crime Prevention Officer, who will be able to advise on making your home more secure.

The higher crime areas carry bigger insurance premiums. Watch out also for subsidence; this is a general problem in London but certain areas – Clapham is one – seem to suffer more than most.

• The British Insurance and Investment Brokers Association can supply a list of insurance brokers in your area.
0171 623 9043

• The Insurance Brokers Registration Council is the trade association for insurance companies and keeps a list of all registered brokers. The Council won't supply a list but they will check that your insurance broker is registered.
0171 588 4387

• **The Streetwise Map Company** publish a map which shows therisk from burglary across Greater London, colour-coding areas to show

where levels are highest and lowest and also listing the risk in each London postcode. They also give borough-by-borough indications of the levels of other crimes – for example, car theft. Available from WH Smith, or contact The Streetwise Map Company
01483 861278

MOVING

If you decide to hire the professionals it is important to assess your needs at the outset. A quote from a small local firm may well differ enormously from an international removals firm but equally if you plan ahead and are flexible on dates moves can be carried out cheaply as part loads. It is also worth checking out temporary and long-term storage costs. The British Association of Removers (0181 861 3331) has a list of approved professional firms.

• **London Women & Manual Trades** publishes a register of qualified tradeswomen including architects, plumbers, electricians and gardeners. A copy is available for £2 from London WAMT, 52-54 Featherstone Street, ECIY 8RT.

LOCAL BOROUGH OFFICES

Either before or as soon as you have moved into a new area, it is well worth making a visit to the local borough's offices to find out where the local One Stop Shop is situated. One Stop Shops carry details of all the neighbourhood's services and amenities available to local residents.

Camden	0171 860 5644
Greenwich	0181 854 8888
Hackney	0181 986 3123
Hammersmith and Fulham	0181 576 5031
Islington	0171 226 1234
Kensington and Chelsea	0171 937 5464
Lambeth	0171 926 1000
Southwark	0171 525 5000
Tower Hamlets	0171 512 4200
Wandsworth	0181 871 6000
Westminster	0171 487 4504

NIGHT SERVICES

A list of late night or 24-hour services.

LATE NIGHT CHEMISTS

BLISS, 5 Marble Arch, W1.
0171 723 6116
9am–midnight every day of the year.

BLISS, 50-56 Willesden Lane, NW6.
0171 624 8000
9am–midnight every day of the year.

BOOTS, 254 Earls Court Road, SW5.
0171 370 2232
Mon–Sat 8.30am–9pm Sun 10am–9pm.

BOOTS, 75 Queensway, W2.
0171 229 9266
Mon–Sat 9am–10pm. Closed Sunday.

WARMAN FREED, 45 Golders Green Road, NW11.
0181 455 4351
8.30am–midnight every day of the year.

WESTBURY'S CHEMIST, 86 – 90 Streatham High Road, SW16.
0181 769 1919
9am–midnight every day of the year.

ZAFASH PHARMACY, 233 Old Brompton Road, SW5.
0171 373 2798
9am–midnight Mon–Sat 10am–midnight Sun.

• The local Family Health Services Authority (FHSA) can provide you with a list of all the chemists in your area and their hours of opening.

• Your local police station carries a list of late night emergency numbers for chemists and doctors in your area.

LATE NIGHT SUPERMARKETS

The best-known stop-offs are the 7-Eleven chain. There are over 40 branches spread all over London, open 24 hours, 7 days a week. A brief selection includes:

7-ELEVEN

112 Westbourne Grove, W2.	0171 727 6342
134 King Street, W6.	0181 846 9154
119 Gloucester Road, SW7.	0171 373 1440
35 Junction Road, N19.	0171 272 1287
271/273 Whitechapel Road, E1.	0171 247 5598
15 Borough High Street, SE1.	0171 357 0277

• Each shop carries a full list of all the branches.

Other late night or 24-hour supermarkets:

Bestway, 107 Edgware Road, W2.	0171 723 6793
Europa Foodstores, Trafalgar Square, W1.	0171 930 5996
Portland Food and Wines,	
152–156 Fulham Palace Road, SW6.	0181 563 1030
Riteway, 57 Edgware Road, W2.	0171 402 5491

Tesco Metro stores

24–25 Bedford Street, Covent Garden, WC2. 0171 240 4342
Mon–Thur and Sat 8.30am–9pm;
Fri 8.30am–10pm; Sun 11am–5pm.

311 Oxford Street, W1.   0171 493 2960
Mon, Tues, Wed, Fri, Sat 8am–8pm;
Thur 8am–9pm; Sun 11am–5pm.

Broadway Centre, Hammersmith, W6.   0181 741 4345
Mon–Sat 7.30am–9.30pm; Sun 10am–4pm.

Portobello Road, Nottinghill Gate, W11.   0181 741 4345
Mon–Fri 8.30am–8pm; Sat 8am–8.30pm;
Sun 10am–4pm.

LATE NIGHT EXTRAS

POST OFFICE

London's late night post office is the branch in William IV Street, WC2. Mon–Sat 8am–8pm. 0171 930 9580

NEWSPAPERS

The first editions of all the main newspapers hit the main line stations well before midnight and can also be bought outside Leicester Square, Piccadilly, Marble Arch and Victoria tube stations.

BOOKSHOPS

The Book Shed is an enormous warehouse-style bookshop which is open till midnight every night of the week; it is open at 8am every day except Sunday, when it opens at 10am.

The Book Shed, 19 Wilton Road, SW1. 0171 233 8383

• The Pan Bookshop is open till 9.30pm Mon–Fri, 10pm on Saturday and 9pm on Sunday.

The Pan Bookshop, 158 Fulham Road, SW10. 0171 373 4997

• All branches of Waterstones are open till 9pm Mon–Fri.

MUSIC

Tower Records in Piccadilly stays open until midnight Mon–Sat, Sun until 10pm.
Tower Records, 1 Piccadilly Circus, W1. 0171 439 2500

CAR BREAKDOWN

AA (Automobile Association) – 24 hours.
Non-members have to join –
Freephone breakdown 01800 887766.

National Breakdown – 24 hours.
Higher charges for non-members –
Freephone breakdown 01800 887766.

RAC (Royal Automobile Club) – 24 hours.
Non-members have to join –
Freephone breakdown 01800 828282.

• When your car breaks down as long as you know which spare part needs replacing Barnet Brake and Clutch Services provide a 24-hour spare parts shop.

Barnet Brake and Clutch Services, 120 Myddleton Road, N22.
0181 881 0847

ALL NIGHT PETROL STATIONS

Cavendish Motors, Cavendish Road, NW6.
0181 459 0046

Chiswick Flyover Service Station, 1 Great West Road, W4.
0181 994 1119

City Petroleum, 316 Essex Road, N1.
0171 226 5991

Dalston Lane Service Station, 156 Dalston Lane, E8.
0171 249 3634

Fountain Garage, 83 Park Lane, W1.
0171 629 4151

Kennington Filling Station, 212 Kennington Road, SE11.
0171 735 2191

Old Kent Road Station, 420/432 Old Kent Road, SE1.
0171 232 2957

Shoreditch Service Station, 168–175 Shoreditch High Street, E1.
0171 739 6599

Star Group Texaco, 63 Fortune Green Road, NW6.
0171 435 2211

Vauxhall Bridge Road Filling Station, 148 Vauxhall Bridge Road, SW1.
0171 828 1371

ALL NIGHT PARKING

With the clamping or towing away of illegally parked cars in the West End on the increase, it is worth knowing some of the Central London 24-hour garages.

Abingdon Street, SW1   0171 222 8621

Brewer Street, W1	0171 734 9497
Broadwick Street, W1	0171 734 8387
Carrington Street, W1	0171 629 9806
Drury Lane, WC2	0171 242 8611
Gloucester Place, W1	0171 935 5310
Great Russell Street, WC1	0171 637 0964
Hyde Park, W1	0171 262 1814
Knightsbridge (Park Tower Hotel), SW1	0171 235 0733
Museum Street, WC1	0171 836 2039
Newport Place, W1	0171 434 1896
Portland Street, W1	0171 437 7660
Semley Place SW1	0171 730 7757
Upper St Martins Lane, WC2	0171 836 7451

If you are clamped the details of where to go and what to do are clearly detailed on the information sheet pasted to your windscreen. It involves going to the pound to pay an 'unclamping fee' and then waiting several hours for the clamp to be removed.

• For a membership fee (about £30) you can join The Car Clamp Recovery Club who will go to the pound, settle the fee and advise you when the clamp will be removed. For an additional amount they will also collect and deliver the car. It's expensive so it depends how important your time is!

The Car Clamp Club, 160 Vauxhall Bridge Road, SW1.
0171 235 9901

• The car is missing! It may not have been stolen so first check with the police to see if it has been towed away. There is now a centralized number to call which will help trace any new admissions to London's various car pounds.
0171 747 4747

Camden Car Pound, Berlin Bank, York Way, NW1. Open 24 hours.
Payment: cash, cheque, mastercard, visa.

City Car Pound, 1-25 Penton Rise, WC1.
Payment: cash, cheque, mastercard, visa, delta, switch.

Hackney Car Pound, Stratford Pound, Blaker Road, E15.
Payment: cash, cheque, mastercard, visa, delta, switch.

Kensington and Chelsea Car Pound, Lots Road, SW10. Open 24 hours.
Payment: cash, cheque, mastercard, visa, delta, switch.

Wandsworth Car Pound, 20 Wandsworth Road, SW8. Open 24 hours.
Payment: cash, cheque, mastercard, visa, delta, switch.

Westminster Car Pound, Old Goods Yard, Paddington, W2.
Open 24 hours.
Payment: cash, cheque, mastercard, visa, delta, switch.

• Too tired or too drunk to drive? Call Designated Drivers who will provide a driver to take you and your car home (see page 29).

ALL NIGHT HOSPITALS

Emergency 24-hour walk-in casualty departments are available at the following hospitals:

University College Hospital   0171 387 9300
Gower Street, WC1 (entrance in Grafton Way).

Charing Cross Hospital   0181 846 1234
Fulham Palace Road, W6 (entrance St Dunstans Road).

Hammersmith Hospital   0181 743 2030
150 Du Cane Road, W12.

St George's Hospital   0181 672 1255
Blackshaw Road, SW17.

Guy's Hospital   0171 955 5000
St Thomas Street, SE1 (entrance Weston Street).

St Thomas' Hospital   0171 928 9292
Lambeth Palace Road, SE1.

Kings College Hospital   0171 274 6222
Denmark Hill, SE5 (entrance Bessemer Road).

Greenwich District Hospital   0181 858 8141
Vanbrugh Hill, London SE10.

Lewisham Hospital   0181 690 4311
Lewisham High Street, SE13.

London Hospital   0171 377 7000
Whitechapel Road, E1.

Hackney and Homerton Hospital   0181 985 5555
Homerton Row, E9.

St Bartholomews Hospital   0171 601 8888
West Smithfield, EC1 (entrance Giltspur Street).

North Middlesex Hospital   0181 807 3071
Stirling Way, Edmonton, N18.

Whittington Hospital   0171 272 3070
St Marys Wing, Highgate Hill, N19.

Royal Free Hospital   0171 794 0500
Pond Street, NW3.

Central Middlesex Hospital   0181 965 5733
Acton Lane, NW10.

LATE NIGHT DENTISTS

The local Family Health Services Authority (FHSA) can provide you with a list of dentists in your local borough and once registered with an NHS dental practice it is required to offer a 24-hour emergency service.

- Other alternatives:

The Royal Hospital's NHS Trust offers an emergency dental unit daily from 7pm-11pm.

The Royal Hospital, Whitechapel Road, E1.
0171 377 7000

If you are really desperate, most of the 24-hour emergency hospitals will have access to an oral surgeon or at least some serious painkillers until the local surgery opens.

OTHER SERVICES

Your local police station will carry lists of late night emergency numbers which include those for chemists, doctors, garages and locksmiths.

In an emergency dial 999 and an operator will connect you to the appropriate service – police, fire or ambulance.

HOME SERVICES

Too busy to shop, too tired to cook, too exhausted to exercise and forgot to go to the dry-cleaners as well? Pick up the phone and all your problems can be solved at the press of a few digits.

HEALTH AND BEAUTY

ALTERNATIVE HEALTH SERVICE

Set up by Camilla Style and Jo Fox over 2 years ago, the Alternative Health Service offers aromatherapy and reflexology treatments in your own home.

Practitioners are all highly qualified and carefully selected. An hour-long aromatherapy massage costs around £35, and a reflexology session between £25 and £30.

The Alternative Health Service operates mainly in south-west London, including Chelsea, Fulham, Clapham, Battersea and Wandsworth.

The Alternative Health Service.
0181 870 9903

ASSOCIATION OF PERSONAL TRAINERS

A wide range of people now work out with a personal trainer, among them people too busy to get to a gym, those who have a specific problem, for example lower back pain, obesity or postnatal depression, or those who just need the motivation a trainer can provide.

The Association of Personal Trainers can recommend a qualified trainer in your area. They grade their trainers according to the level of their qualifications; for example a grade 1 trainer would be a sports science graduate, with a personal trainer's certificate, a fitness qualification, knowledge of first aid, and insurance.

The trainer will draw up a specific programme based on

your goals, medical history and level of fitness and take into account factors like your diet and whether you are under stress.

A session with a trainer typically costs between £25 and £30 if you use a gym and £30–£40 at home.

Association of Personal Trainers
0171 836 1102

• A similar service is offered by the National Register of Personal Trainers
01992 504336

MILLWARD and COMPANY

Gregg Millward set up his 'at-home' hairdressing service several years ago. For a minimum call-out fee of £30 he or one of his colleagues can offer the full range of hairdressing skills including cut and blowdry, blowdry, colour, highlight, lowlight, permanent curl or putting your hair up in the comfort of your own home.

Millward and Company, 31 Upper Tollington Park, N4.
0171 263 1936

FOOD

THE CONTEMPORARY CATERING COMPANY

If entertaining at home is your idea of a nightmare or you're simply a terrible cook, then why not call in a caterer?

A finalist in BBC's Masterchef competition in 1993, Ross Burden has set up his own catering company, which can handle anything from an intimate dinner party to canapés for hundreds.

A New Zealander, Ross's East meets West style includes influences from the Pacific and Asia. He will discuss the occasion with you in advance and offer a varied selection of menus. Canapés can include mouthwatering morsels such as home-cured salmon on dill scones with Japanese horseradish, Thai fish cakes with coriander or tuna tataki on cucumber slices.

A dinner party menu might include warm goat's cheese in walnut crust, duck breast with sweet potato mash and steamed watercress, followed by 24-carat *brûlée,* with mango, preserved ginger and saffron. Dinner party angst is removed and all that is left for the host is to wash the coffee cups.

Canapés from £7 per head, dinner from £30 per person.

The Contemporary Catering Company
0171 385 3671

FOOD FERRY

The Food Ferry were finalists in the Independent Grocer of the Year Award last year and offer a delivery service which takes the pain out of the weekly food shop.

Their catalogue offers 135 pages of items including general groceries, fresh fruit, vegetables and herbs, pet food, prepared food, toiletries, office supplies, postage stamps, stationery, meat, fish, bakery and beverages.

For a minimum order of £20 and a delivery charge of £2.50 a phonecall or a fax before 11am ensures the order will be delivered the same day.

Phone for a free catalogue.

Food Ferry, 31 Glycena Road, SW11.
0171 498 0827   Fax: 0171 498 8009

KATE COLEMAN

Kate Coleman has been part of London's private catering scene for the last 10 years. Her speciality is private dinner parties and her loyal customers cannot praise her cooking, flexibility and pleasant manner too highly.

Kate Coleman, 15 Austral Street, SE11.
0171 582 6655

LOX STOCK AND BAGEL

English solicitor David Evans and his American wife Janet conducted their courtship over ordered-in dinners in the Big Apple, and when they came back to London they decided to set up a business delivering New York style deli treats.

Their bagels are handmade (essential for a good chewy texture) to David's own recipe and come in 8 varieties. A huge range of cream cheese toppings (starting at about £1.99) includes dill mackerel mousse, chilli cheese and jalapena, with rum raisin, ginger or chocolate chip spreads for the sweet-toothed.

Smoked products range from salmon or halibut to pheasant breast, and other deli delicacies include chopped liver, pastrami and herring salad, chicken soup and turkey meatloaf. Among the sweet things are apple strudel, cheesecake and raisin, cheese, apple or pineapple Danish pastries.

For a perfect Sunday brunch, a dozen bagels, with a choice of gourmet cream cheese, half a pound of smoked salmon, fresh juice and a newspaper would cost around £15.

Lox, Stock and Bagel. 7-day delivery from 6.30am until midnight. Orders can be left until 4am for next-day delivery. Delivery free with a minimum order of £15 in SW1, 3, 5, 7 and 10 or £20 in SW4, 6 and 11, NW1, 3 and 8 and W1 and 2. Otherwise cab fare charged on top. Menu and orders 0171 244 6061 or 0171 835 2143.

ROOM SERVICE

If you have a favourite London restaurant, but can't raise the energy to actually go there to eat, Room Service will bring their food to your own kitchen table.

The company operates in central, north-west and south-west London and the City. They can send you their dine-in guide, which features the menus of the participating restaurants in each area (normally numbering about 15, and covering the culinary spectrum from American to Vietnamese.)

Once you have ordered, a bow-tied 'waiter-driver' will then deliver your meal in an insulated bag and for a small extra charge can also stop off on the way to pick up booze, cigarettes or a video for the complete couch potato night-in.

Participating restaurants include the Zen chain, Chutney Mary,

Drones, Chicago Pizza Pie Factory and Ken Lo's Memories of China. You pay the same price as on the restaurant menu plus a delivery charge. Minimum order is £10. What you lose in restaurant ambience you make up for in savings on service and on the restaurant's wine mark-up.

Room Service. Lunch deliveries Mon–Fri 11am–2.30pm. Dinner 7 days a week 5pm–10.30pm (subject to restaurant opening times).
0171 586 5800

WHOLEFOOD EXPRESS

Set up 5 years ago, Wholefood Express has a range of over 1,000 wholefood and green household products in their catalogue and specialize in fresh organic fruit and vegetables.

Delivery all across London, once a week. Minimum order £15.

Wholefood Express
0171 354 4923

• A morsel more:

Alison Price Catering, 5 The Talina Centre, Bagley's Lane, SW6.
0171 371 5133
By Word of Mouth, 22 Glenville Mews, Kimber Road, SW18.
0181 871 9566
Gorgeous Gourmets, Gresham Way, Wimbledon, SW19.
0181 944 7771
Simply Delicious, Unit 5a, 15 Micawber Street, N1.
0171 490 4548

LAUNDRY

LUKE'S

The designers' dry-cleaner, Tony Luke takes care of couture gowns for Bruce Oldfield, Tomasz Starweski and Amanda Wakeley among others.
 Luke's door-to-door service collects and delivers anywhere within the M25 area. They collect from central London on Tuesdays and Fridays, either between 9am and 12noon or between 1pm and 4pm. Garments will be returned, dry-cleaned and hand finished, 3 days later. Collection is also possible on Sundays.
 Minimum order is £25, delivery is free. Silk shirts from £5.50, mens suits from £9.80, women's suits from £8.50. With 35 years of experience, Tony Luke has a good reputation for remedying dry-cleaning disasters.

Luke's
0689 831800

• Other laundries and dry-cleaners who will collect and deliver to your home or office:

5-Star Dry Cleaners	0171 226 9801
Bickmore Services	0171 286 6318
Blossom and Browne	0181 552 1231
Buckingham Dry Cleaners	0171 499 1253
Chevalier	0171 938 4373

Dasini	0171 722 4231
Jeeves of Belgravia	0181 809 3232
Shirt Master	0181 469 2339
Valentinos	0171 240 5879

DELIVERIES

DESIGNATED DRIVERS

It's midnight, your car's parked on a yellow line and you've broken the unspoken promise you made to yourself that you would only stay for 1 drink after work. Now you face a cab journey home plus an early morning trip to retrieve your vehicle before the wardens, clampers and towing trucks get to it. To solve such difficulties Julian Stevenson started Designated Drivers to get you and your car home safely. Ring for one of their drivers who will come to meet you and drive you home safely ensconced in the passenger seat. The driver is then picked up by a shuttle car.

There is a £12.50 flat fee for central London, plus £1.50 per mile to your home. All drivers are aged over 30, have clean licences and are covered (by a large Lloyds insurance policy) to drive any make of car.

Future expansion plans include American-style valet parking.

Designated Drivers
0171 603 9000

CANNON CAR SERVICES

How many times have you wanted to arrange for a delivery in London outside normal office hours and found either that the service was not available or the unsocial hour made it prohibitively expensive?

Cannon Car Services operate a 24-hour, 7-day week, all year round delivery service and overnight or weekend work does not attract higher rates.

The range of services on offer includes the usual minicab, motorbike, van and red star collection or delivery but rather uniquely they also offer an aeroplane service! This provides a small 4-seater plane to carry packages throughout UK and Europe at short notice!

Cannon Car Services
0181 202 6666

FLORISTS

GARLIC SAPPHIRE

Mobile florists Garlic Sapphire specialize in regular deliveries of flowers to a loyal band of customers entranced by their unusual and imaginative blooms. 'We like quite wild-looking, sensual flowers and foliage,' says owner Louise Farman, and their repertoire includes tied bunches of blossom in spring, or hedgerow flowers in summer.

Operating from their homes, plus a garage, Louise and partner

29

Sarah Raven deliver mainly within the Circle-line area. Weekly, fortnightly or monthly delivery can be arranged and prices start at about £22.50 per bunch (including delivery). They can also match flowers to design and colour schemes, and for the truly terribly busy, arrange the flowers and take away the old ones.

Garlic Sapphire 0171 585 2124. Mobile 0850 695 011.

ST SAVIOURS NURSERY

This nursery will only send carnations or freesias but postal boxes are despatched daily and prices range from £8.50 to £21.25. A box of 25 freesias is about £9.50.

St Saviours Nursery,
01481 65521 Fax: 01481 64843

- Other florists:

The Flowersmith	0171 240 6688
Jane Packer	0171 935 2673
Manic Botanic	0171 287 9856
Moyses Stevens	0171 493 8171

INDULGENCES

BASKET EXPRESS

This company can put together a basket for any occasion. Choose from their brochure of special occasion baskets which include 'Wicked Lady', 'Gourmet Basket' and 'Oriental Teatime', or create your own themed basket.
   Champagne baskets, chocolate baskets and booze baskets are also available.

Baskets from £30, delivery from £3.50.

9am–6pm 7 days a week with 24-hour answerphone. Morning calls get same-day delivery.

Basket Express
0171 289 2636

BEVERLEY HILLS BAKERY and GIFT BASKETS

The chance to send an unusual gift – hand-made mini-muffins, cookies and brownies.
   They are made fresh every day to order and without preservatives, and the choice available includes Belgian Chocolate, Georgia Pecans, fresh lemon juice, and buttermilk. Prices start from £17 and include delivery.

Beverley Hill Bakery and Gift Baskets:
0171 584 4401   Fax: 0171 584 1106

CHOCOLATE PARADISE LIMITED

A chocaholic's dream! Chocolate Paradise carry a complete range of chocolate gifts suitable for all occasions including 'no milk', 'no sugar' and kosher chocolates.

Orders are usually sent by post for next-day delvery but special delivery can be arranged. Postage is included in the price but special delivery will carry an additional charge.

Chocolate Paradise Limited, PO Box 6433, N7.
0171 281 6161   Fax: 0171 272 4111

CHAMPERGIFT UK

Champergift offer a choice of champagne from £24.50 a bottle to a 1982 Krug at £84. One rather unique option is to send your gift with a message forever engraved on the bottle (£17.50 plus the cost of the bottle). They also include wine, spirits and chocolates as part of their gift service.

Prices include 2- to 3-day delivery service but next day or specific date delivery can be arranged for an extra charge.

Champergift UK.
01233 662670/660066   Fax: 01233 610721

• Oddbins offer a free delivery in central London if the order is substantial enough – if not, they also offer a gift service with delivery received within 2 working days of despatch.
01992 500612   Fax: 01992 501347

PRESENT SELECT

Present Select provide an ideas and purchase service when you cannot think of a suitable gift. They will suggest presents for all sorts of occasions and charge you £15 for the thought plus, of course, the cost of the present.

Same-day delivery service is offered anywhere in the London Postal District.

Present Select
0181 248 3835

FAX FRUIT

Fax Fruit offer a wide range of baskets with different types of fruit. Prices start from £20 within the M25 area and £29 nationwide.

A same-day delivery service at no extra charge within the M25 area is offered.

Fax Fruit
0181 963 1818   Fax: 081 963 0522

SPECIALIST FOOD SHOPS
• The following shops listed in the Specialist Food Shops section (see page 117) offer a mail order/gift service:

> Algerian Coffee Stores (Tea and Coffee)
> Carluccios (Italian Delicatessen)
> Jeroboams (Cheese)
> Rococo (Chocolate)

MIND, BODY AND SPIRIT

FURTHER STUDY

CAREER COURSES AND CHANGES

Owing to high levels of unemployment over the last 5 years many people have been forced to take a more considered view of their long-term work prospects. Many are choosing work-related part-time courses as a means of improving their qualifications and in some cases changing career completely.

If a career change is in order it is undoubtedly worth considering one of the many agencies that offer a comprehensive careers guidance programme. These courses involve either several sessions or one intensive day session, and comprise a mixture of psychometric tests, analysis and careers counselling. At a cost of about £200 it's expensive but at least it is a course dedicated solely to establishing your own particular strengths and therefore potential opportunities.

Call individual organizations for further details and prices:

Career Management Services, 211 Piccadilly, WIV 9LD.
0171 917 9865

Vocational Guidance Association,
7 Harley House, Upper Harley Street, NW1 4RP.
0171 935 2600

Improving your qualifications is a less dramatic course of action and you will find that nearly all the local boroughs now provide full careers guidance for the long-term unemployed or free comprehensive advice on further education and training.

Hammersmith and Fulham	0181 741 2441
Kensington and Chelsea	0171 938 5311
Westminster	0171 487 4504
Camden	0171 388 0033
Islington	0171 457 5785
Hackney	0181 986 2272
Tower Hamlets	0171 790 5026
Greenwich	0181 312 5140
Southwark	0171 701 4001
Lambeth	0171 737 3221
Wandsworth	0171 350 1790

RETURNING TO WORK

The decision to return to work quite often carries additional worry, whether it be to do with your own self confidence or the need to find suitable childcare.

Listed below are the names and numbers of organizations who offer support and advice (See also London Women's Centre p 265).

WOMEN RETURNERS NETWORK

This organization provides advice and help for women wanting to return to education, training or employment. It publishes *Returning To Work: A Directory of Education and Training for Women* (£15.50), which contains details of over 1500 courses plus advice and pointers on everything from grants to childcare.

Women Returners Network, 8 John Adam Street, WC2.
0171 839 8188

WOMEN'S COMPUTER CENTRE

The Women's Computer Centre offers a variety of computing courses for women of all ages and levels of expertise; they also cover subjects like desktop publishing. Course fees are on a sliding scale according to circumstance.

Women's Computer Centre, Wesley House,
Wild Court, Holborn, WC2.
0171 430 0112

PARENTS AT WORK
(Formerly the Working Mothers Association)

Parents At Work aims to help all working parents and to encourage 'family friendly' working practices among employers.
   Their publications include *The Working Parents Handbook* and *Balancing Work and Home*.
Parents at Work, 77 Holloway Road, N7.
0171 700 5771

THE DAYCARE TRUST

This is a registered charity which can offer advice on all aspects of childcare.
0171 405 5617

THE PRE-SCHOOL PLAYGROUPS ASSOCIATION

Among other activities, this association provides a national helpline for parents seeking advice about childcare facilities.
0171 833 0991

THE KIDS CLUB NETWORK

Offers information on holiday and out-of-school schemes.
0171 241 3009

FULL AND PART-TIME COURSES

Whether you want to study aikido, fashion or watchmaking there is a huge variety of part-time and day and evening classes on offer all over London.

Historically, if enough people wanted to attend a class the local authority would pay most of the cost from public funds with only small fees charged to the individual. Now almost all local colleges are independent, responsible for their own budgeting, and answerable to the Further Education Funding Council for England and Wales.

General day and evening classes with no accompanying qualification are classified by the local councils as leisure and therefore although they do still subsidize part-time adult education for local residents there is far less money available for these sorts of courses. The emphasis is on courses that provide measurable skills for work with nationally recognized qualifications as a goal. Short and weekend courses are also widely available as are crèche facilities for daytime classes.

For the full range of choice you cannot do better than buy *Floodlight* which lists over 14,000 classes under nearly 6,000 different subject headings. There are 3 different books:

• *Full-time Floodlight*, out in October for full-time courses the following year.

• *Floodlight,* out in July for part-time and evening classes.

• *Summer Floodlight,* a guide to summer courses and summer schools, which comes out in March.

All are widely available and local libraries carry course details for their particular borough.

Many colleges have open days near the time of enrolment and it is well worth taking the time to attend – preferably prior to enrolment. Check the local paper or ring the college direct for details.

If you decide on a privately run college check if it is a member of the Conference for Independent Further Education (CIFE) whose purpose is to maintain standards of education and student welfare in member colleges.

Finally, there are voluntary organizations which provide specialist courses. They tend to be registered charities or publicly funded and a fairly thorough list is available at the back of *Floodlight*.

BOROUGH COLLEGES

CAMDEN

Kingsway College

This college offers a general range of more than 500 courses from aromatherapy to word processing plus a wide variety of language courses.

Kingsway College, Gray's Inn Centres, Sidmouth Street, WC1. All course enquiries 0171 306 5760/61

GREENWICH

Greenwich Community College

Offers a broad range of subjects, including music, arts and crafts, clothesmaking, soft furnishings, childcare, cookery, VHF radio for sailing and navigation and bobbin-lace making.

Greenwich Community College, Kidbrooke Centre, Corelli Road, SE3.
All course enquiries 0181 319 8088

Woolwich College

A basic range of courses, including accountancy and word processing but more individual subjects include Chinese and Punjabi and some special courses in freight and transport.

Woolwich College, Plumstead Centre, Vills Road, Plumstead, SE18.
All course enquiries 0181 855 1216

HACKNEY

Hackney Community College

A wide range of skills courses including art and design, building, business studies, community care, languages, the performing arts, science, sport and leisure. Uniquely, this college offers courses on lock and watch repair as well as minority languages such as Amharic, Somali, Yiddish and Yoruba.

Hackney Community College, Brooke House, Kenninghall Road, E5.
All course enquiries 0181 533 5922

Cordwainers College

Specializes in courses on leather arts and craftmanship including the design and making of footwear, saddlery, fashion bags and travel accessories.

Cordwainers College, 182 Mare Street, Hackney, E8.
All course enquiries 0181 985 0273

HAMMERSMITH AND FULHAM

Hammersmith and Fulham Community Learning and Leisure Service

Specialities include a wide choice of languages, philosophy and psychology.

Hammersmith and Fulham Community Learning and Leisure Service.
Cambridge House, Cambridge Grove, W6.
All course enquiries 0181 576 5335

Hammersmith and West London College

Specialities of this college include office skills, building studies and further education teachers.

Hammersmith and West London College, Gliddon Road, Barons Court, W14.
All course enquiries 0181 563 0063

ISLINGTON

City and Islington College Adult Education Service

This college offers a wide range of classes, with good crèche and playgroup facilities.

City and Islington College Adult Education Service, Archway Centre, Mount Carmel School, Holland Walk, N19.
All course enquiries: 0171 607 1132 (same for all Islington adult education).

City and Islington College City Campus

Formerly City and East London College, the City Campus offers specialist courses in electrical engineering, optics, business studies, computing and information technology.

City and Islington College City Campus, Bunhill Row, EC1.
All course enquiries 0171 607 1132

City and Islington College Islington Campus

Formerly North London College. Courses include business, information technology and general education with specialists in media studies, the performing arts and care and nursery courses.

City and Islington College, Islington Campus, 444 Camden Road, N7.
All course enquiries 0171 607 1132

City and Islington College Sixth Form Centre

General adult education courses, including GCSEs and GCE A-levels in art history, dance, music and various languages.

City and Islington College Sixth Form Centre, Annette Road, N7.
All courses enquiries 0171 607 1132

KENSINGTON AND CHELSEA

Kensington and Chelsea College

Specialities of this college include the arts and humanities; painting, drawing, pottery and sculpture, architecture, literature, history and art history, cultural studies and a good range of languages.

Kensington and Chelsea College, Wornington Centre, Wornington Road, W10.
All course enquiries 0181 964 1311

LAMBETH

Lambeth Community Education

Wide range of subjects, from art and antiques to music and massage, with 'mother tongue' courses in African and Asian languages.

Lambeth Community Education, Adare Centre, Adare Walk, Mount Earl Gardens, Leigham Court Road, SW16.
All course enquiries 0181 677 3522

Lambeth College

Offers a wide variety of skills especially in the building trades and uniquely a qualification course for dental technicians.

Lambeth College, Brixton Centre, 56 Brixton Hill, SW2.
All course enquiries 0171 501 5000

SOUTHWARK

Southwark College

This college offers a good basic range of courses, but more individual subjects include canoeing, a range of sports leadership awards, and a specialist fire safety course.

Waterloo Centre, The Cut, SE1.
All course enquiries 0171 620 0567

Thomas Calton Community Education Centre

Nearly 200 courses ranging from book keeping and hotels and catering to Chinese herbal medicine and wall and floor tiling are on offer here. Turkish language courses are held at weekends.

Thomas Calton Community Education Centre, Alpha Street, SE15.
All course enquiries 0171 639 6818

TOWER HAMLETS

Tower Hamlets Community Education Service

A broad, traditional programme of adult education classes and, uniquely, the Kweyol language.

Tower Hamlets, Whitechapel Centre, Stepney West, Myrdle Street, E1.
All course enquiries 0171 377 0640

Tower Hamlets College

Poplar Centre, Poplar High Street, E14.
All course enquiries 0171 538 5888

WANDSWORTH

Wandsworth Adult College

A very wide range of courses are on offer here, including chaircaning, gem cutting, T'ai Chi, gilding, navigation, video editing and Indonesian cookery. There are also many weekend courses.

Wandsworth Adult College,Broadway Centre, Gatton Road, SW17.
All course enquiries 0181 871 8333

South Thames College

Specialist subjects include a range of environment-related subjects, engineering, media studies, languages and computing.

South Thames College, Wandsworth High Street, SW18.
All course enquiries 0181 877 1950

Westminster College

Famed for its catering school and English language centre,
Westminster College offers courses ranging from business,
leisure and tourism to engineering with specialist computing
courses at weekends.

Westminster College, Battersea Park Road, SW11.
All course enquiries 0171 978 1285

WESTMINSTER

Westminster Adult Education Service

One of London's largest adult education services, where you
can study Brazilian, Catalan, Korean and Thai along with many
other languages. Computer courses are offered as weekend options.

Westminster Adult Education Service, Amberley Road Centre, Amberley
Road, W9.
All course enquiries 0171 286 1900

City of Westminster College

Specialities include engineering, electronics, building studies, car crafts
and servicing as well as travel, tourism and leisure industries.

Paddington Centre, 25 Paddington Green, W2.
All course enquiries 0171 723 8826

INDEPENDENT COLLEGES

All the independent colleges listed below specialize in adult education
and carry a huge range of different courses. Weekend and short courses
are widely available. Contact the individual colleges for their prospectus.

THE CITY LIT
Stukeley Street, Drury Lane, WC2.
0171 242 9872

MARY WARD CENTRE
42 Queen Square, WC1.
0171 831 7711

MORLEY COLLEGE
61 Westminster Bridge Road, SE1.
0171 928 8501

WORKING MEN'S COLLEGE (for women as well!)
44 Crowndale Road, NW1.
0171 387 2037

ART COLLEGES

The colleges listed below offer an extensive range of arts-based courses for both the professional and the enthusiast. Short and weekend courses are widely available.

CAMBERWELL COLLEGE OF ARTS
Peckham Road, SE5.
0171 703 3124

CENTRAL SAINT MARTINS COLLEGE OF ART AND DESIGN
Southampton Row, WC1.
0171 753 9090

CHELSEA COLLEGE OF ART AND DESIGN
Manresa Road, SW3.
0171 351 3844

LONDON COLLEGE OF FASHION
20 John Princes Street, W1.
0171 409 2868

LONDON COLLEGE OF PRINTING AND DISTRIBUTIVE TRADES
65 Davies Street, W1.
0171 514 6500

• One of the best fine art bookshops in London is The Atrium Bookshop, 5 Cork Street, W1. 0171 495 0073.

LANGUAGE SCHOOLS

Whether you are looking for a language course to help you in your work or for travel or social purposes, London is choc-a-bloc with choice.

The above colleges and universities cover all the different languages with 4 or 5 different levels, ranging from complete beginners through to total fluency. Birkbeck College, for example, offers part-time BA, BSC and LLB courses in most languages.

There are also specialist institutes which provide maximum flexibility – individual or group tuition, intensive and non-intensive courses – several also run cultural events, but do check the fees before enrolment:

Institut Francais, 14 Cromwell Place, SW7 2JR.
0171 581 2701

Goethe Institute, 50 Princes Gate, Exhibition Road, SW7.
0171 411 3451

The Italian Cultural Institute, 39 Belgrave Square, SW1.
0171 235 1461

The Spanish Institute, 102 Eaton Square, SW1.
0171 235 3317

• For other language courses contact The Institute of Linguists.
0171 359 7445

• The Language Exchange (0181 455 9962) matches those wanting to learn a language for conversational use with a native speaker.

• For language schools look for the Association of Recognized English Language Schools (ARELS) or British Accreditation Council (BAC).

• The biggest selection of foreign language books can be found at Grant and Cutler, 55–57 Great Marlborough Street, W.1. 0171 734 2012

UNIVERSITIES

All these universities have a high proportion of mature students studying part-time degree and non-degree courses. More often than not mature students who have relevant experience, but no formal qualifications, are welcomed. Most of the universities carry a wide range of general subjects but have one area of particular expertise. For example, Roehampton and Greenwich are known for their large specialist programmes for teacher training and practising teachers and the South Bank has a particular bias towards business and the built environment (construction, engineering, land management and urban policy).

If drama and theatre are of particular interest to you the Central School of Speech and Drama and Goldsmiths College carry an excellent combination of creating and performing art courses.

Short courses and summer schools are widely available. Contact the individual universities for their prospectus.

BIRKBECK COLLEGE
Malet Street, WC1.
All course enquiries 0171 631 6390

CENTRAL SCHOOL OF SPEECH AND DRAMA
Embassy Theatre, 64 Eton Avenue, NW3.
All course enquiries 0171 722 8183

CITY UNIVERSITY
Northampton Square, EC1.
All course enquiries 0171 477 8268

GOLDSMITHS COLLEGE
New Cross, SE14.
All course enquires 0171 919 7171

LONDON GUILDHALL UNIVERSITY
Calcutta House, Old Castle Street, E1.
All course enquiries 0171 320 1000

ROEHAMPTON INSTITUTE
Senate House, Roehampton Lane, SW15.
All course enquiries 0181 392 3000

SOUTH BANK UNIVERSITY
Borough Road, SE1.
All course enquiries 0171 815 6109

UNIVERSITY OF GREENWICH
Wellington Street, Woolwich, SE18.
All course enquiries 0181 316 8590

UNIVERSITY OF NORTH LONDON
Tower Building, 166–220 Holloway Road, N7.
All course enquiries 0171 753 5066

UNIVERSITY OF WESTMINSTER
309 Regent Street, W1.
All course enquiries 0171 911 5000

LIBRARIES

In 1994 the Government commissioned a full-scale review of public libraries in England and Wales – who should run them, the services that should be offered, how they are funded and how they can meet the opportunities and challenges of developments in information technology. The committee's findings are due out this year.

With more than 12 million people visiting a public library once a fortnight and an overall figure of 60 per cent of the population using them during the year – the local library is certainly a community asset.

London has a good selection of reference and non-reference libraries. Bigger branches have the better services but in general librarians are obliging and willing to point you in the right direction even if they do not have the exact information you are seeking.

Libraries aim to meet the needs of their local multi-cultural community not just through the lending of books, videos, CDs, cassettes and books on tape but also through language courses, newspapers and magazines, local history and services information, and on-line data and facts. They also carry up-to-date information on courses and careers, including prospectuses and past exam papers, and many can offer a very competitively priced research service.

Local information covers everything from lists of local doctors, sports venues and training schemes to choirs and halls and rooms for hire as well as the full range of services and organizations.
So whether you are looking to source information or study – check out your local library.

MAIN BOROUGH LIBRARIES

CAMDEN

Swiss Cottage Reference Library, 88 Avenue Road, NW3.
General Enquiries 0171 413 6533/6534
Mon and Thur 10am–7pm Tues and Fri 10am–6pm Closed Wed.
Library Community Information 0171 911 1656

GREENWICH

Blackheath Library, Old Dover Road, Blackheath SE3.
0181 858 1131

Eltham Library, Eltham High Street, Eltham SE9.
0181 850 2268

Greenwich Library, Woolwich Road, SE10.
0181 858 6656

Woolwich Reference Library, Calderwood Street, Woolwich, SE18.
0181 316 6663

Mon and Thur 10am–7pm Tues and Fri 10am–5.30pm Sat
10am–5pm Closed Wed.

Library Community Information
0181 858 6656

HACKNEY

Central Library, Mare Street, E8.
0181 985 8262

Mon and Tues 10am–7pm Thur 1pm–7pm Fri 10am–6pm
Sat 9am–5pm Closed Wed.

Library Community Information
0171 739 7600

HAMMERSMITH & FULHAM

Hammersmith Area Library, Shepherds Bush Road, W6.
General enquiries 0181 576 5050
Reference enquiries 0181 576 5053

Fulham Area Library, 598 Fulham Road, SW6.
General enquiries 0181 576 5252
Reference enquiries 0181 576 5254

Mon, Fri, Sat 9.15am–5pm Tues and Thur 9.15am–8pm
Closed Wed.

ISLINGTON

Central Library, 2 Fieldway Crescent, N5.
0171 609 3051

Mon, Wed, Thur 9am–8pm Tues and Sat 9am–5pm Closed Fri.

Library Community Information
0171 609 3051

KENSINGTON & CHELSEA

Central Library, Phillimore Walk, W8.
General enquiries 0171 937 2542

Mon, Tues, Thur, Fri 10am–8pm Wed 10am–1pm
Sat 10am–5pm.

Library Community Information
0171 937 2542

LAMBETH

Tate Brixton Library, Brixton Oval, SW2.
0171 926 1056

Mon 9am–8pm Tues and Fri 9am–6pm Thur 9am–1pm
Sat 9.30am–12.30pm and 1.30pm–5.00pm Closed Wed.

Library Community Information 0171 926 9325

SOUTHWARK

Dulwich (Reference & Information) Library,
368 Lordship Lane, SE22.
0181 693 8312

North Peckham Library, The Civic, 600–608 Old Kent Road, SE15.

Mon and Thur 9.30am–12.30pm 1.30pm–8pm Tues & Sat
9.30am–12.30pm 1.30pm–5pm. Closed Wed and Fri.

Library Community Information
0171 525 1993

TOWER HAMLETS

Bethnal Green Library, Cambridge Heath Road, E2.
0181 980 3902/6274

Mon and Thur 9am–8pm Tues and Fri 9am–6pm Wed and Sat
9am–5pm.

Library Community Information
0181 980 4366

WANDSWORTH

Balham District Library, Ramsden Road, SW12.
0181 871 7195
Mon, Tues, Thur and Fri 10am–8pm Sat 9am–5pm Closed Wed.

Battersea District Library, Lavender Hill, SW11.
0181 871 7466
Mon, Tues, Wed and Fri 10am–8pm Sat 9am–5pm Closed Thur.

Putney District Library, Disraeli Road, SW15.
0181 871 7090
Mon, Tues, Wed and Fri 10am–8pm Sat 9am–5pm Closed Thur.

WESTMINSTER

Victoria Library, 160 Buckingham Palace Road, SW1.
General enquiries 0171 798 2187

Mon–Fri 9.30am–7pm Sat 9.30am–5pm.

Westminster Reference Library, 35 St Martin's Street, WC2.
General enquiries 0171 798 2276

Reference enquiries 0171 798 2034

Mon–Fri 10am–7pm Sat 10am–5pm.

Library Community Information
0171 798 2036

LONDON'S SPECIALIST LIBRARIES

Where an area is known for a specific industry (for example,
law in Holborn) the local library tends to reflect this interest
with a specialist collection or sub-library. The same is true if
an area reflects a specific community – for example, Stamford
Hill carries an extensive range of works about Judaism and of
Hebrew and Yiddish literatures, and Charing Cross offers a full
Chinese library service. Listed below are some libraries that carry
less obvious specialist collections or are self-explanatory through their
name.

   Some libraries ask that you make an appointment prior to using a
specific collection.

BARBICAN LIBRARY
Barbican Centre, EC2.
0171 638 0569
Music enquiries 0171 638 0672

Special collections: art, children's and music libraries. Music
Performance Research Centre collection of non-commercially
available live recordings.

BATTERSEA REFERENCE LIBRARY
Altenburg Gardens (off Lavender Hill) SW11.
0181 871 7467

Special collections: occult, architecture, William Blake,
G.A. Henty, Edward Thomas.

BRITISH LIBRARY
Great Russell Street, WC1.
0171 636 1544

National reference library for humanities and social sciences.
Large collection of older books, foreign literary and scholarly works,
musical scores, maps, official publications from all countries and a
national manuscript collection.

SCIENCE REFERENCE AND INFORMATION SERVICE
25 Southampton Buildings, Chancery Lane, WC2.
0171 323 7494

Special collections: inventions and patents, physics, chemistry,
engineering, technology, industry, companies, markets and products.

• There is another branch at 9 Kean Street, Drury Lane WC2
(071 323 7288) which includes earth sciences and astronomy.

BRITISH LIBRARY NEWSPAPER LIBRARY
Colindale Avenue, NW9.
0171 323 7353

CATHOLIC CENTRAL LIBRARY
47 Francis Street, SW1.
0171 834 6128

CHELSEA LIBRARY
Old Town Hall, Kings Road, SW3.
0171 352 6056

Special collections: costume.

CITY BUSINESS LIBRARY
1 Brewer's Hall Garden, Aldermanbury Square, EC2.
0171 638 8215

COMMONWEALTH RESOURCE CENTRE
Commonwealth Institute, Kensington High Street, W8.
0171 603 4535

FINSBURY REFERENCE LIBRARY
245 St John Street, EC1.
0171 278 7343

Special collections: Sadlers Wells collection, art and design, illustrations and photography.

THE GREAT BRITAIN–CHINA CENTRE LIBRARY
15 Belgrave Square, SW1.
0171 235 6696

GUILDHALL LIBRARY
Aldermanbury, EC2.
0171 606 3030

Special collections: London history and topography. Public and local acts and statutes, Lords debates and journals, Commons papers complete from 1800 (many earlier), maps, prints, drawings and manuscripts.

HOMERTON LIBRARY
Homerton High Street, E9.
0181 985 8262

Special collections: the Americas, Australasia, car manuals pre-1976.

ISLINGTON CENTRAL REFERENCE LIBRARY
Fieldway Crescent, N5.
0171 609 3051

Special collections: the Sickert collection of etchings, drawings and cuttings.

KENSINGTON CENTRAL LIBRARY
Phillimore Walk, W8.
0171 937 2542

Special collections: heraldry, genealogy, biography and folklore.

LIMEHOUSE LIBRARY
638 Commercial Road, Limehouse, E14.
0171 987 3183

Special collections: French, German and Portuguese literature.

MAIDA VALE LIBRARY
Sutherland Avenue, W9.
0171 798 1028

Special collections: military history, criminology.

MARX MEMORIAL LIBRARY
37a Clerkenwell Green, London EC1.
0171 253 1485

MARYLEBONE LIBRARY
Marylebone Road, NW1.
0171 798 1039

Special collections: medicine, dentistry and nursing. Mozart recordings. Sherlock Holmes.

MAYFAIR LIBRARY
25 South Audley Street, W1.
0171 798 1391

Foreign languages, dictionaries, literary histories and literature in French, German, Italian and Spanish.

NATIONAL SOUND ARCHIVE
29 Exhibition Road, SW7.
0171 412 7430

Music recordings of most periods, styles and countries. Oral history, spoken literature, languages and dialects, wildlife sounds and sound effects, BBC recordings. National and international record catalogues.

ORIENTAL & INDIA OFFICE COLLECTIONS
197 Blackfriars Road, SE1.
0171 412 7873

POETRY LIBRARY
Level 5, Royal Festival Hall, South Bank Centre, SE1.
0171 921 0943

POLISH LIBRARY
238–246 King Street, W6.
0181 741 0474

ST BRIDE PRINTING LIBRARY
Bride Lane, Fleet Street, EC4.
0171 353 4660

SHOREDITCH LIBRARY
Pitfield Street, N1.
0171 739 6981

Special collections: furniture and other small manufacturing industries such as clocks and watches.

SWISS COTTAGE LIBRARY
88 Avenue Road, NW3.
0171 413 6527
0171 413 6533/4 (reference)

Specialist collections: *The Times* from 1785 on microfilm; Ordnance Survey maps; philosophy and psychology.

UNIVERSITY OF LONDON LIBRARIES

University of London Library 0171 636 4514
   Daily and weekly newspapers and periodicals – Commonwealth and foreign newspapers (English provincial from 1700; London from 1801).

Courtauld Institute of Art Library 0171 873 2742
Institute of Advanced Legal Studies Library 0171 637 1731
School of Oriental and African Studies Library 0171 637 2388
School of Slavonic and East European Studies Library 0171 637 4934
Institute of Education Library 0171 580 1122
Warburg Institute Library 0171 580 9663

VICTORIA LIBRARY
160 Buckingham Palace Road, SW1.
0171 798 2187

Special collections: fine arts, English literature.

WELLCOME INSTITUTE FOR THE HISTORY OF MEDICINE
183 Euston Road, NW1.
0171 611 8888

WESTMINSTER MUSIC LIBRARY
160 Buckingham Palace Road, SW1.
0171 798 2192

Special collections: books, scores and periodicals in all fields of music.

WESTMINSTER REFERENCE LIBRARY
35 St Martin's Street, WC2.
0171 798 2036

Special collections: British and international maps, theatre, cinema, ballet, painting, sculpture, interiors, ceramics, architecture and antiques.

ALTERNATIVE AND COMPLEMENTARY HEALTH

Perhaps it is a hangover from the indulgences of the Eighties, but the last few years have seen a growing interest in ancient and holistic forms of medicine and therapy. This is no longer an area dismissed as hippy bunkum – even the most hardened sceptics now admit that alternative treatments can work well alone or alongside more orthodox methods.

The range of practitioners of alternative and complementary medicine working throughout London is vast. Acupuncture, aromatherapy and reflexology may be familiar concepts now, but even less well-known treatments like Chinese herbalism, cranial-sacral therapy and polarity therapy are finding a following.

Some alternative treatments are available on the National Health, but most practitioners are private. There are now so many varieties of therapy on offer that it can be rather baffling to know exactly which therapy you feel you need and where to find the best person to treat you.

Jane McWhirter, who founded and runs the All Hallows House Centre For Natural Health and Counselling offers the following advice:

• What you really want to find is a therapist with whom you are going to feel happy having a long-term relationship. Even if you are only actually going to see them infrequently, you should still feel a rapport with them.

• The best way to find a therapist is by word of mouth. You can also ring the professional bodies for a complete list of therapists in the field in your area.

• Ring the centre or the therapist and talk to them. Most people are happy to speak to you before they book you in.

• Use the first session to establish how you feel about the therapist: is this an ongoing thing; do you feel comfortable with them? No good therapist is going to insist you carry on coming to them, so feel free to try someone else until you feel happy.

INSTITUTE FOR COMPLEMENTARY MEDICINE

The Institute runs the British Register for Complementary Medicine, which contains the names of therapists in a wide variety of disciplines, all of whom have reached the Institute's required level of standards of training and competence. They can give you the names of registered practitioners in particular therapies in your area and can also supply details of courses and affiliated training colleges.

Institute for Complementary Medicine,
21 Portland Place, W1.
0171 237 5165

Also: Council for Complementary and Alternative Medicine, 179 Gloucester Place, NW1.
0171 724 9103

PROFESSIONAL ASSOCIATIONS

There are many different professional associations connected with the various disciplines in complementary medicine. This is a selection of some who should be able to provide you with information and a list of qualified practitioners in your area.

BRITISH ACUPUNCTURE ASSOCIATION AND REGISTER
34 Alderney Street, SW1.
0171 834 6229/1012

SOCIETY OF TEACHERS OF THE ALEXANDER TECHNIQUE
10 London House, 266 Fulham Road, SW10.
0171 351 0828

BRITISH CHIROPRACTIC ASSOCIATION
Premier House, Greycoat Place, SW1.
0171 222 8866

CONFEDERATION OF HEALING ORGANIZATIONS
Suite J, 2nd Floor, The Red & White House, 113 High Street,
Berkhamstead, Herts. HP4 2DJ.
01442 870 660

NATIONAL FEDERATION OF SPIRITUAL HEALERS
Old Manor Farm Shop, Church Street, Sunbury on Thames,
Middlesex. TW16 0RG.
01932 783164   Healer Referral Number: 0891 616080

SOCIETY OF HOMEOPATHS
2 Artisan Road, Northampton NN1 4HU.
01604 21400

GENERAL COUNCIL AND REGISTER OF OSTEOPATHS
56 London Street, Reading RG1 4SQ.
01734 576585

**NATIONAL COUNCIL OF PSYCHOTHERAPISTS AND
HYPNOTHERAPY REGISTER**
46 Oxhey Road, Watford WD1 4QQ.
1923 227772

UK COUNCIL FOR PSYCHOTHERAPY
Regent's College, Inner Circle, Regent's Park, NW1.
0171 487 7554

NATIONAL INSTITUTE OF MEDICAL HERBALISTS
9 Palace Gate, Exeter.
01392 426022

**REGISTER OF TRADITIONAL CHINESE MEDICINE
(ACUPUNCTURE)**
19 Trinity Road, N2 8JJ.
0181 883 8431

REGISTER OF CHINESE HERBAL MEDICINE
POB 400, Wembley, Middlesex. HA9 9NZ.
0181 904 1357

THE MAIN ALTERNATIVE AND COMPLEMENTARY THERAPIES

Acupuncture

Acupuncture is one of the oldest forms of Chinese medicine. During treatment, thin sterilized needles are used to stimulate the invisible 'meridian lines' of energy running under the skin. This prompts the 'chi' – the body's vital energy – to make changes in the energy balance of the body and restore health.

Acupuncture can be used to treat sinusitis, asthma, hay fever, digestive disorders, menstrual problems, headaches, stress, anxiety, insomnia and to help with giving up smoking.

Alexander Technique

Bad posture and muscular tension can be the cause of many common complaints such as backache, mental stress, arthritis and breathing disorders.

The Alexander Technique aims to make people more aware of balance, posture and movement. During lessons the dynamic relationship between head, neck, back and limbs is worked on, to bring about improved balance, poise and co-ordination.

Aromatherapy

Aromatherapy is a form of massage using pure oils which are extracted from fruits, flowers, trees and herbs. The oils are highly concentrated and are used in various combinations to stimulate or relax and to treat a range of physical and emotional conditions. Aromatherapy massage isn't as vigorous as Swedish massage, but homes in on pulse points and energy lines.

Aromatherapy can help with stress, insomnia, fatigue, pre-menstrual tension and headaches.

Chiropractic

A chiropractor manipulates the bones of the spinal column and other joints of the body to treat lower back pain and neck disorders. Another version is McTimoney chiropractic which is more gentle and deals with the whole body.

Cranio-sacral therapy

This is a very sophisticated form of tension release. Usually a secondary qualification held by a chiropractor or osteopath, it encompasses slight manipulation of the bone plates in the skull and base of the neck.

Healers

Treatment involves the laying-on of hands as a channel for energy to flow through. Often sought by cancer patients, it is also used for back pain, stress, skin diseases, ME, depression, arthritis and headaches.

The Healers' Code of Conduct does not allow them to diagnose, use manipulation or prescribe drugs.

Herbal Medicine

One of the most ancient of the Chinese arts, herbal medicine uses plants and herbs to heal the body. Herbal medicine is used to treat many types of illness, especially problems affecting the digestive system and joints, and to treat skin complaints, particularly eczema.

Homeopathy

Homeopathy works on the principle of like curing like, using tiny doses of substances that are known to produce similar symptoms to the condition being treated. This then stimulates the body to heal itself.

There are more than 3500 homeopathic remedies including minute dilutions of plant tincture and animal and mineral products. Homeopathy is used to treat stress, anxiety, depression, insomnia, migraine asthma, hay fever, digestive disorders and skin complaints.

Iridology

Iridology is based on the examination and analysis of the iris of the eye, which has a set of individual markings that correspond to the various organs and systems of the body.

An iridologist will offer information about your constitutional strengths and weaknesses as well as information on what diet, nutrition and exercise you need to restore and maintain health.

Osteopathy

Osteopathy uses massage and gentle manipulation to realign the bones, muscles, ligaments and nerves to restore health. Back pain is the most common condition treated by osteopaths, but joint pain, sports injuries and neck and shoulder tension also respond.

Cranial osteopathy is a system of subtle movement which releases inner cranial tensions thus relaxing and balancing tension throughout the body.

Polarity

Polarity therapy aims to find and cure any imbalance of elements in the body's energy system. The therapist will work on the head, feet and central parts of the body, locating areas where energy is blocked as indicated by the body's meridians and then use a series of deliberate but gentle pressure strokes on those areas to free the blockages.

The treatment may also involve other elements, including discussion of diet and nutrition, counselling and exercise.

Reflexology

Reflexology uses the foot as a map of the body to indicate which organs or areas are giving concern. Different parts of the foot relate to certain organs and by massaging the corresponding area on the foot the reflexologist stimulates the healing capabilities of the organs and systems. Like acupuncture it works to clear the body's meridians and restore the free flow of energy around the body.

Disorders which can be treated with reflexology include migraine, menstrual problems, back pain, stress and circulatory problems.

Shiatsu

Shiatsu has its origins in Japanese medicine and acts to rebalance the physical and emotional energies of the body using a combination of gentle stretching, firmer pressure with the thumbs and palms of the hand and breathing exercises to restore the natural flow of life energy.

It can help in particular with muscular pains, colds, tension, menstrual problems and migraine.

• Two annual London events also provide a chance to find out more about alternative and complementary therapies and new age subjects.

The Healing Arts Alternative Medicine and Complementary Therapies Exhibition is in its seventh year and takes place in November. It offers the chance to sample and find out more about a wide range of therapies from the well-known to newer forms like crystal healing and kirlian photography diagnosis. There are over 150 exhibitors and numerous lectures and workshops. The Exhibition takes place at New Hall, The Royal Agricultural Halls, Greycoat Street, SW1. 0171 938 3788.

The Festival of Mind, Body & Spirit has been running each May for 18 years and has over 100 workshops and lectures on a wide range of subjects from cellular regeneration to natural fertility awareness. There are also over 150 exhibition stalls on everything from crystals to cosmic music. It also takes place at The Royal Agricultural Halls. 0171 938 3788.

THERAPY CENTRES

ALL HALLOWS CENTRE FOR NATURAL HEALTH AND COUNSELLING   EC3

Housed in the beautiful spire of a Wren church, the main body of which was destroyed during the war, the All Hallows Centre was founded by Jane McWhirter in 1990.

ˈ The centre aims to provide a cohesive approach to complementary medicine. Jane McWhirter says: 'The vision we had was that, rather than just having a place where therapists rented rooms, we wanted to make it truly holistic and develop it as a team. The practitioners work very closely together, go away for practitioner's week-ends for example, and understand each others' work so we can liaise and cross-refer.'

The therapies on offer include McTimoney chiropractic, aromatherapy, psychotherapy, counselling, cranio-sacral therapy, herbal medicine, homeopathy, polarity therapy, reflexology and shiatsu.

Most therapies cost from around £36 for an hour's treatment, and if you are unsure of your needs, or have a long and complicated history, you can book an initial half-hour consultation costing £12 to discuss the various options.

Amongst the range of conditions the centre treats are many disorders now particularly associated with modern city living and working, including, allergies, asthma, chronic fatigue, repetitive strain injury (RSI) and stress.

The Centre also offers lunchtime and evening self-help courses in a variety of therapies including yoga, aromatherapy and relaxation techniques.

All Hallows Centre for Natural Health and Counselling, Idol Lane, EC3.
0171 283 8908

BRACKENBURY NATURAL HEALTH CLINIC W6

The Brackenbury Clinic in West London was established in 1983 and offers a full range of complementary treatments from acupuncture and Alexander technique through to osteopathy, psychotherapy, reflexology and shiatsu.

Therapists at the centre give talks throughout the year about their particular discipline and a general practitioner is also available to diagnose and refer patients to suitable therapists and to advise if tests are necessary.

Treatment costs between £20 and £50 depending on the type of therapy.

Brackenbury Natural Health Clinic, 30 Brackenbury Road, W6.
0181 741 9264

CLISSOLD PARK NATURAL HEALTH CENTRE N16

There are 30 practitioners operating from the Clissold Park Centre, offering acupuncture, Alexander technique, aromatherapy, dietary advice, herbal medicine, homeopathy, hypnotherapy, massage, osteopathy, psychotherapy, reflexology and shiatsu.

In addition the centre runs a homeopathic drop-in clinic on Mondays, Wednesdays and Fridays to treat acute ailments like throat infections, and digestive upsets. No appointment is needed and the fee is £5.

Homeopathic treatment is also available on Saturdays and alternate Sundays and aromatherapy massage for women is available on Saturdays and Sundays.

The Centre also offers a wide range of courses, including yoga, self-hypnosis and herbal first aid.

Clissold Park Natural Health Centre,
154 Stoke Newington Church Street, London, N16.
0171 249 2990

COMMUNITY HEALTH FOUNDATION EC1

The Community Health Foundation has been running for 18 years from premises in the East/West Centre in Old Street, EC2.

The foundation sees its role as predominantly educational, to encourage people to take the best possible care of their health, and promotes its aims by offering a range of courses in massage, aromatherapy and macrobiotic cooking, as well as yoga classes and a wide range of massage treatments from shiatsu to holistic.

The East/West Centre also houses a bookshop selling a varied selection of books on complementary medicine, a natural foods restaurant and next door is a natural foods store.

Community Health Foundation, 188 Old Street, EC1.
0171 251 4076

LONDON NATURAL HEALTH CLINIC   W8

The London Natural Health Clinic offers osteopathy,
homeopathy and reflexology amongst its therapies, as well as
a form of laser acupuncture used particularly for sports
injuries and to treat smokers who want to give up.

The clinic also holds a children's homeopathy clinic on
Tuesdays and Thursdays.

Fees are £35 for a first visit for adults and £25 thereafter,
£25 for a first visit for children and £15 thereafter.

London Natural Health Clinic, Arnica House,
170 Campden Hill Road, W8.
0171 938 3788

NEAL'S YARD THERAPY ROOMS   WC2

The Neal's Yard Therapy Rooms opened in 1981 and were
initially set up to offer space to practitioners who couldn't
afford the rents for a full-time room in locations like Harley
Street.

The range of therapies on offer is extensive, including
acupuncture, aromatherapy, Chinese herbalism, Japanese
herbalism, chiropractic, osteopathy, hypnotherapy, reflexology,
naturopathy, psychotherapy, and hypnotherapy.

There are 60 therapists working through Neal's Yard, selected by
the manager, Margot McCarthy, on their qualifications and references.
Prices for the various treatments vary and all are by appointment. The
therapy rooms also offer 30 minutes' free consultation for patients
who are uncertain what sort of treatment is most suitable for their
condition.

Neal's Yard Therapy Rooms, 2 Neal's Yard, WC2.
0171 379 7662

NEAL'S YARD PERSONAL DEVELOPMENT AGENCY   WC2

The most recent addition to the Neal's Yard complex is the personal
development agency which puts people in touch with self-
development courses and workshops (everything from aura soma
colour therapy to cranio-sacral sensitivity).

The centre also has some meeting rooms offering yoga classes and
offers taster workshops on such diverse themes as creating your
vision, stress, clowning and outlook transformation.

Neal's Yard Agency for Personal Development,
14 Neal's Yard, WC2.
0171 379 0141

SOUTH LONDON NATURAL HEALTH CENTRE   SW4

Designed to provide a relaxed and friendly atmosphere, the South
London Natural Health Centre offers a varied selection of therapies

including acupuncture, Alexander technique, aromatherapy, colour therapy, colonic irrigation, dietary consultations, herbal medicine, homeopathy, hypnotherapy, iridology, massage and naturopathy, osteopathy, psychotherapy, reflexology and shiatsu.

For those who want advice in choosing the most appropriate therapy for their needs, the centre can arrange a half hour consultation during which the various options can be discussed. You can also meet any practitioner for a free 15-minute chat.

Fees are mostly between £15/£30 per session.

South London Natural Health Centre,
7a Clapham Common Southside, SW4.
0171 720 8817

Also:

• Natureworks, 16 Balderton Street, W1.
0171 355 4036

HERBALISTS

NEAL'S YARD REMEDIES   WC2

Neal's Yard Remedies was started in 1981 with the aim of trying to provide the same sort of service as that available in French pharmacies, where herbs, essential oils and homeopathic remedies are on sale alongside the soap and aspirin.

There are around 235 different herbs on offer, ranging from the familiar to the extraordinary – pellitory-of-the-wall, penny royal, wood betony, blue flaggroot and bladderwrack among them.

The assistants are very helpful in explaining the remedies, but by law are not actually allowed to choose a remedy for you. However, the shop can refer you to a network of practitioners.

Neal's Yard Remedies also stock a wide range of books on alternative therapies and publish 2 of their own books, *Neal's Yard Natural Remedies* and *Natural Healing for Women* The shops also run some courses in herbalism and related subjects.

Neal's Yard Remedies,
15 Neal's Yard, Covent Garden, London, WC2.
0171 379 7222

• Also:

G. Baldwin & Co, 173 Walworth Road, SE17.
0171 703 5550

Chelsea Farmers Market, Sydney Street, SW3.
0171 351 6380
and 9, Elgin Crescent, W11.
0171 727 3398

Culpeper Limited, 21 Bruton Street, W1.
0171 629 4559
and Unit 8, The Market, Covent Garden, WC2.
0171 379 6698

Food for All (London), 3a Cazenove Road, N16.
0181 806 4138

Realfood Store, 14 Clifton Road, Little Venice, W9.
0171 266 1162

• Very basic ranges are now carried by most big chemist stores such as Boots or health food stores Holland & Barrett.

• New regulations are currently underway to restrict what you can buy over the counter. The best safeguard is to ensure that the assistant is registered with NIMH (National Institute of Medical Herbalists).

SPECIALISTS

AROMATHERAPY ASSOCIATES   SW6

Specializing in aromatherapy, the treatment centre was started 4 years ago by Sue Beechy and Geraldine Howard who each have over 20 years' experience as aromatherapists.

Aromatherapy Associates focuses on using aromatherapy to combat stress and as a relaxation therapy.

The centre is open each evening until 8pm and also on Saturdays. Prices are around £35 for an hour-long session.

Aromatherapy Associates, 68 Maltings Place,
Fulmead Street, SW6.
0171 731 8129

CHINESE MEDICINE   NW1/SW15/W2/WC2

The following centres offer Chinese herbal medicine to treat a wide range of conditions from dermatitis to indigestion, constipation and lethargy, or as a tonic to revitalize the system. A mixture of Chinese herbs is usually prescribed to make a herbal tea, taking doses morning and evening. Acupuncture is also available and in some cases is used in conjunction with herbal medicine.

HR Chinese Medicine Centre, 36 Westbourne Grove, W2.
0171 792 8626

Chinese Medicine Centre, 7 Little Newport Street, WC2.
0171 287 1095

Chinese Medicine and Acupuncture Centre,
1 Lower Richmond Road, SW15.
0181 780 1112

Acumedic Centre, 101 Camden High Street, NW1.
0171 388 7604

LONDON COLLEGE OF MASSAGE   W1

Founded in 1987 by Fiona Harrold with the aim of 'putting the energy back into London', the London College of Massage provides a range of massage courses and treatments from shiatsu to reflexology. The courses range from an introductory weekend, which teaches basic massage and the use of essential oils (£90), to a 12-week beginners course on full-body massage (£282). Many of the students on the courses are re-training from other jobs. Students on the courses must be over 21. Treatments include therapeutic massage, remedial massage and sports massage, as well as aromatherapy, acupuncture and postural integration. The college also offers Japanese herbal medicine and nutrition therapy.

Massage treatments cost £40 for the first $1\frac{1}{2}$ hour consultation session and then £30 per hour or £17 per half hour thereafter. The College is open until 10pm each evening.

London College of Massage, 5–6 Newman Passage, W1.
0171 637 7125

FLOATATION THERAPY   NW7/SE1/SW4/W11

Floatation tanks or pools can now be found all across London. Users report a variety of benefits including an easing in back pain, lowering of blood pressure and reduced stress.

Floatation tanks have also been reported to give relief to sufferers of ME, multiple sclerosis and repetitive strain injury.

Floating takes place in a tank with a pull-down lid. The water is some 10 inches in depth, with a high concentration of Epsom salts, which provide natural buoyancy and make it impossible not to float. It is this suspended animation that leads to deep relaxation and enhanced creativity.

Remember the following points:

• The float tank should have a shower in the same room and the door should be lockable.

• There should be a light switch in the tank.

• The water should be filtered thoroughly and needs to be at a temperature of 35–36°C throughout the float.

Floatation tanks typically cost around £20 for a one-hour session.

Acquatonics, 4 Wellington Close, Ledbury Road, Notting Hill, W11.
0171 229 1123

Floatworks, Winchester Wharf, Clink Street, SE1.
0171 357 0111

North London Floatation, 27 Langley Park, Mill Hill, NW7.
0181 959 4989

South London Natural Health Centre,
7a Clapham Common Southside, SW4.
0171 720 8817

or contact:

The Floatation Tank Association on 01296 696300

NEW AGE SHOPS

The past few years have seen the emergence of a wide range of shops (particularly in Chiswick!) offering everything you might need for the New Age lifestyle, from candles and crystals to flower remedies and rainsticks.

Most of the shops also have a handle on psychic matters, offering the services of tarot card readers, astrologers and mediums, and also deal in what might be described as some of the wackier therapies around.

THE ASTROLOGY SHOP   WC2

The Astrology Shop offers Equinox horoscopes, which can be compiled while you wait, using a computerized system. Apparently it took about 10 years to programme the computer with all the different permutations of time, date and place of birth.

You can choose a character portrait, a yearly forecast or a combination of these. Also on offer are child profiles (for babies and children up to the age of 14) and a compatibility profile to see if you and your partner are made for each other. Prices start from £14.

The shop also stocks the largest selection of astrology books in the country as well as many other items, from mugs to candlesticks, with an astrological theme.

They also offer a mail order service.

The Astrology Shop, 78 Neal Street, WC2.
0171 497 1001

CRYSTAL ORACLE   W4

Tucked away behind Stamford Brook tube station, Crystal Oracle is owned by resident clairvoyant and medium Lee Van Zyl. The shop stocks a range of books on self-help and spiritual development, decorative and healing crystals and offers sessions in crystal healing and psychic development.

Crystal Oracle, 3 Wilson Walk, off Prebend Gardens, W4.
0181 563 7505

GAETANO VIVO   W4

Gaetano Vivo is probably the most stylish of the New Age shops, with a high-quality selection of New Age icons, jewellery and so on.

They also run lectures, seminars and workshops on topics like handwriting, astrology, tarot for beginners and developing mediumship.

Gaetano Vivo, 5a Devonshire Road, London, W4.
0181 742 3305

INSPIRATION   W4

Inspiration is a small bright shop with a friendly atmosphere, selling a wide range of books on self-help and therapies, from how to interpret your dreams to channelling. They also have a wide range of items on sale including colour-therapy glasses, relaxation tapes, crystals, Mayan music balls, incense and wind chimes.

There is a tarot reader and clairvoyant working on the premises and they also offer a number of other services, including astrological charts, crystal healing workshops, aura photography and meditation classes.

Inspiration, 28 Devonshire Road, Chiswick, London, W4.
0181 994 0074

MYSTERIES   WC2

Calling itself the New Age Centre of Covent Garden, Mysteries has several tarot readers on site and sittings cost about £15. The cluttered premises also hold a large selection of New Age goods, including a wide range of books on the mystical and the paranormal.

Mysteries, 9–11 Monmouth Street, WC2.
0171 240 3688

• Also:

Abraxas, 7 Shrubbery Road, SW16.
0181 769 4857

Wilde Ones, 49 Kensington High Street, W8.
0171 376 2870
and 283 Kings Road, SW3.
0171 351 7581

Wonders, 31 The Market, WC2.
0171 497 2992

FITNESS

Although finding the time to get fit may present a problem for Londoners, we can't blame lack of opportunity! There are over 20,000 different sports clubs in the capital, and it is possible to take part in any kind of activity from dry-slope skiing to dragon-boat racing, petanque to parascending.

In addition, London has over 200 sports centres and over 500 swimming pools – 30 of these open air. In fact, sport in London generates more jobs than construction and 3 times as many as manufacturing.

The main area of growth in the leisure business has been in private clubs, and the ones that have survived the end of the Eighties, when it was *de rigueur* to be a member, have done so by adopting a Nineties-style approach – less high impact aerobics and more emphasis on fitness as part of the quality of life.

The approach now is one of all-round health, and you are as likely to find massage and aromatherapy on offer as you are state-of-the-art gym equipment. Even public sports centres are following the trend with gyms, exercise studios, steam rooms and saunas now virtually standard features.

Naturally membership of a private club does not come cheap – expect to pay at least £500 a year – so public centres, though less glamorous with queuing at peak times pretty standard, can offer excellent value for money.

PUBLIC SPORTS CENTRES AND GYMS

The Sports Council publishes a directory of all sports centres and facilities in London, *London Sport*, which you can obtain by calling their London regional information line on 0181 778 8600.

Another useful service is Sportsline (0171 222 8000), which has a comprehensive database of all the sports facilities and clubs throughout London. They can put you in touch with someone connected to the sport you are interested in.

Here is a selection of some of the most popular public sports centres.

BALHAM LEISURE CENTRE   SW17

The gym at the Balham Centre has recently been extended and expanded and now offers 2 separate rooms with a wide range of cardiovascular equipment and a weights section. You can also book sessions with a personal trainer. There is also a 25-metre pool, new squash courts and a good range of exercise classes, plus sauna and steam rooms.

Balham Leisure Centre, Elmfield Road, SW17.
0181 871 7176

BRENTFORD FOUNTAIN LEISURE CENTRE   W4

A popular family centre, the Fountain has a 25-metre fitness pool and a leisure pool with wave machine and aquaslide. The gym offers computerized fitness testing and there is a wide range of exercise classes as well as sauna and steam rooms, a sports injury clinic, massage and aromatherapy.

Brentford Fountain Leisure Centre,
658 Chiswick High Road, Brentford, Middlesex.
0181 994 9596

BRITANNIA LEISURE CENTRE   N1

This is a large indoor centre with tennis courts, 5-a-side courts and swimming pool with aquaslide and wave machine. Facilities include sauna, sunbeds and spa bath. A wide range of sporting activities with tuition is available for most as well as lots of club activities for adults and children.

Britannia Leisure Centre, 40 Hyde Road, London N1.
0171 729 4485

BRIXTON RECREATION CENTRE   SW9

Brixton is probably best known for its climbing wall, where you can learn to scale the heights for £3.10 per class.
   A huge range of activities includes everything from basketball, badminton and squash to korfball, martial arts and trampolining. There are a variety of exercise classes on offer and a weights room. The centre has a 25-metre swimming pool, a teaching pool and créche facilities.

Brixton Recreation Centre, Brixton Station Road, SW9 8QQ.
0171 926 9779/9780

CRYSTAL PALACE NATIONAL SPORTS CENTRE   SE19

Opened in 1964, Crystal Palace is the largest multi-sports centre in the country with facilities for over 50 sports, from water polo to dry-slope skiing.
   The swimming pool is Olympic sized and there is also a diving pool. An excellent range of swimming courses are on offer.

Crystal Palace National Sports Centre, Crystal Palace, SE19.
0181 778 0131

FINSBURY LEISURE CENTRE   EC1

This Leisure Centre has both indoor and outdoor facilities for a wide range of sports including netball, badminton, squash, football, martial arts and roller skating. It shares swimming pool, sunbeds, sauna and Turkish bath facilities with Ironmonger Row Baths just round the corner in Old Street.

Finsbury Leisure Centre, Norman Street, London EC1.
0171 253 4490

JUBILEE HALL SPORTS CENTRE WC2

The Jubilee Hall Centre in Covent Garden attracts a cross-section of Londoners and is popular with both office workers and body builders. Although large, it does get very packed at peak times, so that you have to queue to use the equipment in the gym.

The huge indoor area allows for several activities to go on at once, including badminton, basketball and football. Other activities include exercise classes, martial arts training and a sports injury clinic.

The building has just been refurbished, and the crowded changing rooms have been extended.

Jubilee Hall Recreation Centre, The Piazza, Covent Garden, WC2.
0171 836 4835

KENSINGTON SPORTS CENTRE W11

The gym at the Kensington centre was enlarged and refurbished last year and now offers a good range of equipment.

Other facilities include a main swimming pool and a learner pool, sports hall, 3 outdoor tennis courts, sauna and steam room and an exercise studio.

There is also a crèche and the centre runs a good selection of courses.

Kensington Sports Centre, Walmer Road, W11.
0171 727 9747

KINGS HALL LEISURE CENTRE E5

The Kings Hall Leisure Centre was originally a public bathing house.

The original pool (30 metres) still exists alongside a new pool (25 metres), sports hall, weights room and sauna and steam rooms. Activities include basketball, netball, badminton, 5-a-side football, judo, karate, martial arts and aerobics.

There is an activity room, which has excellent crèche and playschool facilities, as well as a Sunshine Safari (loads of inflatables to climb over) for children from 9 months to 12 years old.

Kings Hall Leisure Centre, 39 Lower Clapton Road, E5.
0181 985 2158

MICHAEL SOBELL SPORTS CENTRE N7

One of the older leisure centres in London, the Michael Sobell Sports Centre will celebrate 22 years this year.

Sports include football, badminton, squash, weight training, martial arts, aerobics and climbing. The main arena is huge – the size of a football pitch – and they have a purpose-built room for judo and an ice skating rink.

Michael Sobell Sports Centre, Hornsey Road, Islington, N7.
0171 609 2166

PICKETTS LOCK SPORTS CENTRE N9

This is another Centre with excellent indoor and outdoor facilities, including a campsite (maximum stay 2 weeks!) for families visiting London. Sporting facilities include a swimming pool, Tropical Adventure Trail, soccer, gymnastics, badminton, basketball, roller skating, bowls, hockey, and a 9-hole golf course. Tuition and training in most activities is available.

Picketts Lock Sports Centre, Picketts Lock Lane, N9.
0181 345 6666

QUEEN MOTHER SPORTS CENTRE SW1

The Queen Mother Centre, built in 1981, is bright and modern with 3 pools, a gym, a sports hall, and a sauna and steam complex. There is a good range of sport including squash, badminton, 5-a-side football, volley ball, netball and basketball.
   The Centre also runs a wide selection of exercise classes but the popular ones do tend to have waiting lists.

Queen Mother Sports Centre, 223 Vauxhall Bridge Road, SW1.
0171 233 5837

SWISS COTTAGE SPORTS CENTRE NW3

Built in the Sixties, the Swiss Cottage Sports Centre has 2 swimming pools, a massage room, fitness gym, sun beds and indoor courts. It also has 3 outdoor tennis courts and an outdoor football pitch.
   Sports covered include basketball, badminton, netball, volleyball, gymnastics, weight-training, keep fit, martial arts, karate, boxing and squash.

Swiss Cottage Sports Centre, Winchester Road, NW3.
0171 413 6490

YMCA N8/EC2/WC1/W5

The YMCA sports clubs remain an excellent choice if your cash flow won't run to some of the more exclusive clubs and they offer a wide range of facilities. The largest is the Central YMCA which has a 25-metre pool, sports hall, gym, and a huge range of exercise and dance classes.

London Central YMCA, 112 Great Russell Street, WC1.
0171 637 8131

Barbican YMCA, 2 Fann Street, EC2.
0171 628 0697

Ealing YMCA, Jumpers, 14 Bond Street, W5.
0181 579 1421

Hornsey YMCA, 184 Tottenham Lane, N8.
0171 340 6088

PRIVATE GYMS AND HEALTH CLUBS

In terms of financial outlay, joining a private health club is expensive and fees are usually at least £500 per annum. To make sure you don't waste your money it's important to ensure you choose a club that's right for you. It is not only a question of the facilities on offer; in order to get value for money you have to choose somewhere you will enjoy going.

Health and beauty writer Chrissie Painell has the following tips for choosing and using a club:

• Do you intend to use the club before work, at lunchtime or after work and at weekends? Choose a location that will maximize your opportunity to get the most out of the club.

Realize that you are probably going to have to make real changes in your lifestyle, getting up at least an hour earlier in the morning or allowing around 2 hours in the evening by the time you have been to the club, changed, showered and arrived home.

• Think about what you want to use the club for most – working out, exercise classes, swimming; make sure that you choose the club with the best facilities in your particular area of interest. Remember to try to cross-train as much as possible. The fitness equation is: stamina + strength + flexibility = all-round fitness.

• Many people feel too tired to exercise, and jumping into a workout programme isn't necessarily the magic answer. You may need to look at your diet. If you find you have a lot of difficulty getting up in the morning, you may have low blood sugar. Consider seeing a nutritionist.

• If you have back problems, former injuries such as whiplash, or any other health problems, consider consulting a physiotherapist before you begin. The physiotherapist will look at your whole posture and make much more in-depth recommendations than a fitness instructor can.

• Ask clubs about special deals – corporate membership, couples membership, paying by monthly instalments. Try the club out with a day membership; most clubs will refund the cost against membership if you actually join.

• Exercise is a sure-fire way to help you cope with stress, as it releases mood-enhancing hormones, beta-endorphins. You need to combine aerobic exercise (3 or 4 sessions of 20 minutes each a week) done at the right level for you with weight-bearing and muscle strengthening exercises.

• Check out corporate rates; it might be worth organizing a membership through the office.

ALBANY FITNESS   NW1

Housed in the re-furbished former church of St Bede, the Albany Fitness Centre offers a good range of facilities in a very attractive setting. Aside from the main gym and aerobic studio there is a cardiovascular room, a free weight-training room and a sauna.

Sunbeds and beauty treatments are also available on request.

They offer a 7-day trial for £19 to enable you to try all the facilities, and this is redeemable if you decide to join. The joining fee is £199 with an additional monthly charge depending on the range of facilities used.

Albany Fitness, Albany Street, Regents Park, NW1.
0171 383 7131

THE BROADGATE CLUB   EC2

A favourite with City workers, The Broadgate Club has a light, spacious and airy feel. Clever use of space and glass means you can look down at swimmers in the pool from your perch on an exercise bike in the gym.

Facilities include a 25-metre, 6-lane swimming pool, well-equipped gym and an exercise studio. There is also a Worthingtons Hair and Beauty Salon and a Thayer clinic which specializes in chiropractic work.

Members also give particular praise to the a la carte restaurant – handy for post-workout business deals.

Full membership: £982 plus £160 joining fee. Off-peak £520 plus joining fee.

The Broadgate Club, 1 Exchange Place, EC2.
0171 375 2464

CANNONS   EC4/WC2

The City branch of Cannons is built into the huge arches that support Cannon Street station and, not surprisingly, 90 per cent of its members work in the square mile.

The club has a Nautilus gym, free weights room, vast aerobics studio, squash courts and swimming pool.

There is a second branch of the club in Covent Garden, which also has a physiotherapy and sports injury clinic.

Membership: Gold £545 (plus VAT) per annum, plus £87.50 (plus VAT) joining fee; Silver (excludes gym) £395 (plus VAT) plus the same joining fee. Membership, after 90 days, entitles you to use both clubs.

Cannons, Cousin Lane, EC4.   0171 283 0101
Cannons, Endell Street, WC2.   0171 240 2446

DAVID LLOYD CLUBS Chigwell/Enfield/Finchley/Heston/Raynes Park

As you might expect, the speciality of the David Lloyd Clubs is tennis, with indoor courts (still something of a rarity in Britain) and all levels of coaching, including 'short' tennis to introduce children to the sport.

The clubs have a wide range of other facilities and a good family atmosphere. Some also have tenpin bowling alleys attached.

Full membership (varies slightly between clubs): £588 per year plus £280 joining fee. Separate off-peak and health and fitness memberships also available. Information 01923 213300.

David Lloyd clubs at Chigwell 0181 559 8466, Enfield 0181 364 5858, Finchley 0181 446 8704, Heston 0181 573 9378 and Raynes Park 0181 543 8020.

THE HARBOUR CLUB   SW6

The Harbour Club is possibly London's most exclusive health club. It cost £7.5 million to build, which makes it the most expensive private sports development in London. The facilities reflect the cost, with 10 indoor tennis courts, 4 outdoor courts, a 25-metre swimming pool, 4,000 square foot gym, 2 dance studios and a health suite. The club also has a real tennis court (a version of tennis Henry VIII enjoyed at Hampton Court).

The cost is prohibitive for many people, but for sheer luxury and superb facilities it probably can't be beaten.

Membership: £1020 per year plus £1845 resaleable joining fee.

The Harbour Club, Watermeadow Lane, SW6.
0171 371 7700

THE HOGARTH HEALTH CLUB   W4/W11/WC1

Situated in a leafy road in Chiswick, the Hogarth lacks the high-tech sterility of some other clubs and consequently has a more friendly feel, with plenty of wooden decor and the atmosphere of a country tennis club.

The club recently underwent a £1 million renovation and extension programme to include a new pool and changing facilities.

Other facilities include a gym, with a free weights area, exercise studio with a range of classes, beauty salon, sauna and jacuzzi and 2 outdoor tennis courts.

An alternative medicine clinic is attached to the club, offering a full range of complementary therapies to members and non-members.

No children under 14 except on Sundays.

Membership: £720 per year, plus £175 joining fee.

The Hogarth Health Club. 1A, Airedale Avenue, W4. 0181 995 4600

• The Hogarth Group also operates 2 other clubs:

Lambton Place Health Club, Westbourne Grove, W11. 0171 229 2291
Membership: £700 per year, plus £175 joining fee.

Mecklenburgh Heath Club, Mecklenburgh Place, WC1. 0171 813 0555
Membership: £735 per year, plus £190 joining fee.

HOLMES PLACE CLUBS   SW10/EC1/W5/Kingston-upon-Thames

The newest clubs in this chain have opened in Kingston and Ealing, but the best known is still the Chelsea branch, haunt of King's Road dwellers, where models and celebrities like to work out.

The Kingston club has the first stainless steel swimming pool in Britain and, in common with many of the other health clubs, there is a move away from using chlorine, and towards using an ozone filter instead.

Each club also has a women-only gym as well as a mixed one and a full range of beauty treatments on offer.

Membership varies between clubs. Club policy is not to give

membership costs over the phone but insist you make an appointment to discuss these details! However, Kingston is £600 per annum plus £225 joining fee. (Off-peak £450 plus £225 joining fee.) Figures will certainly be higher for Fulham and the Barbican branches.

Holmes Place Health Club, 188 Fulham Road, SW10.
0171 352 9452
Also: 97 Aldersgate Street, EC1.
0171 374 0091
Level 5, Broadway Centre, W5.
0181 579 9433
3rd Floor, Bentall Centre, Kingston-upon-Thames, Surrey.
0181 549 7700

METROPOLITAN CLUB   SW6/SW11/SW18/W1

The chain of Metropolitan Clubs numbers 15 across the capital, including Battersea, Fulham, Wandsworth and Kingly Street in Soho.
    The amount of space and the facilities on offer at each club vary depending on its location. The West End club is built on lots of different levels in a building just off Carnaby Street and is a popular and friendly club, with lots of regular faces, a small but well-equipped gym and a wide variety of exercise classes. The pool is pleasant, but too small for very serious swimmers.

Membership varies between clubs. Kingly Street: Full, £660 per year plus £180 joining fee.

Metropolitan Club, 27–28 Kingly Street, W1.
0171 734 5002

Also: 252–258 North End Road, SW6.
0171 610 1410
Burns Road (off Latchmere Road), SW11.
0171 228 4400
King George's Park, Burr Road, SW18.
0181 874 1155

RIVERSIDE   W9

There is a long waiting list to join the Riverside – understandable when you consider the facilities on offer, which include 14 outdoor and 12 indoor tennis courts, 2 swimming pools, a gym and 2 dance studios.
    Tennis is the club's main attraction and Pat Cash, Stefan Edberg and Jeremy Bates have all been seen on court here.
    The Riverside is also particularly popular with families and offers a crèche, special activities for the 5 to 12 age group and teenagers, and there is even a Montessori nursery.
    Other facilities include an in-house sports injury clinic, beauty salon and a large sports shop, plus probably the longest opening hours of any club – 6.30am until midnight.

Membership: Full £975 per year plus £1500 resaleable joining fee. Off-peak £653 plus £595 non-refundable joining fee.

Riverside Racquets Centre, Duke's Meadows, Chiswick, W4.
0181 994 9496

HOTEL CLUBS

To keep up with the demands of their clientele, a number of the top London hotels have now built well-equipped and well-designed health clubs on their premises, which are also open to non-residents to join.

CHAMPNEYS, THE LONDON CLUB   W1

Champneys, one of the country's most famous health farms, have opened their London branch in the Le Meridien hotel in Piccadilly. The showpiece of the club is a beautiful pool with marble surround, and other facilities include an exercise studio, steam room and saunas, squash courts and beauty treatment rooms. Needless to say, the luxury and location are firmly reflected in the price.

Membership: £1512 per annum plus £250 joining fee.

Champneys, The London Club, Le Meridien Hotel, Piccadilly, W1.
0171 437 8114

FITNESS ON FIVE   W1

The London Hilton's health club, Fitness on Five aims to combine the advantages of club and personal trainer by including a certain number of one-to-one personal fitness workouts per month in its membership packages.

Much of the equipment has been specially designed for the Fitness on Five gym, and great emphasis is placed on the fact that physiological and psychological well-being are closely linked, with reflexology, hypnotherapy, psychotherapy, shiatsu and nutrition advice all on offer.

There are 3 studios, for cardiovascular work, muscle toning and also a private workout room. The club doesn't have a pool.

Membership: Bronze, £750 per annum, includes a monthly workout with a personal trainer; Diamond, £1,500, includes a personal session every week. No joining fee.

Fitness on Five at The London Hilton, Park Lane, W1.
0171 493 0993/493 8000

THE PEAK HEALTH CLUB   SW1

The Peak Club has one of the best views in London, looking out across the rooftops from the 9th floor of the Carlton Tower Hotel.

The club went through a £1.2 million refit last year and now features an enlarged gym, exercise studio, Clarins beauty studio, therapy rooms and steam rooms. It also has saunas complete with television, and a bar and restaurant.

Membership: £950 per year plus £120. Off-peak, £600 plus £120.

The Peak Health Club at the Hyatt Carlton Tower Hotel,
2 Cadogan Place, SW1.
0171 235 5411

WOMEN-ONLY CLUBS

GYM AT THE SANCTUARY   WC

The Sanctuary has long been an oasis of female hedonism in Covent
Garden, offering a huge variety of beauty and therapy treatments along
with 2 swimming pools, sauna and steam rooms in a warm tropical
atmosphere.

Although small, the gym at the Sanctuary has a good atmosphere and
membership also includes use of the 54-foot swimming pool, sauna and
steam room.

It is also possible to book one-to-one exercise sessions with a personal
trainer at £30 and there are a variety of exercise classes available for an
additional charge of £1.75–£3.

Membership: £120 per year plus £5.50 per visit.

Gym at the Sanctuary, 1 Floral Street, WC2.
0171 240 0695

HEALTH HAVEN   SW

A small but friendly women-only club with exercise classes, steam,
sauna and beauty salon. Health Haven combines a variety of classes
including boxercise, circuit training, stretch and tone with facials,
aromatherapy and Swedish massage.

Membership: Gold £549.00, Silver £449.00.

Health Haven, 40 Vauxhall Bridge Road, SW1.
0171 834 2289

SEQUINPARK   N1/N4/N16/NW

Despite sounding like the club Ru Paul would most like to belong to, the
Sequinpark chain has enjoyed huge success, operating on the principle
that women should be able to exercise in a supportive, friendly and
encouraging environment.

Founded by Nikki Porter and Geraldine Waring, there are now 4 clubs
in the chain, each with a gym, workout studio and health suite.

Membership rates depend on what time you visit and how often but are
between £5.90 and £7.40 per week.

17 Crouch Hill, N4.	0171 272 6857
240 Upper Street, N1.	0171 704 9844
134 Stoke Newington Church Street, N16.	0171 241 1449
81–81, Chalk Farm Road, NW1.	0171 284 0004

• Also:

Camden Mews Health & Fitness Club for Women, 14 Pratt Mews, NW1.
0171 388 9111

PERSONAL TRAINERS

Personal trainers are enjoying a real boom in London. Working out in
your own home can be a lot more convenient and private than going to

the gym and most of us need someone to push us into exercise. Trainers can cost around £35 per hour, but if you book for a number of sessions then you should be able to negotiate a lower price.

The National Register of Personal Trainers will match your needs and fitness goals with a suitable trainer in your area.

National Register of Personal Trainers 01992 504336.
Association of Personal Trainers 0171 836 1102.

DANCE AND FITNESS STUDIOS

DANCE ATTIC   SW6

Dance Attic was opened by former Pan's People dancer Dee Dee Wilde. Primarily a dance rehearsal space, the centre offers a variety of classes for both professional and amateur, in numerous dance styles from classical to contemporary, jazz to flamenco.

As well as the 6 dance studios there is a fully equipped gym.

Dance membership: £30 per annum, plus £2.50–£3 per class. Gym membership: £50 per annum.

Dance Attic, 368 North End Road, SW6.
0171 610 2055

DANCEWORKS   W1

Danceworks has 5 multipurpose studios and runs a huge variety of classes for professional dancers, dance enthusiasts and those who just want to get fit.

Fitness classes range from body sculpting to 'butt attack' and classes are divided into different levels of fitness. Danceworks also holds classes in the latest fitness craze, boxercise, a mixture of non-contact boxing movements and aerobic workout, beloved of actresses and supermodels from Jodi Foster to Cindy Crawford. The classes are run by Paul Connolly, who has his own trademark version of boxercise called box aerobics.

Dance classes range from beginners' classical ballet through to Russian classical ballet for professionals, and you can also try out tap, salsa, merengue and flamenco.

Danceworks has a buzzy, 'Fame'-type atmosphere and a café and dancewear shop on the premises. They also offer Alexander technique, physiotherapy and massage.

Membership: Day £4, month £22, annual £75 plus classes £4 each.

Danceworks, 16 Balderton Street, W1.
0171 629 6183

PINEAPPLE DANCE STUDIO   SW7/WC2

Debbie Moore's Pineapple dance centres offer over 180 classes a week from beginner to professional standard. Covent Garden is the main dance branch; classes include classical ballet, jazz, American funk and modern soul, plus some aerobic and stretch classes. At Kensington, the smaller branch, the classes are more geared towards workout with step and slide, cardio-funk and body sculpting on offer.

Covent Garden also has a treatment centre offering aromatherapy, acupuncture, massage and reflexology as well as a Pilates-based body maintenance studio.

Daily membership: £4, plus class fee. Annual membership: £65, plus class fee. Concessions.

Pineapple, 7 Langley Street, Covent Garden, WC2.
0171 836 4004
38 Harrington Road, SW7.
0171 581 0466

CLUB AEROBICS

Club aerobics is geared towards workout enthusiasts who also enjoy dancing and clubbing.

Nightclubs make excellent workout venues with good sprung floors and decent sound systems. Organizers hire a club for the evening, dispense with the usual inducements of alcohol and cigarettes and instead lay on three 45-minute workouts with live DJs mixing the music and a PA or fitness demonstration between sessions.

Debbie Trotter of Clubland Aerobics, who uses venues like the Electric Ballroom and top London club DJs like Fat Tony, says: 'At the gym you do your class and go. We're offering more than just a workout; people come along for an evening of fun, fitness and entertainment.'

However, it isn't just for the rave generation; all ages from 16 to 60 come along, including men apparently no longer intimidated by the wall to wall mirrors and bright lights of the average aerobics studio.

For details of club aerobics nights in venues like The Fridge and the Electric Ballroom contact:

Definition 0171 228 5628
Clubland Aerobics 0171 266 4816

Usual cost £8 in advance or £10 on the door.

• For Dance classes see page 202.

YOGA

THE LIFE CENTRE   W8

Located just off Kensington Church Street, the Life Centre is one of the newest natural health centres in London, offering a full range of therapies, and particularly specializing in yoga.

A full programme of classical hatha yoga classes runs every weekday from 7.45am through to 8pm (9.30–6.30 on Saturdays) and the range includes classes for beginners, pregnant women, and children, as well as wake-up and relaxation classes and more advanced programmes.

The Life Centre, 15 Edge Street, W8.
0171 221 4602

YOGA THERAPY CENTRE

Yoga therapy differs from traditional ancient Yoga in that it is seen as a healing science. The body's own natural healing resources are promoted through the respiratory system with gentle postures and breathing exercises. It is tailored for particular conditions such as lower back pain, asthma, diabetes and hypertension.

Introductory classes usually last about an hour and a half and exercise sheets are given out to enable you to work on them at home.

Yoga Therapy Centre, Royal London Homeopathic Hospital, WC1.
0171 833 7267

• Other yoga specialists:

Iyengar Yoga Institute, 223a Randolph Avenue, W9.
0171 624 3080
Yoga Biomedical Trust, 156 Cockerell Road, Cambridge, CB4 3RZ.
01223 67301

SWIMMING POOLS

London can boast some of the most architecturally impressive swimming pools in the country, including many with Olympic-standard facilities. Here is a selection of the most interesting and best-equipped.

HIGHBURY POOL   N5

This modern 25-metre pool (there is also a smaller children's pool) carries a full range of classes as well as an extensive lane-only programme for those who want to improve their swimming skills. Women-only sessions are on Tuesday evening from 6.30pm.

Swim £2.00 Adults, £1.00 Children

Highbury Pool, Highbury Crescent, N5.
0171 704 2312 (Recorded opening times 0171 226 4186)

IRONMONGER ROW BATHS   EC1

Built in the 1930s, the Ironmonger Row baths has a 30-metre swimming pool. You can just have a swim or combine it with a Turkish bath or a sauna.

Swim £1.90. Turkish baths £9. Women's days at the Turkish baths, Mon, Wed, Fri and alternate Sundays. Men only the other days.

Ironmonger Row Baths, 1–11 Ironmonger Row, EC1.
0171 253 4011

LATCHMERE LEISURE CENTRE   SW11

The Latchmere, with its huge pool, wave machine and slide, is heaven for children. Adults are catered for too, with swimming lanes and adults-only swimming times. There is also a teaching pool.

Swim £1.90.

Latchmere Leisure Centre, Burns Road, SW11.
0181 871 7470

MARSHALL STREET LEISURE CENTRE   W1

In the heart of Soho, the Marshall Street baths, built in 1931, has a lovely old-fashioned pool which has been beautifully refurbished, showing off the Sicilian white marble surround. There is a second baths at the back which is now derelict.

The baths offer swimming and lifesaving classes, sauna and steam, and weight-training facilities.

Swim £2.25.

Marshall Street Leisure Centre, Marshall Street, W1.
0171 287 1022

POOLS ON THE PARK   Twickenham

The complex at Richmond includes a laned indoor pool, teaching pool and an outdoor pool, which is open from April to December. Other facilities include a sauna and steam room, dance studio and the newly built Park Health and Fitness club. The club has separate membership, starting at £280 per annum, plus £80 joining fee, which includes use of the fitness club, swimming pool, health suite and dance studio.

Among those teaching exercise classes is workout guru, Carolan Brown.

Swim £2.40.

Pools on The Park, Old Deer Park, Richmond, Surrey. TW9 2SF.
0181 940 0561

PORCHESTER CENTRE   W2

An elegant relic from the 1920s, the Porchester Centre remains most famous for its Turkish baths, now incorporated into the Porchester Spa.

A day at the spa (different days are dedicated to different sexes) allows you to use the 3 interconnected hot rooms – hot, very hot and excruciating – the Russian steam rooms, plunge pool, sauna and jacuzzi and relaxation areas. The cost of £15.40 also entitles you to use the swimming pool in the Porchester Centre. Unfortunately, paying for a swim doesn't admit you to the Turkish baths.

A huge range of beauty treatments including seaweed wraps, oxygenating facials, body scrubs and massage are available as extras.

The main Porchester Centre also has a gym with cardiovascular equipment and free weights and runs a variety of exercise classes from step to ski fitness.

Membership of the centre and the spa is also available.

Porchester Centre, Queensway, W2.
0171 792 2919

OPEN AIR SWIMMING

Although appealing to many of us only on the most sultry of summer days, the open air pools in London do good business all year round. Those who indulge swear by the invigorating benefits of a swim in water that is only 42 degrees!

BROCKWELL PARK LIDO   SE24

In their heyday there were over 30 London lidos, but the number has gradually diminished, with 9 lidos, including Finchley, Beckton, Victoria Park and Kennington, having been closed down in the last decade. Some have been demolished, others lie derelict. However, the encouraging story of Brockwell Park Lido should bring hope to any lover of these Thirties water palaces.

  The lido, the last remaining open air pool in the borough, was closed down by Lambeth council in 1991. A group of local residents and lido users started a petition, collecting over 4,500 signatures, and eventually persuaded the council to reconsider the lido's future.

  In January 1994 a 7-year lease was given to Paddy Castledine and Casey McGlue, a former manager at the lido and a sports officer, to re-open the lido. The Lido is open May to September but other activities such as yoga and aerobic classes, sports injury room, holistic centre and café ensures the venue is open all year.

Swim £2.00 weekdays £2.50 weekends. Open May–Sep 7am–7pm daily.

Brockwell Park Lido, Dulwich Road, SE24.
0171 274 3088

HAMPSTEAD MIXED BATHING POND   N6/NW3

There are 3 bathing ponds on the heath: 1 mixed, 1 for men only and 1 ladies only. Swimming at all 3 is free. The mixed pond is at its most popular in the summer. The pools are all hidden by trees, giving a real feel of swimming in the middle of the country. All 3 pools are very deep and not for the inexperienced swimmer although there are attendants on duty.

  May–Sep 10am–4.30pm.

Mixed Pond, East Heath Road, NW3.
0171 435 2366

HIGHGATE MEN'S POND N6

Cut off from view by green corrugated
iron, the men's pond has a reputation as a
gay haunt and in the summer is packed
with men sunbathing naked,
contravening an old heath regulation.
 Apr–Sep 7.30am–8.30pm.
 Oct–Mar 7am–3pm.

Highgate Pond, Millfield Lane, N6.
0181 340 4044

KENWOOD LADIES POND N6

Protected by thick undergrowth, the
women's pond attracts redoubtable old
ladies prepared to endure the weeds and
slime. There is also a small changing hut
with a shower.
 8am–dusk all year.

Kenwood Pond, Millfield Lane, N6.
0181 340 5303

THE OASIS WC2

The open air pool at the Oasis is known as something of a summer pick-
up joint and on hot days does get very over-crowded. Above the pool
there is an upper deck where you can tan yourself and observe the
swimmers below.

 There is also an indoor pool, which has swimming courses, and water
aerobics, a squash court and gym.

Swim £2.30.

Oasis Sports Centre, 32 Endell Street, WC2.
40171 831 1804

TOOTING BEC LIDO SW16

One of the most attractive places to swim in London, the Lido was built
in 1906 and still retains its original features – changing rooms with
brightly painted wooden doors and a fountain at one end.

 The pool, reputedly one of the largest outdoor swimming places in
Europe, is vast – 90 metres by 35 metres – and even in the height of
summer there is still room to swim. There is also a children's play area
and a café.

Easter–Oct 6.30am–7.30pm. Oct–Easter (members only) 7am–5pm.

Tooting Bec Lido, Tooting Bec Common, SW16.
0181 871 7198

SPORT

Sport is not only healthy but it can also provide a fun night out or be a good way of meeting like-minded people.

There is an excellent range of clubs and facilities in London for nearly all types of sport, including: archery, billiards and snooker, bowls, cricket, croquet, fencing, fishing, football, gymnastics, hockey, lacrosse, netball, ice-skating, roller-skating, rowing, rugby, sailing, skating, squash, table tennis, tenpin bowling, volleyball, water-skiing and weight-lifting.

If you are looking for something different to do for a birthday treat or for a night out with friends, why not strap on your skates, climb into a go-kart, dally at the dog track or try your aim at tenpin bowling? (For a group of 10 or more you can often get special deals or group discounts. Ring ahead for special offers.)

If, on the other hand, your New Year's resolution is to fight the flab and get fit, tuition and training in all sports is widely available. So check out local opportunities through the Sports Council (0171 388 1277) or Sportsline (0171 222 8000).

AMERICAN FOOTBALL

American football is now immensely popular in Britain and we have 2 professional teams, the London Monarchs and Edinburgh Claymore. The amateur teams for the over-18s are represented by 70 senior league teams of which the Olympians are the reigning European Club Champions for the second year running, and 29 college clubs from the Universities and Colleges.

The season both for the professionals and senior leagues starts in April and goes through to August – the colleges on the other hand have just started to play during the winter term.

Whether you want to play or watch here are some useful numbers:

National Football League of America 0171 629 1300
Senior League Fixtures 01205 363522

FOOTBALL

Football is by far the most popular British sport from the point of view of both players and spectators, and all 92 clubs attract a loyal following.

The season is from August to May with league matches played every Saturday and most Bank Holidays. There are international matches and the League Cup final – always held at Wembley – but the biggest match has to be the FA Cup final at Wembley Stadium, held in May.

The cheapest way to get information on the different matches is to go along to your local sports centre, which will be able to provide you with details of all the clubs in your particular area. Both the Football Association and the London Football Association publish handbooks which list all the clubs and cost £6 and £10 respectively.

There is also a referees' training course available if you think that this is your particular calling on the sports field!

• Unless you know what you are doing, seats provide a better view than the terraces.

• For information on:
Professional leagues and clubs:
The Football Association, 16 Lancaster Gate, W2.
0171 262 4542

Local amateur leagues and clubs:
London Football Association, Aldworth Grove, SE13.
0181 690 9626

Referees' training courses:
65a Allfarthing Lane, SW18.
0181 870 6958

GOLF

There is one golf course right in the middle of London (below) but on the whole both municipal and private courses are on the outskirts of London. Details and maps of all the courses in around London can be found in the *Daily Telegraph Golf Course Guide* (£9.99).

THE REGENTS PARK GOLF AND TENNIS SCHOOL   NW1

The world's oldest golf school, Regent's Park was founded in 1908 by the then Prince of Wales, who had found himself short of somewhere to practise in central London.

The emphasis is on teaching and the school has a driving range with 11 bays, which are floodlit for night practice. Lessons are about £14 per half hour for members, £18 for non-members, and there is a members' lessons package of 6 half-hour lessons for £70.

The 3 tennis courts, 1 floodlit, are available for hire and you can book tennis lessons.

Other facilities include video diagnosis for both golf and tennis, a pro shop and a computerized club-fitting centre.

Golf club membership from £60; no membership needed for tennis.

The Regent's Park Golf and Tennis School,
Outer Circle, Regents Park, NW1.
0171 724 0643

SPRINGFIELD PARK   SW17

The 9-hole course at Springfield Park is a relative newcomer to the London golfing scene but has become popular since its opening in late 1992.

It costs roughly £5 for non-members to play a round in winter (£7 at weekends) and £7 (£12 at weekends) in summer. Coaching is available at £10 per half hour.

The club also hosts frequent sessions of night golf (open to non-members), an import from the USA where it is extremely popular. Luminous golf balls and illuminated flags help matters, but as you can't see your feet or the club it takes some getting used to.

Full membership of the club is in the region of £1100.

Springfield Park Golf Club, Burntwood Lane, SW17.
0181 871 2468

• Non-membership golf clubs:

Highgate Golf Club, Denewood Road, N6.
0181 340 1906

Lee Valley Golf Centre, Lea Bridge Road, E10.
0181 539 1633

Picketts Lock Centre, Picketts Lock Lane, N9.
0181 803 3611

• For tuition only there is a golf club in All Hallows Lane where the professional, George Robb, teaches, and there are lots of facilities to help you improve your game. Membership is £100.

St Andrew Golf Club, All Hallows Lane, EC4.
0171 626 7107

HOCKEY

With the success of the men's and women's teams in the recent Olympic Games, hockey has now become both fashionable and popular. The season is from September to May and details of the national league games are advertised in the national and local press. In addition London has a large number of clubs, all of whom are affiliated to the Hockey Association and a request to them will provide you with a current list.

• London's senior clubs are:

Hounslow, Chiswick Boat House, Duke's Meadows,
Great Chertsey Road, W4.
0181 994 9470

Indian Gymkhana, Feltham School, Browells Lane, Feltham.
0181 890 8882

Old Loughtonians, Luxborough Lane, Chigwell, Essex.
0181 504 7222

Southgate, Broomfield School, Sunningdale, off Wilmer Way, N14.
0181 361 2932

Surbiton, Sugden Road, Long Ditton, Surrey KT7 OAE.
0181 398 2401

Teddington, Teddington School, Broom Road, Teddington, Middlesex.
0181 977 0598

Willesden Sports Centre, Donnington Road, Willesden, NW10.
0181 459 6605

The officiating bodies of the sport are:

The Hockey Association, Norfolk House, 102 Saxton Gate West, Milton Keynes, Bucks MK9 2EP.
01908 241100

All England Women's Hockey Association, 51 High Street, Shrewsbury, Shropshire.
01743 233572

RIDING

London might not appear to offer many opportunities for horsemanship, but there are several very attractive locations in the royal parks where you can take lessons or saddle up for an accompanied hack.

STAG LODGE STABLES   Richmond

One of the most appealing riding stables is in Richmond Park, where Stag Lodge Stables offers adult group lessons, including a hack through the park for about £18 per hour at weekends or £17 per hour during the week. Private lessons cost approximately £14 for a half hour or £25 per hour.

There are children's group lessons and they also run their own pony club, the Red Riders club on Saturdays from 12.30pm to 2.30pm, which includes learning about pony care.

Rides can also be arranged on Wimbledon Common.

Stag Lodge Stables, Stag Lodge, Robin Hood Gate,
Richmond Park, SW15.
0181 546 9863

ROSS NYE'S HYDE PARK RIDING CLUB   W2

One of the most stylish places to ride has to be Hyde Park, where kings, queens, regiments and lesser mortals have been riding for centuries in a park devised for the 'singular comfort' of the monarch. Ross Nye's Hyde Park Riding Club has 16 horses and takes riders out every day except Monday (the horses' day off). They ride on the park's 6 miles of horse trails, including Rotten Row – a corruption of the original name, Route de Roi.

An hour-long instructional hack is about £20 – group riding lessons cost the same. Private lessons are more expensive. Hard hat and riding boots are supplied free of charge to beginners.

Ross Nye's is also headquarters to the Hyde Park Pony Club.

Hyde Park Riding Club (Proprietor Ross Nye),
8 Bathurst Mews, W2.
0171 262 3791

• Other useful numbers:

British Horse Society, North London, 14 Bigwood Road, NW11.
0181 458 1303

British Horse Society, East London, 67 Hollybush Hill, E11.
0181 989 3256

RUGBY UNION

Twickenham is the home of rugby union and all the important and international matches are staged there.

The rugby season runs from September to May and games are played every Saturday afternoon.

Whether you want to participate or just spectate the opportunities are endless and there is an abundance of clubs which will appreciate your support in either capacity. Tickets for the big international matches are almost impossible to come by unless you belong to a club but it is worth checking out the box office at Twickenham for their list of fixtures and ticket availability at the start of the season.

• The top London clubs include:

Askeans, 60A Broadwalk, Blackheath, SE3.
0181 856 1025

Blackheath, Rectory Field, Blackheath, SE3.
0181 858 1578

Harlequins, Stoop Memorial Ground, Craneford Way, Twickenham.
0181 892 0822

London Irish, The Avenue, Sunbury on Thames.
01932 783034

London Scottish, Richmond Athletic Ground,
Kew Foot Road, Richmond.
0181 332 2473

London Welsh, Old Deer Park, 187 Kew Road, Richmond.
0181 940 1604/2368

Richmond, Richmond Athletic Ground,
Kew Foot Road, Richmond.
0181 940 0397

Rosslyn Park, Upper Richmond Road, Prior Lane, SW15.
0181 876 1879

Saracens, Bramley Sports Ground,
Green Road, Southgate, London N14.
0181 449 3770

Wasps, Repton Avenue, Sudbury.
0181 902 4220

The officiating body for the sport is:

Rugby Football Union,
Rugby Road, Twickenham.
0181 892 8161

TENNIS

Many of London's parks have open air tennis courts in various states of repair. Some of the best are in Regent's Park and 2 of the more interesting places to play tennis are the Market Sports Centre in Spitalfields and The Islington Tennis Centre, where as well as 3 outdoor and 3 indoor courts, there are 3 mini-courts designed to encourage Wimbledon champions of the future.

The Lawn Tennis Association has produced a booklet, *Where to Play Tennis in London*, which gives a rundown of the facilities in each London borough and details of coaching available. (Free on receipt of a self-addressed envelope.)

All England Lawn Tennis Club, PO Box 98, Wimbledon, SW19.
0181 944 1066

Playing venues include:

Lawn Tennis Association, Palliser Road, W14.
0171 385 2366

Islington Tennis Centre, Market Road, N7.
0171 700 1370

London Indoor Tennis Club, Alfred Road,
Off Harrow Road, Westbourne Green, London W2.
0171 286 1985

Market Sports Indoor Tennis Centre,
Old Spitalfields Market Hall, Brushfield Street, E1.
0171 377 1300

Queens Club, Palliser Road, London W14.
0171 381 3301

Regent's Park Golf and Tennis School,
Outer Circle, Regent's Park, NW1.
0171 724 0643

Roehampton Club, Roehampton Lane, SW15.
0181 876 1621

• The Real Tennis headquarters is at the Queens Club.

• The Tennis Network is an organization designed to introduce tennis players to each other. You complete a simple application form detailing your standard of play and availability which will entitle you to receive details of potential playing partners in your area. Membership £15.00. For an application form, write to London Tennis Network, 195 Battersea Church Road, SW11 3ND.

WATERSPORTS

London Docklands offers over 400 acres of sheltered water, making it an ideal location for water sports. Numerous centres have opened up in the area, which, with the new extension to the Docklands Light Railway, is finally becoming more easily accessible to the rest of London.

ROYAL DOCKS WATERSKI CLUB E16

The only waterski club in the heart of London, the Royal Docks offers courses at all levels, plus jump, slalom, mono and tricks for the more experienced. All necessary equipment can be hired.

Royal Docks Waterski Club, Gate 16, King George V Dock, Woolwich Manor Way, E16.
0171 511 2000

PETER CHILVERS WINDSURFING E16

Peter Chilvers invented the windsurfer, building the world's first prototype boardsailor as a 12-year-old on Hayling Island in 1958.

Based at the Royal Victoria Dock, his club and school offers a 1-day Royal Yachting Association Level 1 course for around £35, which will teach the complete novice everything they need to know. Beginners can make some of their early mistakes on a sailboard simulator on the safety of dry land and all equipment can be hired.

The centre has a roped-off practise area and a shingle beach to launch from and the water is regularly checked by chemists.

The school also has a shop with a full range of new and second-hand equipment.

Peter Chilvers Windsurfing, Gate 5, Victoria Dock, Tidal Basin Road, Dock Road, E16.
0171 474 2500

SHADWELL BASIN PROJECT E1

The project offers a range of boating activities, including canoeing, sailing, dragon-boat racing and windsurfing, both within the 7-acre basin and on the tidal waters of the Thames. Other activities include sub-aqua training and angling.

The centre runs a good selection of courses, and can provide wetsuits for beginners.

Shadwell Basin Project, Shadwell Pierhead, Glamis Road, E1.
0171 481 4210

• Other watersport centres:

Jubilee Waterside Centre, Elm Village, 105 Camley Street, NW1. 0171 388 3451

Lee Valley Watersports, North Circular Road, Chingford, E4.
0181 531 1129

Surrey Docks Watersports Centre, Greenland Dock, Rope Street, off Plough Way, Rotherhithe, SE16.
0171 237 4009

Thames Young Mariners, Ham Fields, Riverside Drive, Richmond, Surrey.
0181 940 5550

MAJOR SPORTS GROUNDS

All of the following venues have created bookable tours to enable members of the public to see 'behind the scenes'.

CRYSTAL PALACE

The original Crystal Palace was built in 1851 in Hyde Park for the Great Exhibition of that year and was transferred to the present site in 1852–3. After a disastrous fire in 1936 it was rebuilt and has now become Britain's longest established athletics venue. It hosts a Grand Prix meeting every summer and the sports centre stages major championships in a range of activities from basketball to weightlifting, judo to diving.
Box Office open Mon–Fri 9.30am–5pm.

Crystal Palace, Ledrington Road, SE19.
0181 778 0131

LORDS CRICKET GROUND

Built in 1814, Lords Cricket Ground is the home of Marylebone Cricket Club (the MCC) and Middlesex County Cricket Club. County and international matches are a permanent fixture from April through to September.

Ticket and membership enquiries:
0171 289 8979

Lords Cricket Ground, St Johns Wood Road, NW8.
0171 289 1611

THE OVAL

Originally a market garden, the Oval was transformed into a cricket ground in 1845, and is the home of the Surrey County Cricket Club and the English international team. Matches are held from April through to September.

The Oval, Kennington, SE11.
0171 582 6660

TWICKENHAM

This is a very spacious ground which provides a venue for England's home international matches and finals of club, county and divisional competitions. The seating capacity is currently being increased to 75,000 and should be finalized by the end of the year.

Rugby Internationals: 0181 892 8161.
Twickenham, Rugby Road, Twickenham.
0181 891 4565

WEMBLEY

The Wembley Complex comprises an arena, stadium, conference centre and exhibitions halls.

The stadium seats 80,000 and has to be one of the world's most famous sporting grounds. It plays host to the FA Cup finals, the Rugby League Challenge Cup Final, and many other major international sporting events. There is also dog racing 3 nights a week. The stadium is London's foremost venue for megastar concerts but in truth it is too big and you normally end up staring at a video with the performers hardly visible in the distance. The acoustics are pretty dreadful as well.

At the arena you will find the Horse of the Year show, and lots of big sporting events including ice hockey, top level gymnastics, boxing and basketball. There are pop concerts on throughout the year; regular acts currently include Phil Collins, Take That, Wet Wet Wet, and Status Quo. During the winter months there are also ice-skating shows.

The conference centre carries a similar range of sports and music but the smaller seating capacity reflects a less starry line up.

Greyhound racing takes place every Monday, Thursday and Friday, starting at 7.30pm (see page 87) and there is a weekly Sunday market.

You can subscribe to a monthly mailing list for details of all the different events.

Box Office hours: Mon–Sat 9.30am–9pm Sun 10am–6pm.
Wembley Stadium, Empire Way, Wembley, Middlesex.
0181 900 1234 (24 hours)

WIMBLEDON

The home of the Wimbledon Lawn Tennis Championships. Tours are not available but you can visit the Wimbledon Lawn Tennis Museum.

Museum hours: Tues–Sat 10.30am–5pm Sun–2pm–5pm.

Closed Mondays, bank holidays, Fri, Sat and Sun prior to the Championships and throughout the Championships except for ticket holders.

Wimbledon Lawn Tennis Museum, Church Road, Wimbledon, SW19.
0181 946 6131

SOCIAL SPORTS

GO-KARTING

Many of the world's top racing drivers, Nigel Mansell and Alain Prost included, have been involved with karting at some point in their careers, but it really took off as a recreational sport in the early 1990s. In 1990 there were just 4 circuits in the country; now there are about 120.

Lightweight karts, 3cm above the ground, and powered by 5.5 horse-power engines, make 40mph feel a good deal faster and bends are named after those on the big circuits. All clothing and equipment is provided and there is a thorough briefing.

Much of the business comes from corporate events, the mix of fun and competition being most companies' idea of a perfect night out. Corporate packages vary between circuits but are usually organized to mirror a real grand prix as closely as possible, right down to the traditional champagne-spraying session for the champion.

The National Karting Association (01926 812550) was set up to regulate and inspect the circuits and can offer advice about the sport and details of your nearest circuit.

In all cases you need to pre-book sessions and opening times vary. Prices are only a guide and can vary depending on the time of day and the type of event. Call individual centres for full details.

ATLANTA RACEWAY   Croydon

The circuit has a bridge feature and computerized lap-testing. They also run open grand prix sessions and endurance races.
Practice sessions £12 for 15 minutes, £20 for half an hour.

Atlanta Raceway, 4 Peterwood Way, Croydon.
0181 688 4215

DAYTONA AND INDIANAPOLIS RACEWAYS   W12

The circuit here was designed by Damon Hill. They also have an Indianapolis Raceway, featuring Formula One replica cars for Indycar racing. Practice session £30 per person.

Daytona and Indianapolis Raceways, 54 Wood Lane, W12.
0181 749 2277

PLAYSCAPE PRO RACING   SW4/SW11

In addition to the adult sessions they run a cadet school on Saturday mornings for 8 to 12-year-olds which costs about £25.
Sessions: 9.30am–1pm 2pm–5.30pm 6pm–9.30pm. £37.50 per person.

Playscape Pro Racing, Clapham Kart Raceway, Triangle Place, SW4.
0171 498 0916
Their other branch is Battersea Kart Raceway, Hester Road, SW11.
0171 498 0916

RACEPRO   E16

An outdoor, fully floodlit circuit. Endurance races. Practice, plus briefing, £15 per half hour, £25 per hour.

Racepro, Gate 14, Royal Albert Dock Basin Southside. Gallions entrance, off Woolwich Manor Way. 0171 476 9572

SPITFIRE KARTING   Feltham

Open daily from 10am to 5pm for practice sessions. £10 for 15 minutes.

Spitfire Karting, Browells Lane, Feltham, Middlesex. 0181 893 2104

DOGS

A night out at the dogs tends to conjure up visions of *Minder*, cashmere overcoats and a whiff of spiv, but, like horse-racing, the dogs appeal to everyone and you can have a wonderful time watching the highly trained greyhounds in pursuit of the elusive hare.

The action comes fast and furious with a race every 15 minutes and 12 races in a meeting. Each race features 6 dogs, normally running over a 460-metre course. Betting is the same as at the horses: you can opt for a win or a place or choose a more complex trio or forecast.

Most of the grandstands have restaurants, so if you want to make a big night of it book a table to watch the racing over dinner. The Wimbledon Stadium has the Broadway Restaurant where you get a good view of the track plus a monitor on every table and a tote messenger to place your bets.

There are normally good deals on admission and food for parties of 10 or more who book in advance.

Meetings every Tues, Wed, Fri and Sat, starting at 7.30pm.

Wimbledon Stadium, Plough Lane, SW19. 0181 946 5361

• Other London Greyhound stadia (call for details of forthcoming meetings):

Catford Stadium, Ademore Road, SE26.   0181 690 2261
Hackney Stadium, Waterden Road, E15.   0181 986 3511
Walthamstow Stadium, Chingford Road, E4.   0181 531 4255
Wembley Stadium, Stadium Way, Wembley.   0181 902 8833

HORSE RACING

London has several racecourses within easy reach of the capital. The best-known events are Derby Day at Epsom in the first week of June, the Royal Ascot meeting later the same month, and the annual Boxing Day meeting at Kempton, which includes the King George VI Chase.

A great way to spend a warm summer's night is at an evening race meeting. Both the extremely pretty course at Sandown Park (take the train from Waterloo to Esher, journey time about half an hour) and the Kempton Park racecourse host evening meetings, as does Windsor race course. Call the courses for dates. (Epsom, Kempton Park and Sandown Park are all owned by United Racecourses and any one of them can send you the list of fixtures for all 3 courses.)

Ascot	01344 222211
Epsom	01372 726311
Kempton Park	01932 782292
Sandown Park	01372 463072
Windsor	01753 864726

ICE SKATING

BROADGATE   EC2

London's equivalent of New York's Rockefeller Plaza, Broadgate is the only open-air ice-rink in the country.

The circular rink is open 7 days a week throughout the winter season and is used by 40,000 skaters each year. The location is very attractive, set among the high-rise City buildings and overlooked by the Corney and Barrow wine bar.

Several evenings a week the ice is taken over to play broomball. The game originated in St Petersburg 200 years ago and is similar to ice hockey, but is played wearing trainers instead of skates.

Nov–March Mon–Fri 12noon–3pm Tues–Fri 4pm–7.30pm Sat–Sun 11am–1pm 2pm–4pm 5pm–7pm. Tuition available.

Broadgate Ice Rink, Eldon Street, EC2.
0171 588 6565

QUEENS ICE SKATING CLUB   W2

Trainee Torvills and Deans pack the ice at Queens alongside tourists and tentative first-timers. Since the much-lamented demise of the Richmond Ice Rink, Queens is now the most famous ice-skating venue in the capital.

There is also a tenpin bowling alley, video games centre, plus a new cafeteria.

Mon–Fri 10am–4.30pm and 7.30pm–10pm. Sat–Sun 10am–5pm and 7.30pm–10pm. Lessons also available.

Queens Ice Skating Club, 17 Queensway, W2.
0171 229 0172

• Other London ice rinks:

Alexandra Park Ice Rink, Wood Green, N22.
0181 365 2121

Lee Valley Ice Centre, Lee Bridge Road, Leyton, E10.
0181 533 3154

Sobell Ice Rink, Michael Sobell Sports Centre,
Hornsey Road, N7.
0171 609 2166

Streatham Ice Rink, 386 Streatham High Road, SW16.
0181 769 7771

LASER

Dubbed 'serious fun with a laser gun', zap game centres are springing up all over the capital. The 2 main players in the laser league are Quasar and Laser Quest, each with several centres in the London area. Quasar's centre at the Trocadero is billed as one of the largest in the world.

After an instruction video and briefing, you're fitted with a body pack and laser gun and let loose inside the zap zone. Dimly lit, smokey and usually designed with a futuristic theme, the arenas feature different levels, hiding places, flashing lights and loud music.

The aim is to avoid being zapped by your opponent while making sure you score some direct hits, shooting the harmless red ray of your laser gun to hit the discs on the front or back of their body packs. A direct hit disables your opponent's gun for a few seconds, enabling you to make your getaway. A computer printout at the end tells you who has triumphed.

Laser combat is suitable for anyone over the age of 8. The manager of Laser Quest at Raynes Park found that the customer who got most over-excited at her complex was a 70-year-old granny – supposedly accompanying her grandchildren for a treat – who had to be asked to stop running!

Don't wear white, unless you want to be a particularly easy target. Average cost is about £3–£5 for a game lasting around 30 minutes. Most centres are open from around 10am until 10pm, but it's wise to check opening times and special offers.

These are some of London's most popular laser locations:

Quasar

249–289 Cricklewood Broadway, NW2.	0181 208 4141
13 Junction Road, N1.	0171 281 5001
Frobisher Road, N8.	0181 348 9798
124 Ladbroke Grove, W10.	0171 243 8088
Trocadero Centre, 12 Coventry Street, W1.	0171 734 8151

Laser Quest

155 Clarence Street, Kingston, Surrey.
0181 974 8484

David Lloyd Centre, Bushey Road, Raynes Park, SW20.
0181 543 8057

London Road, Wembley, Middlesex.
0181 795 1000

Pulsar

34a–36, Kilburn High Road, NW6.
0171 328 0981

POLO

Elitist and exclusive it may be, but a summer afternoon spent watching polo can be very enjoyable.

There are 2 polo grounds within easy reach of London:

HAM POLO CLUB

Matches are played every Sunday afternoon from May to September, beginning at 2.30pm. Admission is free if you are on foot, £4–£5 for a car. The polo field is close to the river and the recently restored Ham House.

Ham Polo Club, Richmond Road, Petersham, Surrey.
0181 940 2090

GUARD'S POLO CLUB

The season runs from May to September with matches virtually every Saturday and Sunday afternoon at 3pm. Spectators are welcome. The biggest event is the Cartier Tournament in July, with a large selection of invited UK and US celebrities. Cars £10 each.

Guard's Polo Club, Smith's Lawn, Englefield Green,
Windsor, Berks.
01784 434212

• Bicycle Polo: Believe it or not Bicycle Polo is over 100 years old and in its heyday there were leagues all over the country! Its now enjoying a revival in London due to the efforts of 2 teams – Herne Hill and the Chelsea Paddlers. Competitors use a very basic bike, no gears, no brakes just a fixed-wheel transmission. Venues are Herne Hill Velodrome and Chelsea Paddlers, Hurlingham Park, Fulham.

Bicycle Polo Association of Great Britain
0181 656 9724

TENPIN BOWLING

Forget the complicated score cards and the rather grim interiors, Nineties-style bowling alleys have computerized scoring, brightly coloured bowls, MTV playing in the background and prefer to think of themselves as bowling centres.

Children are encouraged with special bumper lanes to improve their chances of scoring a strike and the atmosphere is bright and friendly.

Many of the centres keep very late hours and have bars and restaurants. Some, like the Lloyds Lanes Centres, also have private lanes for corporate hire.

Here are some of the best bowling bets:

GX SUPERBOWL

Daily 10am–midnight. 22 Lanes.

GX Superbowl, 15–17 Alpine Way, Beckton, E6.
0171 511 4440

HARROW SUPER BOWL

Sun–Thur 10am–10.45pm Fri–Sat 10am–11.45pm. 28 Lanes.

Harrow Super Bowl, Pinner Road, North Harrow, Middlesex.
0181 863 3491

HOLLYWOOD BOWL

Daily 10am–midnight. 38 Lanes.

Hollywood Bowl, Broad Lane, Tottenham, N17.
0181 365 1992

LEWISHAM BOWL

Mon–Fri 10am–11pm Sat–Sun 10am–midnight. 24 Lanes.

Lewisham Bowl, 11–29 Belmont Hill, SE13.
0181 318 9691

LLOYDS LANES

Daily 10am–midnight. 40 Lanes/20 Lanes.

Lloyds Lanes, 180 Carterhatch Lane, Enfield,
Middlesex. EN1 4LF.
0181 364 5178
Also: Bushey Road, Raynes Park, SW20.
0181 544 8020

ROWANS TENPIN BOWLING

Mon–Fri 10am–3am Sat 10am–6am. 24 Lanes.

Rowans Tenpin Bowling, 10 Stroud Green Road, N4.
0181 809 5511

STREATHAM MEGABOWL

Daily 10am–midnight (1am at weekends). 36 Lanes.

Streatham Megabowl, 142–144 Streatham Hill, SW2.
0181 671 5021

• The Trocadero's Lazer Bowl arcade has Bowlingo, a compact version of tenpin bowling which can be played by up to 4 people and is particularly good for kids.

The Trocadero, 13 Coventry Street, W1.
0171 734 3859

SELF-DEFENCE

Night-time safety is a continuing worry in any major city but London is safer than many and there are lots of ways to reduce your vulnerability. Opting not to go out at all in the evenings is not the answer!

Self-defence classes won't make you invincible – and the aim in any difficult situation should always be to find a way to escape – but they can help to increase self-confidence, which in turn can make you appear less vulnerable.

Here are some central London venues offering self-defence classes. Contact the extremely helpful, and free, Sportsline service for details of classes in your area: 0171 222 8000.

University of Westminster (Recreation Unit),
309 Regent Street, W1.
0171 911 5000 ext 2034

Seymour Leisure Centre, Seymour Place, W1.
0171 723 8019

London Central YMCA, 112 Great Russell Street, WC1.
0171 637 8131

Drill Hall Arts Centre, 16 Chenies Street, WC1.
0171 637 8270/ 0171 485 4619

Livingwell Premier Health Club, 4 Millbank, SW1.
0171 233 3579

Queen Mother Sports Centre, 223 Vauxhall Bridge Road, SW1.
0171 798 2125

Some forms of martial arts are also useful self-defence tools. Contact Sportsline or your local sports centre for details of judo, karate, aikido or ju jitsu classes.

• Don't take shortcuts down unlit side roads and passageways.

• Always have your doorkey in your hand before walking home. A rolled-up newspaper is also a confidence-giving 'weapon'.

• Send for the information pack from The Suzy Lamplugh Trust (see page 268).

RELIGION

Whether you have an interest in ecclesiastical architecture, a love of church music or a service to attend, London has something for everyone. Here are a selection of religious centres for a number of different faiths:

RELIGIOUS CENTRES

BAPTIST

Bloomsbury Central, 235 Shaftesbury Avenue, WC2.
0171 836 6843

BUDDHIST

Buddhapadipa Temple, 14 Calonne Road, SW19.
0181 946 1357

CATHOLIC

Brompton Oratory, Brompton Road, SW7.
0171 589 4811

Westminster Cathedral, Ashley Place, SW1.
0171 798 9055

CHRISTIAN SCIENTIST

Eleventh Church of Christ Scientist, 1 Nutford Place, W1.
0171 723 4572

CHURCH OF ENGLAND

St Paul's Cathedral, Ludgate Hill, EC4.
0171 248 2705

Westminster Abbey, Dean's Yard, SW1.
0171 222 5152

EVANGELICAL

All Souls Church, Langham Place, 2 All Souls Place, W1.
0171 580 3522

ISLAMIC

London Central Mosque, 146 Park Road, NW8.
0171 724 3363

East London Mosque, 84-98, Whitechapel Road, E1.
0171 247 1357

JEWISH

Liberal Jewish Synagogue, 28 St John's Wood Road, NW8.
0171 286 5181

West Central Liberal Synagogue, 109 Whitfield Street, SW1.
0171 636 7627

METHODIST

Westminster Central Hall, Storeys Gate, SW1.
0171 222 8010

Wesley's Chapel, City Road, EC2.
0171 253 2262

PENTECOSTAL

Assemblies of God Pentecostal Church, 141 Harrow Road, W2.
0171 286 9261

PRESBYTERIAN CHURCH OF SCOTLAND

Crown Court Church of Scotland, Russell Street, WC2.
0171 836 5643

QUAKERS

Religious Society of Friends, Friends House,
173-77 Euston Road, NW1.
0171 387 3601

UNITARIAN CHURCH

Rosslyn Hill Unitarian Church, Rosslyn Hill, NW3. 0171 435 3506.

• One of the best selection of new religious books and backlist titles is at Church House Bookshop, Great Smith Street, SW1.
0171 222 9011

CAROL SERVICES

Some of the most popular annual carol services take place at the following churches. Many also have other special Christmas events, including performances of the *Messiah*. Telephone for exact dates and details.

• St Bartholomew's, West Smithfield, EC1
(London's oldest church).
0171 606 5171

• St Martin-in-the-Fields, Trafalgar Square, WC2.
0171 930 1862

- St Paul's Cathedral, Ludgate Hill, EC4.
0171 248 2705

- Westminster Abbey, Dean's Yard, SW1.
0171 222 5152

- Southwark Cathedral, Montague Close, SE1.
0171 407 3708

Other special Christmas concerts take place at The Royal Albert Hall (0171 930 1862) and The Royal Festival Hall (0171 928 3002). Ring for details.

- For details of lunchtime concerts, see Music Section, p184.

CHURCH MUSIC AND CHOIRS

It is worth checking church notice boards for details of lunchtime and evening concerts but the following are noted for their high musical standards.

All Saints, Margaret Street, W1.
Brompton Oratory, Brompton Road, SW7.
Central Hall, Storeys Gate, SW1.
Christ Church, The Green, Southgate, N14.
St Alban' s Holborn, Brooke Street, EC1.
St Bride, Fleet Street, EC4.
St Giles, Cripplegate, Fore Street, EC2.
St James, Spanish Place, W1.
St Martin-in-the-Fields, Trafalgar Square, WC2.
St Mary the Virgin, Bourne Street, SW1.
St Mary the Virgin, 7 Elsworthy Road, NW3.
St Michael, The Grove, Highgate, N6.
St Michael-upon-Cornhill, Cornhill, EC3.
St Pauls Cathedral, Ludgate Hill, EC4.
St Peters, Mount Park Road, W5.
Southwark Cathedral, London Bridge, SE1.
Westminster Abbey, Dean's Yard, SW1.
Westminster Cathedral, Ashley Place, SW1.

SHOPPING
FASHION

London has always been one of the style-setting capitals of the world. In the Sixties it was the miniskirt and flower power, the Seventies had punk and throughout the Eighties everything was designer dressing and shoulder pads!

London's fashion scene is as exciting as ever. New young designer partnerships, like Flyte Ostell and Sonnentag Mulligan, bring a new generation of innovation, and even international designers like Christian Lacroix travel to London to pick up inspiration from our street fashions.

Despite the continuous burgeoning of new talent, there are also shops devoted to the fashions of previous eras, like The Cavern in London's East End, which specializes in Sixties and Seventies gear, and Dave Carroll's stall in Portobello market, which does a roaring trade to those leading the way in the current punk resurgence. Revivalists travel from all over the world to pick up second-hand punk Seditionaries clothes from Acupuncture in Soho, where an original pair of bondage trousers can now sell for £1,000. The fashions of today are the collector's items of the future.

So whatever your fashion weakness there is something for you somewhere in the capital – at a price! However, for the financially challenged it is possible to get the pick of the designer crop for less money – designer sale shops, dress agencies, sample sales, individual designers and second-hand – the ways are endless.

Here we put you on the inside of London's fashion track to make sure you get the best.

DESIGNER DRESS AGENCIES AND EXCHANGE SHOPS

Second-hand designer agencies or exchange shops provide a great way of designer-label dressing for less. More and more of these shops are opening up across London, each with its own individual character, reflecting both the location and the clientele it attracts.

The shops work by accepting clothes on a sale or return basis, deciding a price for each garment and then taking a percentage from the sale. The best shops are strict about the condition of the clothes and their age.

In the hard-pressed Nineties even those whose wardrobes boast nothing but designer labels can no longer afford to leave things languishing once they are bored with them and there are great bargains to be had. Designer clothes depreciate fast in value, but with the best in cut, design and fabric, their style doesn't diminish and the thrill of picking up a virtually new Jasper Conran jacket for a fifth of its original price is unbeatable!

Dress agencies are also a great way of getting rid of good-quality clothes that you may have become bored with, or of getting some money back on something that may have turned out to be a fashion mistake for you, but could be someone else' s dream buy. Most shops accept clothes by appointment only.

Some of the best agencies and shops are the following:

CATWALK W1

The owner of Catwalk, Carmen Boulton, used to deal in second-hand designer clothes from her home as a sideline to her day job in advertising. After being made redundant she went into the business full-time and opened her shop in Marylebone.

The clothes are a mixture of familiar names and the more exotic, and include Hermes and Jean Muir. The stock is not quite as fashionable as at some of the other shops, but there are some good buys to be had. Sample buys: Gucci silk blouse at £62 and a Ferregamo silk jacket at £45.

Mon, Wed, Fri 10.30am–7pm Thur 10.30am–8pm Sat 10.30am–5pm.

Catwalk, 42 Chiltern Street, W1.
0171 935 1052

THE DESIGNER SALE AND EXCHANGE SHOP W11

This blue-fronted shop, owned by Judy Bank and Lucy Lister, is located a few yards away from Portobello Road, in the heart of Notting Hill, and offers the range of current, up-to-the minute fashionable merchandise you would expect from its location.

The stock includes a wide range of clothes, from high-street labels such as Jigsaw and Next, to designers like Rifat Ozbek, Arabella Pollen and Jasper Conran. Most of the clothes are second-hand but there are also some samples and pieces from fashion shows.

There is a particularly good selection of leather jackets and all the clothes feel very current, with quite a few eccentric one-offs. They also stock shoes, hats and belts.

Sample buys: fabulous Jasper Conran leather jacket for £165 and a beautiful Timney Fowler printed silk shirt for £75.

Mon 12noon–6pm Tues–Sat 10am–6pm.

The Designer Sale and Exchange Shop, 61D Lancaster Road, W11.
0171 243 2396

DESIGNS NW3

Established 12 years ago by Dominique Cussen, Designs numbers Moschino, Hermes, Chanel, Donna Karan, Issey Miyake and Ralph Lauren among its top-notch labels.

Turnover is very quick with up to 700 garments coming in each week, many apparently from very well-known people. However, discretion is paramount at Designs and sellers are given a code number and never referred to by name in the shop.

The stock strongly reflects the seasons: March, April and May are the best times for the pick of spring and summer outfits, September and October for autumn and winter.

Sample buys: Christian Lacroix black suit £345, Kenzo linen jacket £85, Jaeger suit £85.
Mon–Sat 10–5.45pm. Thur closes 6.45pm.

Designs, 60 Rosslyn Hill, NW3.
0171 435 0100

THE DRESSER   W2

Sally Ormsby worked in the music business before opening her first designer second-hand shop 8 years ago. Many of her customers, both buyers and sellers, work in the music, media and PR industries, where a fast-turnover wardrobe is essential. This makes for an up-to-date selection.

Designers on sale include Comme des Garcons, Edina Ronay, Paul Costello and Jean-Paul Gaultier. Clothes are rarely more than 2 seasons old and there is an in-house alteration service.

The Dresser also stocks an extensive range of menswear downstairs, including Versace, Armani and Paul Smith.

Sample buys: Jasper Conran black and cream wool jacket £58, Ozbek silk skirt £38, Arabella Pollen gold silk dress £68, man's Comme des Garçons suit £95.
Mon–Sat 11am–5.30pm.

The Dresser, 10 Porchester Place, W2.
0171 724 7212

THE FROCK EXCHANGE   SW6

One of the oldest established dress agencies, the Frock Exchange has been running since 1972.

The stock changes very rapidly and features clothes from the high street as well as designer labels. Designers on the rails include Kenzo, Ben de Lisi and Jean-Paul Gaultier as well as Wallis, Marks and Spencer, and Next.

Frock Exchange is particularly good for working clothes, with good shirts, skirts and suits. Sample buys: Equipment shirt £18, Kenzo shirt £24.
Mon–Sat 10am–5.30pm.

Frock Exchange, 450 Fulham Road, SW6.
0171 381 2937

HANG UPS   SW10

Just over the bridge from Chelsea Football ground, Hang Ups has murals painted on the walls and the clothes are an eclectic mixture of designer and high street labels, with a wide selection of one-offs and quite a lot of club gear.

Sample buys: leather bikers jacket £40, Joe Casely Hayford Suit £65. There is also a good variety of shoes, with classic Charles Jourdan and satin pumps.

Downstairs is Dingly Dells, which sells a wide range of second-hand children's wear.

Mon–Fri 11am–6.45pm Sat 10.30am–6pm.

Hang Ups, 366 Fulham Road, SW10.
0171 351 0047

PANDORA SW7

Tucked away in a quiet street close to Harrods, Pandora is one of the largest of the second-hand designer shops and one of the most famous. Its rails are packed with over 5000 garments, including every designer name you can think of, among them Valentino, Thierry Mugler, Ferregamo and YSL. There are clothes to suit all age groups and the atmosphere is friendly and unsnobby.

Pandora is where Knightsbridge ladies bring their designer cast-offs and there are rails devoted solely to Chanel, Versace and Azzedine Alia. Each item is helpfully labelled with the exact details of the garment, its original cost price and often some very helpful additional information, e.g. 'Gianni Versace trouser suit, worn once for an hour'. Nothing is more than 2 years old and everything is dry-cleaned before going on display.

One of the most tempting rails is that devoted to Chanel. Sample buys: a fabulous short black evening dress £252, or a perfect cream wool boucle suit at £705 – still outrageous, but then remember it was £1600 originally. Other garments from around £40 upwards.

Mon–Sat 10am–5pm. Call to make an appointment if you want to sell.

Pandora, 16-22 Cheval Place, SW7.
0171 589 5289

For children:

CHEEKY MONKEYS W11

Nearly new clothes and equipment for children, from birth to 14 years. Designer kids' labels include Cacherel, Kenzo and Oililly, as well as Next and Hennes. New shoes include Start-Rite and Kickers. There is also a children' s hairdresser.

Mon–Fri 9.30am–5.30pm Sat 10am–5.30pm.

Cheeky Monkeys, 202 Kensington Park Road, W11.
0171 792 9022

• Second-hand children' s clothes and equipment can also be found at the following:

Change of Habit, 25 Abbeville Road, SW4.
0181 675 9475

Encore, 53 Stoke Newington Church Street, N16.
0171 254 5329

Swallows and Amazons, 91 Nightingale Lane, SW12.
0181 673 0275

For men:

L' HOMME DESIGNER EXCHANGE W1

Andrew Torz used to have stalls in Portobello and Camden, where demand for his second-hand menswear was so great that he decided it was time to open premises of his own.

The range of men' s suits, jackets and ties includes Paul Smith, Armani and Versace, with Armani suits starting at £180. He also stocks ties, shoes and waistcoats.

Mon and Fri 11am–6pm Tues–Thur 11am–7pm Sat 11am–5pm.

L' Homme Designer Exchange, 50 Blandford Street, W1.
0171 224 3266

• Other second-hand designer shops and agencies:

Anything Goes, 16 Webbs Road, SW11.
0171 924 6220
Butterfly, 3 Lower Richmond Road, SW15.
0181 788 8304
Change of A Dress, 1a Woodsome Road, NW5.
0171 482 1904
Distractions, 35 Monmouth Street, WC2.
0171 240 3807
Dressage, 299 New Kings Road, SW6.
0171 736 3696
Dress You Up, 190 Battersea Road, SW11.
0171 720 2234
Dynasty, 12A Turnham Green Terrace, W4.
0181 995 3846
Pzazz, 153 Church Road, Barnes, SW13.
0181 748 1094
Second Sinns, 34 Moreton Street, Pimlico, SW1.
0171 834 7485
Sharp Shop, 1a Hollywood Road, SW10.
0171 376 2137
Sign of The Times, 17 Elystan Street, SW3.
0171 589 4774
Upstairs Downstairs, 46 Chalcot Road, NW1.
0171 483 2499

• If you need some style guidance, Laurel Herman offers a free advisory service along with a choice of 5,000 nearly new designer outfits including shoes and accessories. Prices are reasonable and sizes range from 8 to 18. They employ 2 full-time fitters and service is by appointment only.

Laurel Herman, 18a Lambolle Place, NW3.
0171 586 7925

FACTORY SHOPS

Factory shops – manufacturers selling their brand goods at low prices straight to the public from their factory site – are a relatively recent phenomenon. The lack of a middleman means big savings for the customer.

Due to the space required, most of the factory shops are outside of London, but there are a couple of fashion shops in the London area working on the same principle.

THE BRAND CENTRE   Enfield

The Brand Centre aims to be a new concept in British retailing. By buying clothes direct from the manufacturer and then selling in an out-of-town, low-overhead warehouse, it aims to knock 20 to 50 per cent off normal retail prices. It stocks names like YSL, Christian Dior and Pierre Cardin for men; Mondi, Betty Barclay and Morgan for women, as well as small collections from top-of-the-range designers like Sara Sturgeon, Ally Capellino and Jasper Conran.

The surroundings – an industrial estate in Enfield – may not match up to the West End as a shopping backdrop and it is probably not worth making a special trip – the reductions are really only what you would expect in the virtually round-the-year sales in the main stores – but if you are out that way it is worthwhile dropping in.

Some typical price reductions have included Warners and Gossard underwear for around half price, Sara Sturgeon knitwear down from £145 to £99. Timberland boots about £5 off and Jasper Conran jackets reduced from £415 to £330. The Brand Centre also stocks shoes, handbags and children's clothes.

There is also a free on-site alteration service and a café.

Mon–Fri 10am–8pm Sat 10am–7pm Sun 10am–6pm.

The Brand Centre, Mollison Avenue, Enfield.
0181 805 8080

DISCOUNT DRESSING   W1/N12/ILFORD/BUCKHURST HILL

A team of buyers all over Europe purchase mostly European designer stock directly from the manufacturer. By cutting out importers and wholesalers they are able to charges prices between 50 per cent and 90 per cent below the normal retail outlets.

Brand names are not advertised (part of the suppliers agreement) and the stores have a policy that if you can find the same item of clothing cheaper elsewhere they will give you the outfit free!

Discount Dressing, 39 Paddington Street, W1.
0171 486 7230

Other branches:

16 Sussex Ring, Woodside Park, N12.   0181 343 8343
521 Cranbrook Road, Gants Hill, Ilford.   0181 518 3446
164 Queens Road, Buckhurst Hill, Essex.   0181 559 1025

IN-WEAR   SW18

Based at their Wandsworth factory, the In-Wear shop also stocks their

Part Two and Radio ranges and Matinique for men. There is a fairly even split between women's and men's clothing made up of samples and ends of lines. Sample buys: In-Wear cream jacket £45, black diaphanous shirt £20, Part Two burnt-orange tunic top £10, Matinique men's jacket £55, shirt £20.

Mon–Fri 10am–5pm Sat 10am–4pm.

In-Wear, 100 Garratt Lane, SW18.
0181 871 2155

NICOLE FARHI/FRENCH CONNECTION E3

Located at the company's manufacturing headquarters in the East End, this small shop has stocks of both the main Nicole Farhi line and her Diffusion range, including jackets, skirts, knitwear, shirts and dresses.

Also on sale is a good selection from Stephen Marks' cheaper French Connection label. In both cases the merchandise is a mixture of last season's collection and seconds. Reductions are around 40 per cent. Sample buys: Nicole Farhi long wrap-over wool skirt £75, full-length black wool crêpe dress £130, French Connection oatmeal wool sweater £25.

Tues 10am–3pm Thur 11am–6.30pm Fri 10am–5.30pm Sat 10am–3pm.

Nicole Farhi/French Connection, 75–83 Fairfield Road, E3.
0181 981 3931

T.K. MAXX Hatfield

T.K. Maxx have brought their successful US off-price retailing to the UK. The Galleria's no-frills shopping warehouse environment offers famous brand men's and women's fashions as well as lingeries, accessories, shoes, gifts, home goods and kitchenware for 20 per cent to 60 per cent less. The men's fashionwear is particularly good.

T.K. Maxx, The Galleria, Comet's Way, Hatfield, Herts.
01707 26006

• Also worth trying:

Burberry, 29–53 Chatham Place, E9.
0181 985 3344

DESIGNER SALES

DESIGNER WAREHOUSE SALES N1

There are several types of designer sales but the biggest are the Designer Warehouse Sales which take place over a weekend 5 times a year each for both the women's and men's sales.

The organizers work with between 75 and 80 designers who supply whatever stock they may have available, including ends of ranges, samples and stock supplied to shops that have subsequently gone into liquidation.

Among the designers whose clothes you can find are Betty Jackson,

Ally Capellino, Bella Freud, Artwork, Nicole Fahri and Sara Sturgeon for women, and Christopher New and Joe Casely Hayford for men. Expect to pay around a third of shop prices, with stock ranging from £2 up to about £200.

The sales always take place at the same venue and if you contact the organizers they will put you on the mailing list to keep you informed of the dates of the next sale. Admission is £2 to each sale.

Once a year, usually at the end of October there is also a fabric sale, with fabric from the same range of designers on sale from 50p per metre.

Usual opening times for the sales: Fri 10am–8pm Sat 10am–6pm Sun 11am–5pm.

The Designer Warehouse Sale, The Worx, 45 Balfe Street, N1.
0171 704 1064

DESIGNER SALE ROADSHOW   NW1

Run 4 times a year, the Designer Sale Roadshow was started 4 years ago by Elaine Foster who used to work in PR for Jasper Conran.

The sale features samples, ends of lines and leftover stock from a host of young designers including Rifat Ozbek, Xavier Foley, Sonnentag Mulligan, No Such Soul and The Duffer of St George.
Prices from £5 with reductions of up to 80 per cent on both the women's and menswear.

Admission £2 to each sale. Contact the organizers to be put on the mailing list. Sale days Fri, Sat, Sun.

Designer Sale Roadshow, Blank Space Studios, 10a Belmont St, NW1.
0171 226 7437

LONDON DESIGNER SALE   SW7

The London Designer Sale runs 4 times a year, in March, May, September and November, and organizer Francesca Eggling says she aims to 'appeal to all ages, all sizes and all pockets', with prices ranging from £15 to £350 and sizes from 6 to 20.

Clothes are a mixture of big names and less well-known designers and there are also handbags, belts, shoes and jewellery. The sales take place in The Polish Hearth Club in South Kensington, and entrance to each sale is £2. To put your name on the mailing list, ring 081 670 4745.

Polish Hearth Club, 55 Princes Gate, SW7.
0171 589 4670

SAMPLE SALES

Many of the big designers, usually based in Soho, hold sample sales from time to time. These are sometimes advertised in the *Evening Standard,* but it is also worth writing to your favourite designer to ask if they have a sample sale coming up. Most operate on a mailing list, but once you've been to one sale you will normally be circulated.

This is where the fashion cognoscenti tend to pick up the big bargains and those in the know make sure they are there for the first hour on the first day when the real scrum takes place. The clothes hang on rails around the room and there are rarely any changing rooms. Payments are usually cash and cheque only – no credit cards.

JASPER CONRAN W1

Sample sale twice yearly. Fantastically well-tailored suits, dresses, jackets etc.

Jasper Conran, 12 Great Marlborough Street, London W1.

PAUL COSTELLO W1

Sample sales are held twice yearly. Costello, along with current British Designer of the Year John Rocha, has put Ireland firmly on the fashion design map. Great Irish design; timeless classics.

Paul Costello, 76 Wells Street, W1.

NICOLE FAHRI W1

French-born Nicole Fahri creates elegant, wearable clothes, which her customers find still look current 10 years on.

Nicole Fahri, 16 Foubert's Place, W1.

FENN WRIGHT AND MANSON W1

This company creates beautiful silk separates and knitwear.

Fenn Wright and Manson, Moray House, 23–31 Great Titchfield Street, W1.

GHOST W10

There is an annual sale of the current year's spring/summer and autumn/winter collections each December.

Ghost, The Chapel, 263 Kensal Road, W10.

BEN DE LISI W1

This designer's speciality is wonderful evening wear.

Ben de Lisi, 6a Poland Street, W1.

PERMANENT SALES

DESIGNER SALE STUDIO SW3

Stylishly situated on the King's Road, the Sale Studio specializes in Italian designers and operates by buying cancelled orders and over-production direct from the designers' own factories in Italy. Clothes are usually from the current or previous season.

The cream of Italian designers are featured, including Byblos, Krizia, Complice and Romeo Gigli, with Armani and Versace also represented. There is a menswear department downstairs.

Sample buys: Complice suit, full price £633, sale studio price £275; Byblos trousers, full price £175, sale studio price £80.

Designer Sale Studio, 241 King's Road, SW3.
0171 351 4171

VIVIENNE WESTWOOD   W1

Our most influential designer, Westwood has her own discount shop
in Conduit Street, which sells a mixture of clothes from her past 4
collections, including her inimitable corsets. Expect to save around 40
per cent on the original price.

Vivienne Westwood, 40–41 Conduit Street, W1.
0171 439 1109

BROWNS   W1

The basement at top designer outlet Browns in South Molton Street
houses a permanent reduction room where last season' s unsold stock
from designers like Comme des Garçons, Donna Karan and Romeo
Gigli is sold at around 60 per cent off.

Browns, South Molton Street, W1.
0171 491 7833

FASHION COLLECTIVES

The original fashion collective – really just meaning lots of designers
housed together under one roof – was probably Kensington market,
which has been around since the 1960s and has reflected every street
style, from hippy to punk.

More recently, other collectives have sprung up, usually associated
with young designers and featuring street fashions. Notable are Hyper
Hyper, also in Kensington, and the Bluebird Garage (formerly The
Garage) on the King' s Road.

The latest recruit to the fashion collective family is The Chelsea
Collections, a rather upmarket example of the breed featuring 10
young designers with a particular emphasis on evening wear and
modern classics.

BLUEBIRD GARAGE   SW3

Home to the rave generation, The Bluebird Garage, now rumoured to
be owned by Mark Knopfler, stocks a wide range of young designers
and brand-name club clothes. Shoppers here know the names that
matter now.

There are around 50 stalls in the former ambulance station,
featuring names like Stussy, Dolce Vita, Diva and Junior Gaultier. The
clothes are in the main well priced.

Bluebird Garage, 350 King' s Road, SW3.
0171 352 7215

THE CHELSEA COLLECTIONS   SW3

Rather a different animal to its collective brothers and sisters, The
Chelsea Collections stands on the same parade of Fulham Road shops
that houses top British designer Amanda Wakeley.

The look here is far less street, and more exclusive couture house,
with 10 resident designers showing their wares within the marble and
gilt portals.

The Chelsea Collections was opened by Joyce O' Regan and Laura Jamieson, a designer herself, with the aim of showcasing up-and-coming new designers, including Maria Grachvogel, Paola Kovacz, Ed Bentley Baker and Christine Hammond. Milliner, Rachel Trevor-Morgan, also has space and there is a selection of clothes from Vivienne Westwood.

It remains to be seen whether the collective idea will work as well in this sector of the fashion market as it has in the more street-fashion oriented collectives.

The Chelsea Collections, 90 Fulham Road, SW3.
0171 581 5792

HYPER HYPER W8

Hyper Hyper opened 10 years ago and in that time has been a launch pad for designers like Pam Hogg and Ghost.

Owned by businesswoman Loren Gordon (whose company also owns Kensington Market and used to own the Bluebird Garage when it was just The Garage), Hyper Hyper now has its own label line as well as stocking the creations of over 70 designers including Rina da Prato, No Such Soul, Signs of the Times and Sue Rowe.

The set-up is less basic than at The Bluebird Garage and there is much to covet, whether you want to be at the front end of a fashion trend or a more subtle reflection. Hyper Hyper shows no sign of slipping from its secured place as a house of innovation.

Hyper Hyper, 26–40 Kensington High Street, W8.
0171 937 6964
Hyper Hyper (own label shop), 131–133 King' s Road, SW3.
0171 352 6340

KENSINGTON MARKET W8

At various times in the last 30 years the axis of fashion has turned on Kensington Market: flares and loons in the early Seventies, bondage trousers and safety pins for punk in '76 and the work of designers like David Holah of Body Map and the Littman sisters of English Eccentrics in the early Eighties.

Now the market seems to be going through one of the phases where tourist tat seems to dominate everything else, and design is quite thin on the ground. There are, however, some stalls still worth a look, like Western Styling for their cowboy boots, and Rock-a-Cha, where you can find Fifties suits.

Kensington Market, 49–53 Kensington High Street, W8.
0171 938 4343

PAUL SMITH W1

Paul Smith' s classic menswear designs can be bought at great reductions at his well-stocked constant sale shop, tucked away just behind South Molton Street.

Suits reduced from £650 to £295, trousers from £29, jeans from £19 and jackets from £69. Also shoes, belts and accessories.

Paul Smith, 27 Avery Row, W1.
0171 493 1287

SOULED OUT

W10/W1

Souled Out offers easy, alternative glamour rather than couture chic! With more than 100 young designers represented, styles range from recycled classic Seventies attire to new club-kitsch design.

A concession has opened at Top Shop, Oxford Circus with nothing costing more than £100.

Souled Out, Unit 25, Portobello Green Arcade, 281 Portobello Rd, W10.
0181 964 1121
and Top Shop, Oxford Circus, W1.
0171 636 7700

BEST FASHION SHOPPING STREETS

NEWBURGH STREET

W1

Located in the rather artificially named 'West Soho', Newburgh Street boasts some of the best and most innovative fashion names in London. Helen Storey, Pam Hogg, John Richmond and Junior Gaultier all have outlets here.

BROMPTON CROSS

SW3

Another artificial creation, Brompton Cross is really the junction of the Fulham and Brompton Roads. The delights on offer include Joseph and The Conran Shop and it's easy to see why the area's nickname is Amexville.

Nearby is Betty Jackson's shop and the designer delights of Walton Street and Draycott Avenue.

KENSINGTON HIGH STREET

W8

Names include Jigsaw, Hobbs, Pied a Terre, Hyper Hyper and Red or Dead and celebrity mums can be seen eyeing up the charming children's clothes at Trotters, owned by former Sock Shop supremo Sophie Mirman.

Check out Amazon at 1–22 Kensington Church Street – 10 floors of fashion, where names include Nicole Fahri, Equipment, Joseph and Soap Studio. They seem to have a nearly permanent sale, always with great bargains.

FLORAL STREET

WC2

French fashion stars Nicole Fahri and Agnes B. have shops here, but Floral Street is really Paul Smith Row, with his menswear at several outlets and the long-awaited Paul Smith Women at no. 40.

ST CHRISTOPHER'S PLACE, (through South Molton Street)

W1

Start off at Whistles in St Christopher's Place, then work your way down via The Hat Shop and Mulberry. Cross Oxford Street and join up with South Molton Street for the various Browns shops, including the new (and cheaper) Browns Own Label. Try Agatha for stylish French jewellery. Turn left at the end of South Molton Street for Fenwicks in Bond Street – fabulous for accessories, the best designers and the new Joe' s restaurant, beloved by *Vogue* journalists from nearby Conde Nast publishing HQ.

INDIVIDUAL DESIGNERS AND TAILORS

Most of us can only dream about the joys of couture outfits, but there are a number of young designers who have struck out on their own with small shops, and who will make up their designs to your individual size as well as selling off the peg.

KATHARINE BIRD   SW11

After graduating from the London College of Fashion, Katharine Bird sold her designs from a unit in Hyper Hyper for 6 years before opening her own shop in Battersea 4 years ago.

Her aim of creating young classic designs is reflected in the simple cut of her suits, jackets and dresses, and in her use of pure fabrics: silks, wool and linens.

Any of the designs on display can be made to measure. Skirts are from £75, jackets £150 and a full-length green velvet evening dress is £150. The shop also stocks complementary designers like Fenn Wright and Manson and Sara Sturgeon.

Katharine Bird, 20 Battersea Rise, SW11.
0171 228 2235

TWICE THE SIREN   SE1

Tucked away behind Waterloo Station amongst the market stalls in Lower Marsh is Caroline Scott's stylish shop, which she opened 3 years ago to augment her flourishing Camden market stall.

She works mostly in silks and velvet and her designs include a classic range of simple, well-cut, stylish dresses and jackets which are augmented by a more seasonal collection. The Thai silk fitted dresses would be a particularly versatile addition to any wardrobe.

The shop also gives house room to a hat designer, shoe designer (see below) and a hand-picked collection of Egyptian and Indian jewellery.

Twice the Siren, 28 Lower Marsh, SE1.
0171 261 0025

• For more evening and wedding orientated fashion, try Prudence Wright, 21a Upper Tachbrook Street, SW1.
0171 932 0880

SHOES

CLAIRE NORWOOD   EC1

Claire Norwood is a bespoke shoemaker and proud owners of her creations swear by their comfort! Commissions take on average 4 to 6 weeks and prices range from around £110 to £250 depending on whether it's a shoe or boot and the detail required.

Claire Norwood, 398 St John Street, EC1.
0171 837 2355

• Miriam Gribble's work is currently shown at Twice the Siren.
0181 567 2493

VINTAGE CLOTHES SHOPS

Treasure troves of potential delights, vintage clothes shops combine the thrill of the antiques rummage with the pleasure of acquiring something new to wear.

For creating an individual style, making a statement or simply buying something from an age when cut and fabric really mattered, the best vintage clothes shops are unmatched.

CORNUCOPIA   SW1

It would be impossible to calculate just how many garments are crammed into Cornucopia. Every single rail is jammed, clothes hang on racks from the ceiling, and hats, bags, shoes and jewellery are all squeezed in to every available space.

Almost every era is covered and you could spend hours inside this dark shop toying with, for example, silver platform shoes at £15, a white sequin minidress at £25, or Twenties beaded evening gowns.

Mon–Sat 11am–6pm.

Cornucopia, 12 Upper Tachbrook Street, SW1.
0171 828 5752

DOLLY DIAMOND'S   W11

The real Dolly Diamond does exist and set up her eponymous shop in 1993 after running a stall in Covent Garden for many years.

Fashions from the Twenties onwards make up the stock and are acquired from contacts all over the UK and abroad. The high-quality garments range from feminine Forties day and evening dresses, silk slips and camiknickers up to Seventies skinny-rib jumpers. There are also traditional classic English styles for men.

Among the gems on offer were a blue Fifties lace jacket for £35, black wool Fifties coat with Persian Lamb trim for £125 and a beautiful green satin full-length evening gown with embroidered bodice for £85. The shop also sells bags and jewellery.

Mon–Sat 10am–6.30pm.

Dolly Diamond' s, 51 Pembridge Road, W11.
0171 792 2479

THE CAVERN   E1

Specializing in Sixties and Seventies gear, The Cavern features such time-warp items as Afghan coats, flares and platform soles for both men and women.

Psychedelic and flower-power prints are everywhere and during last year's Seventies revival, business was especially brisk. Almost all the stock is brand new, much of it still in its original packaging and includes such crucial accessories as lava lamps and sew-on hippie patches.

Tues–Thurs 12noon–6pm Fri 12noon–7pm Sat 12noon–6pm.

The Cavern, 154 Commercial Road, E1.
0171 247 1889

GALLERY OF ANTIQUE COSTUME AND TEXTILES NW8

The Gallery is a Pandora's box of original antique clothes and fabrics. To augment their range they also recreate original designs with antique material or a modern one that bears more than a passing resemblance to the original. Garments sell from between £75 and £500.

Gallery of Antique Costume and Textiles, 2 Church St, NW8.
0171 723 9981

GLORIOUS CLOTHING COMPANY   N1

This popular shop has the knack of anticipating the next big revival and being ready for it.

Old clothes and modern street style mix happily, with 1920s lace dresses selling alongside brand new 'God Save the Queen' T-shirts bought in for the current punk revival. Also on offer are snakeskin platform boots and those brightly coloured Seventies lycra disco trousers that many of us would prefer to forget about.

Menswear is upstairs and also on sale are feather boas, gloves and bags. Mon–Sat 11am–6.30pm.

Glorious Clothing Company, 60 Upper Street, N1.
0171 704 6312

• Other places to look for vintage clothes include:

Stoke Newington Church Street – look out for Filberts at no. 142 and Ribbons and Taylor at no. 157 – and in and around Camden Lock, including Modern Vintage Clothing at 65 Chalk Farm Road, NW1.

Greenwich is also a good area, both in the market and at The Emporium (330 Creek Road) and The Observatory (20 Greenwich Church Street).

Portobello is probably the best hunting ground of all. The huge collection of stalls along Portobello Green and shops, including no. 295 and the Antique Clothing Shop at no. 282, are some of the best places to look. Also worth seeking out is The Old Haberdashery in the Red Lion Arcade at no. 165 Portobello Road, for antique ribbons, laces, textiles and trims.

Radio Days is full of collectables and memorabilia from the 1920s to the 1960s, and this includes clothing, accessories and costume jewellery.

Radio Days, 87, Lower Marsh, SE1.
0171 928 0800

• For pre-Eighties clothing that can be bought or hired:
Blackout 11, 51 Endell Street, WC2.
0171 240 5006

SPECIALIST SHOPS

For creating, adapting or enhancing your clothes and accessories, the following suppliers have everything you need.

THE BUTTON QUEEN   W1

The Button Queen has been owned by the Frith family for 40 years and they pride themselves on a very personal service; as Martyn Frith says, 'Buttons can totally change the character of a garment and we work with the customer to find the right button for an outfit.' The Button Queen stocks a huge range of antique and modern buttons, all neatly stored in small cardboard boxes stacked on shelves around the shop.

Designers like Vivienne Westwood and Victor Edelstein choose their buttons here, as do fashion students and costume designers from *The House of Eliot, Blackadder* and films like *The Mirror Crack' d* and *Murder on the Nile.*

Antique buttons include rare eighteenth-century Wedgwood and Victorian mother-of-pearl. Modern ranges of horn, wood and leather complement the current vogue for natural looks.

Prices range from 2p for a backing button to £37 for a gilt and diamante creation and into the hundreds for antique collector buttons.

The Button Queen, 19 Marylebone Lane, W1.
0171 935 1505

BOROVICK FABRIC LTD   W1

Taffeta, tulle, Thai silk or tweed – whatever the fabric, Borovicks are bound to stock it, as fashion, costume, interior and set designers throughout London and as far as Australia now.

The family business began trading in 1932 and is now run by Martyn Borovick who dismisses any attempt to work out how many fabrics he stocks as 'incalculable.' Third generation brides come to Borovicks to choose material for their wedding dress, and the shop has recently shipped a tonne of fabric to the Kirov in Russia for some new costumes. Martyn reckons there isn't a film, television or theatre company that Borovicks hasn' t supplied at some time and everyone, whether they are buying for an entire production or just need 20cm of trim, is guaranteed the same helpful, knowledgeable and entertaining service.

Borovick Fabric Ltd, 16 Berwick Street, W1.
0171 437 2180
Also:

• Joel & Son Fabrics, 77–81 Church Street, NW8.
0171 724 6895

JANET COLES BEAD EMPORIUM   W11

Janet Coles stocks thousands of different beads from all over the world, among them Peruvian ceramic, Venetian glass, Czech foil and beads made of wood from the Philippines and India.

All the beads are displayed in wooden trays and the huge array of styles, colours and designs makes a dazzling display. The current fashion for large pendants means you can choose several large silver or glass beads, plus some leather thread and make up your own version in minutes. There are also ready made-up pieces of jewellery.

A wide variety of jewellery kits are also on sale with all the pieces you need to make a blue filipiattine necklace or a pair of aqua zephyr earrings, or you can go freeform and do your own thing. The assistants will advise you and the shop sells 'how to' books as well as all jewellery fittings from clasps and clips to thread and tools.

Prices range from 7p for tiny glass lettered beads to £8.20 for a large crystal bead.

Mail order catalogue also available.

Janet Coles Bead Emporium, 128 Notting Hill Gate, W11.
0171 727 8085

V.V.ROULEAUX   SW6

V.V. Rouleaux stocks over 4,000 ravishing ribbons, from delicate flower-patterned organzas to silks, satins and taffetas.

The ribbons come in a vast range of colours and the designs include stars, moons, cherubs and tartan patterns. The shop also stocks tassels, fake-fur trim and wired ribbon for tying perfect bows for a clientele that ranges from top fashion designers to interior designers and the enthusiastic amateur dressmaker.

Prices range from 15p a metre to £60.

V.V. Rouleaux, 201 New King' s Road, SW6.
0171 371 5929

DRESS HIRE

When you need something special to wear, and a look in your wardrobe or purse only highlights their limitations, one option on offer is to hire an outfit.

AMAZING GRACE   W14

Amazing Grace carries a range of dresses, both long and short, bought directly from the designers in sizes ranging from 8 to 18.

Set up three years ago and run from home, Juliet Stocks offers her local clients a free home collection and delivery service.

Amazing Grace also hire out handbags, jewellery and gloves and offers a free alteration service. Prices range between £50 and £70 per one evening's hire.

Amazing Grace, 83a Elsham Road, W14.
0171 602 7704

RITZY NIGHTS   W10

In addition to a range of ballgowns and cocktail dresses, Ritzy Nights also offer a maternity evening wear range. Sizes range from 8 to 18.

Ritzy Nights, 41 St. Quintin Avenue, W10.
0181 968 7371

• Further selections:

After Dark, 6 Ashbourne Parade, Finchley Road, NW11.
0181 209 0195.

Biddulph & Banham, 8 Ludgate Square, St. EC4.
0171 489 0727

The Fashion Clinic, 180 Wandsworth Bridge Road, SW6.
0171 736 4425

Frock Around the Clock, 42 Vardens Road, SW11.
0171 924 1669

One Night Stand, 44 Pimilico Road, SW1.
0171 730 8708

20th Century Frox, 614 Fulham Road, SW6.
0171 731 3242

Youngs Formal Wear, 16 Ludgate Hill, EC4.
0171 236 6927

THE MERCHANT OF EUROPE W11

If you are looking for a more unconventional outfit The Merchant of Venice hires out original clothing, including accessories, from the 1920s to the 1970s.

The Merchant of Venice, 232 Portabello Road, W11.
0171 221 4203

• Check out the dress agencies listed on Page 97 and the vintage clothes shops (Page 110) some of whom offer hire facilities.

• Best for men are the Moss Bros Group plc and Youngs Formal Wear.

Moss Bross: 4-10 Blomfield Street, EC2.	0171 588 7550
6 Grays Inn Road, WC1.	0171 831 9867
27 King Street, WC2.	0171 240 4567
Youngs: 16 Ludgate Hill, EC4.	0171 236 6927
1-2 Berners Street, W1.	0171 580 7179
19-20 Hanover Street, W1.	0171 437 4422
275a Kensington High Street, W8.	0171 602 5225

FOOD

For die-hard foodies, or anyone who simply likes eating, London is now a paradise of choice. Delicious delis proliferate, specialist cheese shops thrive and some of the best food shops are to be found serving their local communities – the Polish delicatessen in Balham, Spanish stores in Portobello Road, Italian delicatessens in Soho and Clerkenwell or Turkish grocers in Stoke Newington!

The range and quality of food on sale in the capital is now better than ever before. Many of the quality shops have been in existence for decades, but they are now being joined by a new generation of exciting newcomers, like the huge Japanese superstore on the Edgware Road, which offers sushi, seaweed and 70 varieties of sake, or Simply Sausages, devoted solely to bangers.

One of the best things about London's smaller specialist food shops is the enthusiasm and expertise of their owners and staff. Whether crazy about cheese or fanatical about fish, it is impossible not to be inspired by their enthusiasm and it is well worth asking their advice and making use of their knowledge.

For culinary inspiration, London also has some excellent specialist food bookshops. Try Books for Cooks at 4 Blenheim Crescent, W11 (0171 221 1992) or Food for Thought, 27 Cecil Court, WC2 (0171 379 8171).

SHOPPING LIST

AMERICAN
The American Dream, SW6
Beverley Hills Bakery, SW3

BAKERS
Bliss Bakery & Patisseries, EC1
Clarke's Shop, W8
Coughlans, SW11
Dunns, N8
Lois Hot Bread, NW1/N1
Maison Blanc, SW3/W11/NW3/Richmond
Neal's Yard Bakery, WC2
The Irish Bakers, NW2/NW6

BUTCHERS
R. Allen, W1
F. Godfrey, N5/N16
Lidgate, W11
M. Moen & Sons, SW4
Randalls, SW6
Simply Sausages, W1/SW1/EC1

CHARCUTERIE
Randall and Aubin, W1

CHEESE
Barstow & Barr, N1
Hamish Johnston, SW11

Jeroboams, SW1/SW7/W11
Neal's Yard Dairy, WC2
Paxton & Whitfield, SW1
Rippon Cheese Stores, SW1

CHINESE
Loon Fung Supermarket, W1

CHOCOLATE
Rococo, SW3
Gerard Ronay, SW1/NW3

DELICATESSEN
Clarkes, W8
Rosslyn Deli, NW3
Tom's, W11

FISHMONGER
J. Blagden, W1
Chalmers and Gray, W11
Steve Hatt, N1
Jeffersons, W9
H.S. Linwood & Sons, EC3
Richardsons, W1

GREEK/CYPRIOT
Athenian Grocers, W2

HONEY
The Hive, SW11

IRANIAN
Reza, W8

ITALIAN
I Camisa, W1
Carluccio's, WC2
Fratelli Camisa, W1
Gallo Nero, N16
G. Gazzano, ECI
Lina Stores, W1
L. Terroni, EC1

JAPANESE
Yaohan Plaza, NW9

POLISH
Panadam, SW17

SPANISH
R. Garcia & Sons, W11

TEA AND COFFEE
Algerian Coffee Stores, W1
H.R. Higgins, W1
The Tea House, WC2
Monmouth Coffee Company, WC2

THAI
Talad Thai, SW15

TRAITEUR
Traiteur Pagno, NW1

WHOLEFOODS/HERBALIST
Baldwins, SE 17
Cornucopia Health Foods, W5
Freshlands Wholefoods, EC1
Neal's Yard Wholefood Warehouse, WC2
Peppercorns, NW3
Wild Oats, W11

SPECIALIST SHOPS

ALGERIAN COFFEE STORES   W1
(Tea and coffee)

Stocking over 50 coffees and 100 teas, as well as stylish coffee-drinking
accoutrements, the Algerian Coffee Stores is a Soho essential. Customers
include local businesses like Patisserie Valerie as well as a loyal clientele
that extends worldwide by mail order. Amongst the connoisseur coffees
on offer are Java, Boston, velluto nero and the Turkish gourmet mulatte.
For an unusual post-dinner brew, there are flavoured coffees like peaches
and cream, and southern pecan. The house specials include Lebanese
with cardamoms and Arabic with spices.

The Algerian Coffee Stores, 52 Old Compton Street, W1.
0171 437 2480

• Other coffee specialists:

H.R. Higgins, 79 Duke Street, W1. 0171 629 3913

Monmouth Coffee Company, 27 Monmouth Street, WC2.
0171 836 5272

R. ALLEN   W1
(Butchers)

For traditionalists, R. Allen is the place for meat. The interior remains
virtually unchanged from when the shop first opened in 1866, with
glazed tiles, huge butcher's blocks, an oak counter and sawdust. Game
is a major speciality, and top London hotels like Claridges and The
Connaught come to Allens for their grouse and pheasant as well as
Scottish beef and English lamb.

R.Allen, 117 Mount Street, Mayfair, W1.
0171 499 5831

• Other butchers:

F. Godfrey Ltd., 7 Highbury Park, N5.
0171 226 2425
and 220 Stoke Newington High Street, N6.
0171 254 0123

Randalls, 113 Wandsworth Bridge Road, SW6.
0171 736 3426

THE AMERICAN DREAM   SW6
(American)

For US expats with food cravings! Americans come from as far away
as Cornwall to stock up on oreo cookies, Hershey' s kisses, clamato,
hamburger helper, Betty Crocker cake mixes, Captain Crunch cereal
and the other 500 imported American products available.

Among the best sellers are Pam's spray – the spray–on cooking oil
to which Oprah Winfrey attributes her diet success – and of course all
the Hershey' s chocolates. And who could resist Goobers peanut
butter, with its stripes of strawberry jelly?

The American Dream, 183 New Kings Road, SW6.
0171 384 3025

ATHENIAN GROCERS   W2
(Greek/Cypriot)

This traditional Greek Cypriot grocers is located close to the Greek
cathedral on Moscow Road. They sell a good selection of olives and
cheeses, sweet halva and delicious small soft breads studded with huge
squashy black olives. At Easter-time they stock tsoureki and flaounes,
the traditional Cypriot Easter biscuits.

Athenian Grocery, 16a Moscow Road, W2.
0171 229 6280

BALDWINS   SE17
(Wholefoods and herbalist)

Established in the area since 1844 this health food shop is well stocked
and has friendly staff, but most interesting is their herbalist section.
Herbs are displayed in wooden cases and the original signs on the
walls advertise Tonic and Nerve mixture, the forerunner of today' s
vitamin supplements.

Aromatherapy products sell especially well and both the health food
shop and the herbalist' s stock a good range of books on the subject.
Herbs range from horsetail to hemlock and the shop has a factory
making the herbal tonic Sarsaparilla, a root concentrate herbal drink,
which is still a big seller, alongside Nineties pick-you-ups like gurana.

Baldwins, 171–173 Walworth Road, SE17.
0171 703 5550

• Other good health food shops include:

Cornucopia Health Foods, 1 Devonshire Road, W5.
0181 995 0588

Freshlands Wholefoods, 196 Old Street, EC1.
0171 250 1708
A magnet for macrobiotic for customers.

Neal' s Yard Wholefood Warehouse, off Shorts Garden, WC2.
0171 836 5151

Peppercorns, 2 Heath Street, NW3.
0171 431 1251
Small and cosy – good for takeaways.

BARSTOW & BARR   N1/NW7
(Cheese)

This small shop opened in the summer of 1993, selling over
100 different cheeses from Britain, Ireland, France and the
rest of Europe.

Many of the cheeses come from individual farms and herds,
including Beenleigh Blue from Devon, Maroilles, a French
cheese invented in the tenth century by monks in Flanders, and
Dunloppe, handmade on an Ayrshire farm.

To complement their cheeses, Barstow and Barr also stock a range of
home-made pickles and chutneys, cheese biscuits, Provence olives and
sundried tomatoes.

Barstow and Barr, 24 Liverpool Road, N1.
0171 359 4222
and Unit 90, Camden Lock, Chalk Farm, NW7.
0171 428 0488

BEVERLEY HILLS BAKERY   SW3
(American)

If you want memorable muffins, then the Beverley Hills Bakery is the
place to go. Tempting flavours include blueberry, lemon, carrot and
raisin, pecan and orange, and banana bran.

The shop sells brownies and cookies as well, and the muffins also
come in mini-sizes – miniature morsels of temptation that have
compelled expat American customers to pop in. The bakery runs a gift
and delivery service (see Page 30) and their muffins can also be bought
at Harrods, Fortnums and Selfridges.

Beverley Hills Bakery, 3 Egerton Terrace, London, SW3.
0171 584 4401

CARLUCCIO'S   WC2
(Italian delicatessen)

Most of the products on sale are made or imported especially for
Carluccio' s, and the expertise of Antonio and his wife Priscilla results
in the best from the various Italian regions: truffles from Piedmont,
olive oil from Luguria, biscuits from Puglia, risotto rice from the Po
Valley and chocolate from Turin.

Dried pastas come from Sardinia, Puglia and Naples and fresh pasta
is made in the Carluccios' own kitchens using double zero flour from
Emilia-Romagna and coloured with beetroot, spinach or cuttlefish
ink. Seasonal pastas are flavoured with wild garlic or wild horseradish.

Field, oyster and chantarelle mushrooms are joined by dried morels,
fairy rings and the foodie favourite – dried porcini.

Prepared dishes include wild mushroom pancake purses, grilled
polenta, stuffed squid, tiramisu and panna cotta, and they sell an
extensive range of Italian wines.

A gift, delivery and party service is available.

Carluccio's, 28a Neal Street, WC2.
0171 240 1487

CHALMERS AND GRAY

W11

(fishmonger)

Activity in this turquoise-tiled shop revolves around the huge marble slab where swordfish, tuna, snapper and bourgeois join the more familiar cod, skate and sole. Chalmers and Gray cook live crabs and lobsters on the premises, and sell a wide range of fish and poultry that has been smoked for them in Norfolk, including trout and pheasant.

Mediterranean, tiger and Indian prawns sit alongside fresh scallops in their shells and Irish rock oysters.

Chalmers and Gray also stock their own range of sauces and marinades. Chalmers and Gray, 67 Notting Hill Gate, W11.
0171 221 6177

• Other popular fishmongers include:

H.S. Linwood & Sons Ltd, 67 Grand Avenue, Leadenhall Market, EC3.
0171 929 0554

Richards, 21 Brewer Street, W1.
0171 437 1358

J. Blagden, 65 Paddington Street, W1.
0171 935 8321

CLARKE'S SHOP

W8

(Baker)

It is unfair to refer to Sally Clarke's shop as simply a baker's as they also carry a fine range of cheeses, puddings and bottled goods. But it is the range of bread that provides the highest level of interest and diversity.

Sun dried tomato bread, hazelnut and raisin bread, brioche current bread, three different types of foccacio are just a few of the treats on offer and the shop assistants are all too willing to make suggestions as to which bread goes best with what.

Clarke's Shop, 122 Kensington Church Street, W8.
0171 353 6211

• Some other choices:

Bliss Bakery & Patisseries, 428 St John Street, EC1.
0171 837 3720

Coughlans, 315 Lavender Hill, SW11.
0171 738 9039

Dunns, 6 The Broadway, N8.
0181 340 1614

Lois Hot Bread, 98 Robert Street, NW1.   0171 388 9033
              137 Newington Green Road, N1.   0171 226 7168

Maison Blanc, 11 Elyston Street, SW3.   0171 584 6913
              102 Holland Park Avenue, W11.   0171 221 2494
              62 Hampstead High Street, NW3.   0171 431 8338
              The Merchant Centre, New Street Sq, EC4. 0171 353 6211
              27b The Quadrant, Richmond. TW9   0181 332 7041

Neals Yard Bakery, 6 Neals Yard, WC2.   0171 836 5199

R. GARCIA & SONS   W11
(Spanish)

Catering for the large local Spanish community (the Spanish
School is just nearby), this 40-year-old family business sells
Manchego cheese, a wide variety of olives and olive oils,
chorizo sausage and, best of all, churros: piped twists of
doughnut, delicious dipped in hot chocolate.

   The shop is also well known for its range of Spanish wines and
spirits and also sells Spanish music tapes.

R. Garcia & Sons, 250 Portobello Road, W11.
0171 221 6119

G. GAZZANO   EC1
(Italian)

Gazzano' s was founded in 1901 and remains a family business,
currently run by the grandson of the original owner. Salamis and
other meats hang from the ceiling in this packed shop, which also
sells hot and spicy Tuscan, Genovese and Neapolitan sausages.
Gazzano' s offer 10 varieties of fresh olives, several varieties of
pecorino cheese and, in addition to a huge selection of dried pastas,
they sell their own fresh varieties. Try the delicious tortellini with
parma ham. There is a good selection of Italian wines and special
occasion cakes in huge pink boxes.

G.Gazzano, 167–169 Farringdon Road, EC1.
0171 837 1586

STEVE HATT   N1
(Fishmonger)

Steve Hatt is one of the best-known fishmongers in London,
attributing his continued success to 'consistent hard work' .
Assistants dart about serving such fishy delights as red sea bream and
red snapper, fresh anchovies, sardines from France and Rossmore
oysters flown in from Ireland.

   A particular speciality of this fourth generation family business is
their own smoked haddock and mackerel – smoked on the premises in
the old-fashioned way and not just 'shown to the smoke' as many
modern smoked products are. Steve Hatt also sells court bouillon
ready for poaching, as well as a range of ready-made fish soups.

Steve Hatt, 88–90 Essex Road, N1.
0171 226 3963

THE HIVE   SW11
(Honey)

Devoted solely to the sweet delights of honey, The Hive is heaven for
anyone with the same tastes as Winnie The Pooh.

   The owner, Californian James Hamill, is a third generation
beekeeper who inherited his obsession from his grandfather. He now
has 60 hives, producing 4-5 tonnes of honey a year. Contrary to what
you might expect, London is a bee' s paradise, producing all-year-
round supplies of nectar. The result is an annual harvest of 240lb of

honey from each of James's Tooting hives, around 4 times what the country beekeeper would expect.

On sale are numerous seasonal varieties of honey: dark and light, lime tree, blackberry and floral, many of them first prize winners at the National Honey Show and all of them miles away from the sticky sweet syrup that often graces the supermarket shelves. In addition, James and his wife Ute make and sell such culinary combinations as honey with white chocolate, orange, almonds, walnuts, cognac or ginger. The Hive also stock their own honey and royal jelly based beauty products, hold honey tasting evenings and James Hamill also runs beekeeping courses for adults and children.

A fascinating feature of the shop is the observation glass hive built into the wall, where 20,000 bees dance attendance on the queen.

The Hive, 53 Webbs Road, SW11.
0171 924 6233

THE IRISH BAKER'S   NW2/NW6
(Baker)

If you have never tasted Irish soda bread then there is a treat in store for you. The Irish Baker's was founded 4 years ago by Roger Ryan for the homesick Irish community, and there are now 3 stores selling soda bread, barnbrack and potato bread to the discerning bread-loving community!

The Irish Bakers, 267 Kilburn High Road, NW6.   0171 372 7167
                    328 Kilburn High Road, NW6.   0171 625 7399
                    155 Cricklewood Broadway, NW2.   0181 450 4080

C. LIDGATE   W11
(Butchers)

David Lidgate is the fourth generation to take on his family butcher's business in Holland Park, founded by his great grandfather Alexander in 1850.

Lidgate's success seems to lie in mixing old-fashioned service and quality with an up-to-date range of products and ideas. All the beef and lamb is grass-fed or organic, from Scotland, the West Country and the Prince of Wales's Highgrove estate in Gloucestershire.

As well as all the standard cuts, Lidgate's sells marinated and stuffed meats, chicken kebabs in lemon and coriander, lamb in oil, rosemary and garlic, pork stuffed with apricots and prunes, and specialities like osso bucco and wild boar cutlets. Their range of home-made pies includes steak and kidney, lamb and leek, game and the latest addition, the coq au vin pie, which recently won a Smithfield gold medal.

The shop itself is also a delight – tiled walls, staff in brown-and-white check uniforms and a beautiful wood and mirrored cash desk.

C. Lidgate, 110 Holland Park Avenue, W11.
0171 727 8243

LINA STORES   W1
(Italian)

One of Soho's best-loved delicatessens, Lina Stores is
particularly famous for its raviolis. Displayed on the counter
are interleaved sheets of freshly made pumpkin and ricotta or
4-cheese ravioli and your choice is lovingly packed into a box
for careful transport home.

   Fresh basil plants and different sized hunks of parmesan sit on the
counter, and there is a good choice of olives, sauces and salamis, as
well as fresh ciabatta and focaccia bread. The owners are friendly and
the atmosphere relaxed and chatty.

Lina Stores, 18 Brewer Street, W1.
0171 437 6482

• Other popular London Italian delicatessens:

I Camisa, 61 Old Compton Street, W1.
0171 437 7610

Fratelli Camisa, 1a Berwick Street, W1.
0171 437 7120
and 53 Charlotte Street, W1.
0171 255 1240

Gallo Nero, 45 Newington Green Road, N16.
0171 226 2002

LOON FUNG SUPERMARKET   W1
(Chinese)

The Loon Fung supplies local restaurants in Chinatown and stocks a
wide range of Chinese vegetables, like chow chow and bitter melon,
fresh lemon grass and other herbs. Tinned and dried goods include
shark's fin soup and they also have a good selection of ready-to-steam
dim sum.

   Well worth a look is their large range of Chinese cookware – bamboo
steamer baskets, woks, pans, cooking implements and china, all at
good prices.

Loon Fung Supermarket, 42–44 Gerrard Street, W1.
0171 437 7332

M. MOEN & SONS   SW4
(Butchers)

Citizens of Clapham and far beyond crowd into Moen's for the quality
and variety of the meat, which includes wild boar, venison and hare as
well as poultry, beef and lamb.

   The shop also has a charcuterie with chorizo imported from Spain, a
cheese counter with Italian dolcelatte and on top of the counter are
baskets of fresh duck and goose eggs. The Scottish influence is here
too, with fresh haggis, also in a vegetarian variety, and Scottish black
pudding.

M.Moen & Sons, 19 The Pavement, SW4.
0171 622 1624

NEAL'S YARD DAIRY

WC2

(Cheese)

Concentrating on cheeses from Britain and Ireland, Neal' s Yard has a
friendly atmosphere and the helpful and knowledgeable staff positively
encourage you to try before you buy.

Huge cloth-bound Cheddars and Cheshires line the shelves and
downstairs is a cellar where the cheeses mature. Hearing the details of
the cheeses and the farmers who make them gives a strong sense of
the individuality of our traditional cheeses.

Neal' s Yard Dairy, Short's Gardens, WC2.
0171 379 7646

PANADAM

SW17

(Polish)

Close to the local Polish church and almost opposite the club,
Panadam has been supplying the Polish community in Balham since
1980.

Owner Mr Brzeski specializes in Polish sausages, among them white
sausage, tuchowska and wiejska. Breads include Ukranian rye bread
and cheese yeast babka. For the sweet-toothed, the 5 varieties of
cheesecake on offer include poppy seed mazurka and cracovia, made
by Mr Brzeski's wife to recipes handed down from his mother.
Panadam also sells sweet Polish halva, stuffed cabbage leaves and
dumplings, with flavours like sauerkraut and mushroom, and cream
cheese and potato. The walls are hung with strings of wild Polish
mushrooms, graduated by size.

Panadam, 2 Marius Road, SW17.
0171 673 4062

PANZER

NW8

(Continental delicatessen)

A delicatessen crossed with a supermarket, the shelves of Panzer
groan with a truly international selection of foods: American, Italian,
Greek and Japanese to name a few. Outside, strings of garlic and
onions hang from the green canopies and fruit and vegetables include
uglis, paw paw and Jamaican ortaniques.

If there is a prevailing emphasis it is probably Jewish: gefilte fish,
Bloom's kosher viennas and chopped herring are all on sale in the deli,
as are fresh gravadlax and a huge selection of breads.

Panzer, Circus Road, St John's Wood, NW8.
0171 722 8596

RANDALL AND AUBIN

W1

(Charcuterie)

Randall and Aubin first opened in 1906 when it was the only
charcuterie in Britain. For 10 months in the early 1990s the premises
stood empty after the previous owner's death, but were then bought
and rescued by Rod Lane, who also runs a club at 2 Brydges Place.

The interior was restored, preserving the original marble central
counter and wooden-doored fridges, and now Randall and Aubin

thrives once again. The butchery counter features many French cuts, like carre d'agneau and contre filet and there are French and English cheeses, olives, patisserie and charcuterie on sale. Specialities include cooked hocks of ham, their own home cooked ham and scotch eggs as well as duck and turkey eggs.

Randall & Aubin, 16 Brewer Street, W1.
0171 437 3507

REZA   W8
(Iranian)

Mr Reza opened his first Iranian deli some 10 years ago and his empire now includes a grocer, a butcher, patisserie and a greengrocer.

Fresh herbs are flown in throughout the year and they carry a splendid selection of dried fruits and nuts all priced at £3.50 per pound, which makes them extremely good value. The patisserie is famous for its selection of Iranian sweetmeats – try *zoulbia*, a pastry dipped in syrup and honey flavoured with rosewater.

Reza, 347 Kensington High Street, W8.
0171 603 0924

RIPPON CHEESE STORES   SW1
(Cheese)

Philip Rippon and his wife Karen opened their cheese shop 3 years ago and now stock possibly the largest selection of cheeses in London – over 550 different types at the last count, and the list is still growing.

Philip Rippon possesses an impeccable cheese pedigree, having spent 8 years as manager of Paxton and Whitfield, and his aim is to run the best cheese shop in Europe.

The cheeses are lovingly nurtured, the more robust kept at the front of the shop and the fragile at the back in a cooler room. All are displayed on straw mats, which keep the air circulating and help the cheese to breathe.

Among the stock are over 100 types of goat cheese of all maturities, Irish cheeses like Milleen and Gubbeen, Swedish Prastost and Greve and English cheeses like Cotterstone and Cornish Yarg. The Welsh are represented by Llanboidy and Pencarreg and the Scots by Strathkinness and Tobermory Truckle.

Rippon Cheese Stores, 26 Upper Tachbrook Street, SW1.
0171 931 0628

• Other cheese shops include:

Hamish Johnston, 48 Northcote Road, SW11.
0171 738 0741

Jeroboams,	51 Elizabeth Street, SW1.	0171 823 5623
	24 Bute Street, SW7.	0171 225 2232
	6 Clarendon Road, W11.	0171 727 9359
	mail order service	0171 727 9792

Paxton & Whitfield, 93 Jermyn Street, SW1.
0171 930 0259

ROCOCO
SW3
(Chocolate)

Chantal Cody's chocolate emporium attracts chocoholics from all over the world, drawn irresistibly to the King's Road by the temptations of pink champagne truffles, orange confites and the sensual sounding Nipples of Venus.

Chocolate know-alls will be able to wax lyrical over the cocoa content of the chocolate and the quality of the beans used, which include the world's rarest cocoa bean, the Cziollo, grown on the shores of the Indian Ocean. They will probably be moved to tears by the sheer perfection of the Truffes Maison – price £20 per pound – whose manufacture involves rare manjari chocolate, Normandy cream and butter.

The traditional English selection includes rose and violet creams, while banana cream and pistachio marzipan appear on the hand-dipped list. Chocolate bars include poivre rose, feuilles de menthe, juniper and chocolat extra brut.

Rococo is no chocolate-snob shop though – they also stock plenty of children's sweets, including gummi bears and flying saucers, and for those who like their chocolate with a sense of humour there are chocolate fishes, frogs, mushrooms and spears of chocolate asparagus.

A gift delivery service is available.

Rococo, 321 King's Road, SW3.
0171 352 5857

GERARD RONAY
SW1/NW3
(Chocolate)

Currently the hottest young chocolatier in London, Gerard Ronay, stepson of Hungarian food critic Egon, has made his name with the bizarre and imaginative selection of flavours he creates for his chocolates. Smoked lemon, dill and rose, chestnut, red wine truffle and tomato (yes, tomato) all feature among the flavours on his chocolate chart.

All the chocolates are made by hand in his workshop in Acton, using the finest ingredients and couverture chocolate. The results are an expensive £22 per pound, but are definitely the chocolate lover's current fave rave.

Gerard Ronay chocolates are available from Harrods, SW1; Theo Broma, Camden Lock, NW3; Rococo, SW3. Enquiries: 0181 743 0818.

ROSSLYN DELI
NW3
(General delicatessen)

Catering to the cosmopolitan tastes of Hampstead, the Rosslyn has a massive selection of international goods – brie oozing with flavour, Swiss cheeses for raclette and fondue, charcuterie, breads and home-made jams and sauces, as well as a large selection of meals prepared in their own kitchens.

Among the more exotic goods are raspberry and chocolate fettucine, blackcurrant and blueberry vinegars and a special American section, featuring such calorie-packed delights as oreo cookies and marshmallows.

The Rosslyn Delicatessen, 56 Rosslyn Hill, NW3.
0171 794 9210

SIMPLY SAUSAGES   W1/SW1/WC2/EC1
(Butchers)

With over 37 varieties on sale, Simply Sausages is raising the
once humble banger to gourmet status.

   Traditionalists can choose the Cumberland, Lincolnshire or
breakfast sausage, while for the more adventurous, pork,
prune and cognac, beef and guiness or creole smokey may appeal.
They also make smoked salmon sausages and the vegetarian selection
includes chestnut and orange and mushroom and tarragon.

   Up to 7,000lb of sausages are produced every week and they can be
poached, pan-fried or grilled, but forget popular wisdom: they should
never be pricked – apparently you lose the flavour.

Simply Sausages, 93 Berwick St, W1.	0171 287 3482
34 Strutton Ground, SW1.	0171 976 7430
Villiers Street, WC2.	0171 839 5439
341 Central Markets, Farringdon St, EC1.	0171 329 3227

TALAD THAI   SW15
(Thai supermarket)

Thai food has become increasingly popular in the capital and this
supermarket serves local Thai restaurants as well as being popular
with Thais attending the temple in nearby Wimbledon. They also sell
Thai newspapers and magazines and hold cookery courses to cater for
the growing interest in Thai cooking.

   All the ingredients for a Thai meal are on sale, from imported tilapia
fish to several varieties of coconut milk, chopped salted radish and
tamarind. Fresh fruit and vegetables include a wide selection of
chillies and herbs, and tinned soups like tom yap and tom kha line the
shelves along with pickled ginger, sauces and pastes.

   Thai food takeaway is available and Thai cookery demonstrations are
every Sunday morning at 11am – £2.

Talad Thai, 320 Upper Richmond Road, SW15.
0181 789 8084.

THE TEA HOUSE   WC2
(Tea)

Our tastes in tea have grown more adventurous over the years, but
The Tea House aims to enliven our tea taste buds even more.
Over 100 different teas are on sale, from Chinese chun mee and
chrysanthemum to sencha bancha from Japan, kandy from Sri Lanka
and Russian tea grown on the slopes of the Caucasus.

   Fruit teas and herbal infusions have become increasingly popular,
among them Caribbean fruit, Moroccan orange, hibiscus and marigold
flowers.

   Novelty teas include rum-flavoured sailor' s tea, and lovers' tea. The
shop also stocks a wide variety of bizarre teapots, tins and infusers.

The Tea House, 15 Neal Street, WC2.
0171 240 7539

L. TERRONI

EC1

(Italian delicatessen)

Under a green awning on the Clerkenwell Road, L. Terroni, established in 1878, stocks a vast and varied selection of Italian goods, including probably the largest selection of dried pastas in London.

Pasta sauces include fresh pesto, mushroom and carbonara. There is a huge range of cakes and biscuits, meat and cheeses, tinned fish, and everything from salted capers to several types of Marsala sherry. Fresh breads include casareccio as well as ciabatta and olive.

Italian gossip at full volume entertains while you browse.

L. Terroni, 138 Clerkenwell Road, EC1.
0171 837 1712

TOM'S

W11

(Delicatessen)

Son of restaurant magnate Sir Terence, Tom Conran is a former winner of Deli of The Year for his stylish food emporium. Tom's is dramatically decorated in orange and turquoise with a food mural on the ceiling, and equal care has been taken over the choice of products.

Downstairs you can find Irish soda bread, black fig jam and liquid veal stock, while upstairs the cheese selection includes mimolette, a speciality of their French supplier in Lille.

Champagne, chocolates and charcuterie all feature and the choice of ready-prepared meals is especially appetizing: chestnut and potato gnocchi; puy lentils with bacon lardons; or Moroccan root vegetables with lemon, garlic and parsley. Follow with an apple, pear or lemon tart from the patisserie.

Tom's, 226 Westbourne Grove, W11.
0171 221 8818

TRAITEUR PAGNOL

NW1

(Home-made specialist delicatessen)

The difference between a traiteur and a delicatessen is that at the traiteur all the food is cooked with the freshest ingredients on the premises. The Traiteur Pagnol opened in June 1994 and is the first of its kind to open in London.

Specialities include a delicious garlic soup, confit, cassoulet, gratin dauphinois and crème brûlée. They also sell their own home-made jams, pickles and Christmas puddings.

Shelf stock is all specialist and personally tested. Traiteur Pagnol is one of the few places where you can find the Elvas plum (greengages soaked in sugar syrup and then sun-dried) – a mouth-watering but expensive Christmas delicacy!

Orders will be walked round if you live close to Regents Park Road or they will organize a cab for specially requested deliveries.

Traiteur Pagnol, 170 Regent' s Park Road, NW1.
0171 586 6988

WILD OATS
(Wholefoods)

W11

One of the biggest and best-stocked health food shops in London, Wild Oats offers a huge array of wholefoods and, unlike some health food shops, the layout, packaging and produce actually make you want to start eating more healthily.

Downstairs are numerous varieties of pulses, pasta and dried goods, a Japanese section, organic produce including tomato ketchup, ratatouille and baby foods and a selection of herb teas which includes liquorice-flavour yogi tea and 'smooth move' tea.

Upstairs is devoted to a vast range of vitamin and mineral supplements and natural beauty products including tea tree oil toothpaste, Tisserand essential oils and Herbatint natural hair colourings.

Organic fruit and vegetables, including fresh dates and shitake mushrooms, are available.

Wild Oats, 210 Westbourne Grove, W11.
0171 229 1063

YAOHAN PLAZA
(Japanese)

NW9

'All Japan under one roof' declares the Yaohan Plaza slogan, and indeed, the Plaza, sandwiched between Asda and Do It All on the Edgware Road, offers the widest selection of Japanese foods and goods in London 7 days a week.

Inside the airport-terminal-sized building are a variety of stores, culminating in a huge and excellent Japanese supermarket, which offers over 20 varieties of soy sauce, fresh fish, beef shabu shabu, pork thinly sliced ready for stir frying, amazing vegetables, a huge variety of noodles, green tea, dried seaweeds – nori, kombu and wakame among them – and soups.

Much is completely inexplicable to non-Japanese, but many of the products have helpful English translations on white slips of paper by the shelves, explaining the uses of goods like alimentary yam paste.

Just outside the supermarket is a brilliant sushi stall, and then a food court, selling Japanese and Western foods, with Japanese satellite television beamed in. Other shops in the complex include a vast Japanese bookstore, a children's toy shop and shops selling Japanese goods such as good-luck daruma dolls and sake bottles. There is also a Segadome games centre.

Upstairs are 2 restaurants: the vast 400-seater Zen CX, which has a huge Chinese buffet with dim sum, crispy duck, seafood and also Thai and Malaysian dishes; and Abeno, which makes okonomiyaki, the Japanese equivalent of pizza, a doughy base with toppings like squid, steak or seaweed.

Yaohan Plaza, 399 Edgware Road, Colindale, NW9.
0181 200 0009

MARKETS

REGULAR MARKETS

The oldest of London's 50 markets – Brick Lane, Petticoat Lane and Portobello – carry with them much of the city's history, vividly reflecting not just the changing mood in what we eat and wear, but the ethnic mix and economic fortunes of each area. The newer ones – the crafts at Gabriel's Wharf or the organic produce at Spitalfields, say something too about London in the Nineties.

Many of the markets have changed dramatically over recent years. The original Covent Garden fruit, vegetable and flower market was moved out in 1974 to Nine Elms and the area earmarked for office development. After vigorous campaigning by Londoners, plans were finally agreed to preserve and restore the original buildings and so make way for the thriving area Covent Garden is today.

Of the original produce markets, only Smithfield meat market remains at its original location; Spitalfields has become an organic food and craft market (fruit and veg have moved east to Leyton) and Billingsgate moved its fish to the Docklands in 1982.

The 5am start at Bermondsey and New Caledonian market is well worth while for anyone interested in antiques, and if you want to fill your home with fresh flowers at wholesale prices then an early morning trip to the New Covent Garden market will save you pounds.

Whatever it is you need, there's bound to be a market somewhere in London to provide it – and usually at a price far lower than you'd pay in the shops. Market culture is fun and carries with it the ever-inspiring possibility of saving money or getting a bargain!

BERMONDSEY NEW CALEDONIAN MARKET SE1
Fri 5am–1pm

Bermondsey is a splendid sight at 5.30 in the morning when trade, by torchlight, is well underway.

Known as a dealers' market, there are an average of 300 open-air stalls each week, covering everything the specialist, generalist and browser might be interested in, including jewellery, china, wooden boxes, prints and collectables. Silver is a particular speciality, with any number of stalls selling everything from rare eighteenth-century pieces to more modern items.

Bermondsey is where most dealers display their wares for the first time after a week's astute bidding at house clearances, auctions and fairs around the country, and the early hours are mainly taken up with inter-dealer trading. Most of the stallholders take as much money before 8am as they do in the 4 or 5 hours after.

As a dealers' market the quality of goods on offer is high, though that doesn't necessarily mean expensive. Depending on your interest you can spend anything from a few pounds to a few thousand, and there are plenty of quirky bits and pieces on offer too.

The general feeling is that this is the place for genuine antiques with fewer reproductions on offer than, say, Portobello. It also feels like one of the most exciting markets and it's worth trying to get there early both for the best bargains and the atmosphere.

There is also a smaller indoor market on the corner of Bermondsey Street and Long Lane.

Bermondsey New Caledonian Market, Bermondsey Square, SE1.

• Refuel after an early start with a fry-up at Rosa's Cafe, close to the indoor market on Bermondsey Street. Bacon, egg and bubble is £2.50. Or try M. Manze at 87 Tower Bridge Road for traditional pie and mash, or eels.

• Bermondsey dubs itself 'the heart of London's antique trade' and it is also worth looking around some of the 18 massive furniture warehouses in the area. They are widely used for export, and VAT is added for UK customers. Most of the warehouses are on Bermondsey Street, Newhams Row and Tower Bridge Row.

• The Old Cinema's antiques are displayed on 3 vast floors and include everything from antique beds, bookcases and wardrobes to art deco cocktail cabinets, a vast Eureka bath and baby grand pianos.

The Old Cinema, 157 Tower Bridge Road, SE1.
0171 407 5371

BERWICK STREET MARKET   W1
Mon–Sat 9am–6pm

Berwick Street Market is generally thought to offer some of the best quality and best-priced fruit and veg in central London.

Although Berwick Street is predominantly a fruit and veg market, stalls include fish, herbs, exotic fruits and spices, dried fruit and nuts, cheese, bags, material, clothing, hardware and light electrical goods.

The market stretches from the junction with Broadwick Street up to the point where Berwick Street is crossed by Peter Street. Prices tend to be more expensive at either end of the market and slightly cheaper in the middle. It is here that the decibel level reaches maximum volume as the traders compete with each other to shout out the best price for their produce.

Look out for the occasional fruit and veg stall piled high with just 1 or 2 items – these tend to be offering the best prices, especially if you want to buy in bulk! As with most markets prices can dramatically drop come late afternoon as the stallholders clear produce for the next day's stock.

Near the top of the market, at the Broadwick Street end, there is an excellent fish stall (Tues–Sat 8am–3pm) which the owner has run for 25 years and boasts the freshest of fish bought daily. He regularly carries fresh salmon, prawns, smoked salmon and dover sole as well as the more common fish. Slightly further on is the specialist stall in exotic fruits and spices and a little further down a comprehensively stocked herb stall (Tues–Sat) where you can buy every form of dried herb. They also carry fresh herbs with the biggest range limited to Fridays and Saturdays. Like all the specialist stalls, they will order in specific requests.

A wide range of cut flowers and plants can be found for very reasonable prices in the middle. They will always order in special requests, work to budgets large and small, and if you are local they are happy to make a delivery.

Again at the Broadwick Street end the bag stall is quite famous for carrying quite an extensive range including good 'seconds' of Tula and Hidesign. The clothing stall tends to specialize in suits and smart jackets with a top price of £80 for the top of the range. One suit costing £38 was found in one of the main London stores for £75.

Many of the stallholders can boast over 20 years of trading which attracts a repeat trade of approximately 80 per cent from residents and local office workers and reflects their high standards.

While you're in Berwick Street don' t miss Simply Sausages at no. 93 (see page 127).

Berwick Street Market, Berwick Street, W1.

BRICK LANE   E1
Sunday 5am–2pm

Brick Lane, in Spitalfields, has one of the most varied histories of any London street. It is probably best summed up by the building on the corner of Brick Lane and Fournier Street, which at various times has seen service as a French church, a Methodist chapel, a synagogue and a mosque.

From the Huguenot silk weavers to today's Bangladeshi-owned clothing factories, Spitalfields has always had strong local trades, but has also suffered great poverty. Although people tend to bang on about the great bargains to be had in the market, you get the feeling that many of the people selling things here are existing at something close to subsistence level.

Nevertheless the market is packed to bursting on a Sunday. To score in the bargain stakes you need an eagle eye, plenty of creative imagination and the knack of being able to rummage through piles of junk to spot a potential find.

The market begins at the junction of Brick Lane and Bethnal Green Road, stretching up to Shoreditch station, and branching off down both Cheshire and Sclater Streets, which are the busiest areas.

At the Bethnal Green end the market continues along Bethnal Green Road and winds along Commercial Road, where much of it is made up of people selling just a few items on the pavement. On Cheshire Street you'll find plenty of old records, furniture, old typewriters and anything from a stethoscope to an African carving. Blackman's is great for Doc Marten's and Ratzker's Yard has good second-hand books, old linens and clocks.

Sclater Street has more modern goods, from fishing rods to pet foods and stationery, and Bacon Street is good for bikes. Everywhere seems to have stalls stacked with second-hand Black and Decker and Bosch tools.

Goods are also sold underneath the arches under Shoreditch station. On the Grimsby Street side it is mainly junk, though if you forage hard enough and don't mind the vaguely intimidating atmosphere you might come across something. In the other arch there is more to see: old books, furniture, art catalogues and bric-a-brac, including old porcelain door handles and clothes.

If you are interested in a bargain, then you need to get there early, preferably around dawn, which is when the true Brick Lane devotees claim to pick up the best buys.

Brick Lane Market, Brick Lane, E1.

Also worth visiting in Brick Lane and the surrounding area are:

• Beigel Bake, no. 159. Open 24 hours daily, this bagel shop does a non-stop trade to locals, all-night ravers, cab drivers and market folk. Plain bagels are 10p, with smoked salmon and cream cheese they are 85p and coffee is 30p.

• Atlantis European Ltd, no. 146. Housed in the former Truman's Brewery, Atlantis is the largest art materials shop in the UK and is much used by the local artistic community in Spitalfields as well as attracting professionals, art students and amateur dabblers from all over the country.

Last year Atlantis opened up the 4th floor of its building as a new gallery space for shows of twentieth-century British and European art. The white painted space is vast, covering 12,000 square feet, and makes an imposing and impressive exhibition setting. There is also a smaller middle gallery and a third gallery is being built.

Mon–Sat 9am–6pm Sun 10am–5pm.

Atlantis European Ltd, 146 Brick Lane, E1.
0171 377 8855

• Ambala Sweet Centre, no. 55. The best-known purveyor of Indian sweets in London, the Ambala is part of a 25-strong shop empire. Among the delicacies are halwa (not to be confused with the Turkish sweetmeat of the same name), ladoo, jalabee and barfi.

Ambala Sweet Centre, 55 Brick Lane, E1.
0171 247 8569

• Indian restaurants. Brick Lane is known as one of the best places in London for a good and well-priced Indian meal. Among the most popular curry houses are The Clifton at no. 126 and the Nazrul at no. 130.

• Tubby Isaacs. Near to Aldgate East station, Tubby Isaacs is one of the most famous shellfish and jellied eel stalls in London.

• Bloom's. Jewish cult comedienne Sandra Bernhard praised the latkes at Bloom's, which still can't be beaten for a kosher blowout. Morris Bloom opened his first restaurant in Brick Lane in 1920 to cater for local immigrants, and never looked back. If you haven't time to sit down, try take-away salt beef from the front.

Blooms, 90 Whitechapel High Street, E1.
0171 247 6001

BRIXTON MARKET   SW9
Mon–Sat 8.30pm–5.30pm

Brixton market is probably the best weekday market south of the river. The strong Afro-caribbean influence in the area has ensured sweet yuca, chow chow, hot peppers, white aubergine, sava sava and every type of yam can be found alongside the more conventional English vegetables as well as offering one of the biggest and best ranges of fish outside Billingsgate.

The market spreads from Brixton Station Road through to Electric

Avenue encompassing the surrounding roads, railway arches and three arcades.

Brixton Station Road gets started a bit later than the rest of the market and carries a wider choice of items including hardware, general household goods, jewellery and shoes as well as the least interesting range of fruit and vegetable stalls. At the far end, past the junction with Pope Road, the stalls both under the arches and lining the roads are given over to second-hand clothes with one or two also throwing in some general bric-à-brac. Prices are low and this area can be a good hunting ground for bargains, but it will take a fair amount of searching.

• Stall 10 carries a good range of herbs and spice and dried beans and pulses.

• After a hard mornings browse John's Café amongst all the second-hand cloth stalls is a popular greasy spoon or try The Bushman Kitchen for fried dumplings, fried snappers, salt cod fritters or a range of fillings offered inside soft sweet cocobread washed down with a large glass of carrot juice.

The crowd density increases in Popes Road and gives a taste of the richness of choice on offer in Granville Arcade and Electric Avenue. Granville Arcade is a surprisingly light and airy building which offers a wealth of fruit, vegetables and groceries. One of its more unique shops is the Afro-Caribbean baker, D. Bess, situated on the corner of 4th and Ist Avenue. Their mouth-watering display includes Toto, a deliciously heavy but moist current cake, Gizarda, coconut pastry tarts, wonderfully dark brown bread pudding and delicious hard dough bread. Try the Coconut Drips, fragments of coconut coated in dark brown sugar, if you want a real treat. Nearby, Harry Otto and Son, the fishmongers, used to cure fish on the premises but health regulations put a stop to all that and now they can only boast salt mackerel as their own home-cured produce. This is offered with a wide range of fresh fish.

Electric Avenue, named thus because it was one of the first streets in the 1880's to get electricity, has the biggest range of fishmongers, butchers and fruit and vegetables and always seems to be the busiest part of the market. In amongst the produce stalls near Brixton Road there is a good selection of clothes and a haberdashery stall.

• Ginger's Stall, No. 3, is famous for his very competitively priced dress fabrics. The Atlantic fabric shop at No. 28 also carries an extensive range.

• Chaffer's displays hats of every size shape and colour at very affordable prices.

Market Row runs between Electric Avenue and Coldharbour Lane. A smaller version of Granville Arcade but with a good selection of clothing and a pet shop that specializes in tropical fish!

• Check out under the arches at No. 3 Atlantic Road: A & C Continental Grocers is a Greek, Italian, Portugese and Spanish delicatessen. Specialities include the carrot torte, a good choice of deliciously fresh Greek bread, and the Spanish specialities dried Sarrano ham and Manchego cheese.

CAMDEN LOCK MARKET N1
Sat–Sun 8am–6pm

There is still a very hippy feel to Camden Lock: plenty of tie-dye and ethnic jewellery on offer and a combined smell of incense and lentil dahl in the air.

The market is incredibly popular with tourists, and coachloads of Norwegians, Italians and especially Japanese unload every week. It gets very packed, particularly on Sunday afternoons, with log jams of people building up between the stalls.

There are over 200 stalls at Camden Lock, which is divided into several sections – Middle Yard, West Yard and the Dingwall Gallery among them. The main hall features a huge variety of arts and crafts stalls on 3 floors. The selection is rather hit and miss: everything from the impressive work of young jewellery designers to perfectly useless objects.

Best buys at the market include hats, jewellery and old clothes. There are also some good second-hand books, and plenty of tempting refreshments.

Some of the stalls and shops worth looking for in the market include:

• Liz Burrows. Liz has been running her leather stall in the middle of Middle Yard for 12 years and sells a mixture of new and old leather jackets. The new jackets are based on classic designs and the second-hand are a mixture of British and European jackets from the Sixties and Seventies. New jackets range from £75 to £160, second-hand cost about £25 to £35. She also sells waistcoats, trousers and jerkins.

• Norma Greenaway. Midddle Yard, opposite the Trading Post. Norma Greenaway designs and makes her own hand-knitted and crafted hats in wool and cotton. Skull caps and pointed hats in a wide variety of colourways. £9 to £30. She will also take commissions.

• Henry and Daughter. 17–18 Camden Lock Place. A great selection of vintage clothes, including beautiful silk and lace evening dresses, beaded dresses and a range of their own made-to-measure designs.

• Dingwall Gallery. Good for suede, leather and sheepskin.

Camden Lock Market, Chalk Farm Road, N1.

CAMDEN PASSAGE N1
Wed 7am–2pm Sat 9am–3pm

Camden Passage is one of London's largest antiques markets with over 350 shops and stalls packed into 200 yards along the narrow street. The market is open on Wednesdays and Saturdays. Wednesdays are when the dealers turn up to do business with each other and Saturday is the main day for browsers, tourists and locals.

The dealers are to be found in the various arcades which branch off the passage, The Georgian Village at the top nearest to Islington Green, the Mall on Upper Street, the Pierrepoint Arcade and Fleamarket in the centre and the Angel and York Arcades. The stalls also spill out onto the pavement around the Arcades. As a general rule the most expensive items are in the permanent shops along the passage, next most expensive are in the Arcades and any bargains are probably to be found on the pavement stalls. Among the best for browsing are the Georgian and Pierrepoint Arcades, with the Mall Arcade being rather more exclusive.

Most of the dealers specialize in certain items, for example, old teddy bears, Staffordshire figures or art nouveau, and if you are collecting a certain item, the Camden Passage Traders Association (0171 359 9969) will be able to put you in touch with a dealer. The market is also popular with film prop buyers who come to search out particular period items, like marcasite jewellery for *Scarlett*, the recent sequel to *Gone With The Wind*.

On Saturdays the basement of the Angel Arcade is given over to the London Military Market, an almost exclusively male preserve of medals, memorabilia, uniforms and badges, relating to every regiment and battle one could imagine. There are some salutary sights, such as an unexpurgated edition of Hitler's *Mein Kampf* on sale for £35.

The market never gets uncomfortably crowded, though many of the tiny stalls in the arcades are so packed with goods that there is only room for either the dealer or the customer inside.

Look out for:

• Hollywood Deco, York Arcade. Owner Tim Maddison, a self-confessed 'Late night double bill junkie', opened his shop, which is devoted to Hollywood film posters, in 1993. Hollywood Deco is the only shop of its kind in Britain, but in the USA, film posters are recognized collectors' items, with large scale auctions at Sotheby's and Christie's. Some samples from his stock include the Saul Bass poster for *Vertigo* retailing at £600 and the stunning poster for *Breakfast at Tiffany*'s – since Audrey Hepburn's death even more sought after at £750.

• The Bookstalls Market at the Islington High Street end of Camden Passage, which takes place every Thursday, 9.30am–3.30pm.

Camden Passage, N1.

CHAPEL STREET MARKET   N1
Tues–Sun. Early closing Thur and Sun.

One of the best general street markets in London, Chapel Street caters well for its mixed Islington clientele; stalls selling herbal teabags exist happily alongside those selling shellfish and jellied eels.

The market has a large range of very good fruit and veg stalls, mainly concentrated towards the Liverpool Road end of the market. There are also several good flower stalls and well-priced fashion and general goods.

Chapel Street Market, off Liverpool Road, N1.

CHELSEA ANTIQUES MARKET   SW3
Mon–Sat 10am–6pm

Chelsea Antiques Market calls itself Britain's oldest antique market and as soon as you walk down the passage, you step into another world far removed from the bustle of the King's Road. Quirky and eccentric, and now rather rundown, it offers a host of delights if you like what the trade refers to as 'small collectables' .

The ground floor is a showbiz buff's heaven, with 2 stalls selling entertainment memorabilia. One specializes in old theatre programmes, bills and posters, and is packed with a huge array of boxes and files containing everything from a 1930s Royal Variety Performance programme to a poster from Jimmy Edwards' appearance at the Liverpool Playhouse.

The second is devoted to old and modern movie stills, with plenty of up-to-date movie posters and some oddments like the Belgian poster for the Michael Caine movie *Billion Dollar Brain*.

The market also has a number of antiquarian book stalls, a specialist in telescopes and a number of stalls dealing in china, glass and jewellery.

The variety of items makes it a great place for browsing and it would seem to be a lot easier to strike a deal for a bargain here than at a lot of the other antiques markets. Peculiarly there is also a clairvoyant, though whether she can tell you if you and your purchase will end up making history on *The Antiques Roadshow* remains unclear!

Chelsea Antiques Market, 253 King's Road, SW3.
0171 352 5689

COLUMBIA ROAD   E2
Sun 8am–1pm

During the week Columbia Road is a quiet, pretty, residential street of flat-fronted Victorian houses, but on Sundays it is transformed into a lively botanical street party for the weekly flower market. Depending on the season, there are bedding plants, bulbs, shrubs, fresh cut flowers and indoor house plants on offer, all at some of the best prices in London.

The market has around 50 stalls and attracts a wide variety of customers, from locally resident artists to docklands dwellers and people from the suburbs. The feel of the area is a mixture of the traditional and the trendy, and the atmosphere at the market is relaxed, friendly, fragrant and very Sunday-morningish.

The stallholders are helpful and if you are after something especially obscure or exotic they can usually get hold of it for you. The market officially opens at 8am, but things really get going from 6.30am. The closing time of 1pm is strictly enforced and is probably the best time to get involved in some haggling as the traders pack up to get home for Sunday lunch.

Some of the stalls to look out for include:

• Mick Halcro's indoor and tropical plants stall in the middle of the market. Very good-quality palms, yuccas, and weeping figs, as well as exotics like banana and pineapple plants.

• The Grover family stall, on the corner near Ezra Street. Known as the Grover bunch, the family have been selling fresh cut flowers in the market for years. They sell all varieties of flowers in season, including some of the most perfect roses you'll find. Tulips £2.50 for 10, longiflora lilies at £3 a bunch.

Columbia Road Market, Columbia Road, E2.

- For trendy bits and pieces, stylish garden accessories or an enjoyable Sunday munch, the wooden-fronted shops running along the street are also well worth a look.

- No. 93, Paris and Rio's delicatessen. A great delicatessen and a good place to pick up some delicious comestibles to take home for lunch.

- No. 94, sells a range of jewellery by 4 young local designers, Susan Small, Simon Rees, Anna Lovell and Vicky Davies from £10 up to £90; they also stock clocks and T-shirts.

- No. 118, Fred Bare. Hat designers Fred Bare specialize in wearable titfers in a range of up-to-the-minute designs.

- No. 134, Lee's Seafoods. Takeaway cartons of whelks, cockles and eels.

- No. 138, Cafe Columbia. Filled or plain bagels and coffee to sustain you.

- No. 144, Classic Terracotta. A good range of well-priced terracotta pots and planters from France and Italy.

- No. 146, The Garden Studio. Garden sculptures made from old taps, beautiful window boxes and old-fashioned green iron watering cans with silver spouts (£24.50) are among the merchandise on sale.

- It might also be handy to know that the local pub, The Royal Oak, opens at 8am on Sundays. If a drink is too daunting a prospect they also serve tea, coffee and rolls and bagels to keep the traders going.

The Royal Oak, 73 Columbia Road, E2.
0171 739 8204

COVENT GARDEN WC2
Mon–Sun 9am–4pm

Covent Garden leads the pack in the Eighties arts and crafts markets boom.

The Apple Market, located in the restored arcades of the Piazza, still has a wide selection of good quality jewellery and handicrafts on sale. However, the prices are aimed at tourists, as are quite a lot of the goods, some of which, like the clowns and novelty clocks, now look a bit passé.

Jubilee Market is not much better and again is very touristy. The best day for both is probably antiques day on Monday, when a good selection of dealers offer Victoriana, silver, china and paintings.

Opera House Market deals in good second-hand clothes on Mondays but the rest of the week is a mixture of cheap jewellery, leather items, African memorabilia, and so on.

Covent Garden still definitely wins the best busking and street entertainment award, whether you like a superb rendition of *O Sole Mio* or a good mime artist.

Covent Garden Piazza: Mon antiques Tues–Sat crafts.
Jubilee market: Mon antiques Tues–Fri general Sat–Sun crafts.
Opera House market: Mon clothes Tues–Sun general.

Covent Garden Market, WC2.

• If you visit Covent Garden on a Saturday it's quite interesting to pop along and see the weekly Collector's Fair where badges, coins, stamps and medals are exchanged underneath the arches of the Embankment tube station!

Sat 8.30am–5pm
Charing Cross Collector' s Fair, WC2.

GRAYS ANTIQUE MARKET   SE1
Mon–Fri 10am–6pm

Historic interest at Grays doesn't just lie with the antiques: this market also has to be the only antiques emporium in London with an indoor river.

The water is a tributary of the River Tyburn, originating just south of Hampstead Heath, and once the last stretch of water seen by condemned men on their way to the gallows at what is now Marble Arch.

When Benny Gray bought the redbrick Victorian building in 1977, he decided to make a feature of the Tyburn tributary and the water is now channelled through the middle of the basement, overlooked by dealers' stalls and crossed by an ornamental bridge. At lunchtime, the dealers draw up chairs and eat their lasagne gazing into the waters.

Grays market is split over 2 sites, Davies Street and Davies Mews, and each contains over 200 dealers. Grays has a huge selection of antique jewellery dealers, with specialists in jet, Edwardian and Victorian pieces, Scottish agate and marcasite. There are also specialists dealing in fine oriental antiquities.

The large number of specialist dealers and the location means that bargains are rare, but the range of dealers is fascinating, from Art Deco to dinky toys, lalique to old London bus timetables.

There are also 2 cafes; the one in the Mews building is particularly attractive.

Look out particularly for:

• No. 10, The Golf Gallery. Sarah Fabian Baddiel, mother of comedian David Baddiel, first started collecting golf memorabilia 18 years ago and has since become a renowned authority on the subject, travelling all over the world to buy and sell. Her books on the subject include *Miller's Guide to Golf Memorabilia*. The collection of golfiana on display includes clubs, balls, trophies, books and postcards.

• No. 134, The Thimble Society of London. Started in 1981, the Thimble Society has over 1,000 members worldwide. The selection of thimbles on sale includes Staffordshire enamel, nineteenth-century porcelain, silver, gold, medieval and old Spanish thimbles, plus old advertising thimbles from the Twenties and Thirties.

Grays Antique Market, 558 Davies Street, and 1–7 Davies Mews, W1. 0171 629 7034

GREENWICH MARKET   SE10
Sat–Sun 9am–6pm

Historic Greenwich plays host to both an arts and crafts market and an antiques market each weekend.

The arts and crafts market is held in the middle of Greenwich in the former fruit and veg market, which was built in 1737. Designs on offer are high quality and more original than many such items you find elsewhere. There are approximately 100 stalls selling jewellery, handmade lace underwear, prints, painted china, ironwork candle holders, rugs and clothes. There is even a gargoyle stall. Worth looking out for are:

• No. 66. Zara Siddiqui describes her cushions as 'camp, opulent and lavish'; they feature cupids, violins, poodles and unicorns on screenprinted and handpainted silk, calico and cotton. There are over 60 designs and prices start at £13.

• Sara Reilly's mirrors, jewellery and lamps are made from beaten bronze, silver and copper on steel. Brooches from £10, mirrors £45 upwards. Sara also undertakes commissions.

The open air antiques market on Greenwich High Road is quite small, and made up of stalls selling jewellery, bric-à-brac, old pine and silverware.

A better bet for unusual items is the much larger market in the yard at Stockwell Street. Once you get past the burger stands and standard market fare at the front, things start to get interesting, with a good selection of Sixties and Seventies clothes in a big lock-up at the back.

Lock-ups Nos. 12 and 13 have a good selection of art deco, and no. 10 was selling a huge old butcher's block for £35. There is plenty to rummage through on the ground, including old brass portholes if you want to keep up the maritime theme.

The best fun and nostalgia, however, is to be had at no. 9 where James Lowe specializes in Fifties and Sixties kitsch: there is a splendid selection of curtains, cocktail glasses, yellow formica kitchen tables and chairs, flying ducks and lava lamps.

Tucked away in Thames Street, Sundays only (8am–4pm), there is a small bric-à-brac market which is worth a potter round if you are just browsing.

Greenwich Market, SE10.
0171 240 7405

LEADENHALL MARKET EC3
Mon–Fri 7am–3pm

The first Leadenhall market began in the Middle Ages, selling meat and fish, and taking its name from the lead-roofed mansion which stood nearby. In the fifteenth century, Dick Whittington, by then into his third term as Lord Mayor of London, bought the site and presented it as a gift to the City of London.

After the destruction by the Great Fire, the present building was redesigned and constructed in 1881 by Horace Jones (who also created Tower Bridge). The market has been sympathetically restored, retaining the cobblestones and many of the original shop fronts.

At lunchtimes, Leadenhall is packed with City workers flocking to the wine bars and takeaways, shopping for their supper or having their Oxfords shone up by the red-and-black uniformed boot boys. The market specialized in butchers, fishmongers and fruiterers but has now been joined by interlopers, such as the fashion chain Jigsaw, but it still retains plenty of character. Beware – the market keeps City hours and most of the shops shut by 3pm. Take a look at:

• No. 6–7, H.S. Linwood & Sons (established 1883). Despite the ravages of the recession there is still plenty of money about in the City, as the displays of smoked and fresh salmon at this traditional fishmonger serve to demonstrate.

• No. 64–72, Farringdons Records. A huge (over 20,000 titles) and excellent selection of classical, opera, jazz and blues CDs and tapes. Beautifully suited brokers and bankers tune out of the stresses of City life and into Maria Callas at the listening posts.

Leadenhall Market, off Gracechurch Street, EC3.

MERTON ABBEY MILLS   SW19
Sat–Sun 10am–5pm crafts
Sat 8am–2pm car boot sale
Thur 8am–2pm antique market

Converted from the former Liberty silk printing works, with the original Victorian waterwheel still in place, Merton Abbey Mills has become a thriving weekend craft market, attracting around 100 stalls on a Saturday and up to 250 on a Sunday.

There is a good and varied selection of crafts, including Victoriana, handpainted pottery, plaster busts, home-made jerk seasonings, old records, lace and clothes. There are a number of permanent shops on the site, as well as stalls, and the market is particularly good for second-hand books. Look out for:

• Abbey Books. Excellent selection of good-quality second-hand fiction paperbacks. They also specialize in Irish literature and cover film, art and poetry.

• Books and Lyrics. Books, records and tapes, sheet music and ephemera.

• Kenny's Komics. Bill Kenny says 'I don't sell comics, I sell memories,' and whether your favourite was *Wizard* or *Hotspur*, *Dick Barton* or *Bunty*, you're transported straight back to childhood among the 25,000 comics and annuals on offer. Bill can sell you an 1800 *Punch* annual or a 1975 *Wombles*.

There are also a number of food stalls, including Thai, Phillipine and hog roast, a tea room and a branch of the Gourmet Pizza Company, which overlooks the water.

On Saturdays a car boot sale also operates, regarded by aficionados as good for bric-à-brac and on Thursdays there is an antiques market.

Merton Abbey Mills, Watermill Way (A24), SW19.

NEW COVENT GARDEN FLOWER MARKET   SW8
Mon–Fri 4am–11am, Sat 4am–9am

For early birds, the most spectacular flower bargains in London are to be caught at the wholesale flower market in Nine Elms.

Based at this site since 1974, the market supplies the floristry trade, market stallholders and plant professionals, but is also open to the public.

At the entrance in Nine Elms Lane go in through the 'cash only' side, pay £2 entrance fee and find a parking space. Once you're through the automatic plastic doors, prepare to be amazed by the hectic profusion of plants, flowers and people.

This is a wholesale market and so bulk buying is the order of the day. The flowers are not marked with prices, so you' ll need to ask the stallholders, and VAT is added on when you pay. The market is busiest up until 7am, then things suddenly quieten down. The pick of the blooms are to be had earliest, but even towards closing there is still a huge selection.

The larger the amount the better the bargain. Bunches of 50 perfect Dutch tulips, literally fresh off the boat are £11; 15 lilies around £9; 10 marigolds £3. Birds of Paradise are £15.00 for 10, single amaryllis blooms £1.20 each and sunflowers 50p per head. A half-box of single jewel-coloured gerberas is £7.50 for 20 blooms. All the flowers are at their absolute best, and it shows.

The market is catering to all ends of the trade, so you'll find mixed bunches alongside extremely exotic blooms, and rarities like orange trees and beautiful corkscrew-trunked bay trees.

Smaller plants are sold by the box – for example, £16 for 8 azaleas – but the larger plants like palms, yuccas and jasmine can all be bought individually.

Stallholders are helpful as long as you don't hold things up; this is probably not the place to ask what might go best with the irises!

New Covent Garden Market, Nine Elms Lane, SW8.
0171 720 2211

There are 4 other wholesale markets which cater for serious bulk buying:

• For vegetables try further along Nine Elms Lane, provided you are prepared to buy by the crate and don't just want a couple of pounds of spuds.

• Or try Borough Market (the oldest fruit and veg market) which has far greater character. Mon–Sat 5.30am–10am.

Borough Market, Borough High Street, SE1.

• Billingsgate fish market will happily sell you a whole salmon or seabass. Wear wellingtons as it's wet and slippery. Tues–Sat 5am–9am.

Billingsgate Market, Trafalgar Way, Poplar, E14.
0171 987 1118

• Smithfield Meat Market is still operating from its original site and although trying to store, let alone eat, an entire carcass is unlikely, a visit to the poultry section can be very worthwhile.
Mon–Fri 5am–10.30am.

Smithfield Meat Market, EC1.

NINE ELMS SUNDAY MARKET   SW8
Sun 10am–3pm

If you like big, bold, brassy markets, then Nine Elms should
hit the spot. Taking place at the Covent Garden vegetable
market every Sunday, all the stalls sell modern goods,
including toys, trainers, T-shirts, tapes and toiletries.

You won't find anything here that you can't get elsewhere,
but it is a chance to see inside the modern monolithic
structure of the fruit and vegetable market. Unfortunately
that means that there is always a faintly pervading smell of
greens, which mixed with the odour of hot-dog onions isn't wildly
appealing.

Nine Elms Sunday Market, Nine Elms Lane, SW8.

• Other big, modern Sunday markets also take place at
Wembley Stadium and Western International.

NORTHCOTE ROAD ANTIQUES MARKET   SW11
Mon–Sat 10am–6pm Sun 12 noon–5pm

A pretty indoor arcade with an upstairs gallery and glass roof,
Northcote Road Antiques Market provides a cosy home for 30 dealers.
Goods on offer include silver, furniture, glass, china, prints and
paintings.

The market is particularly good for old pine, Victoriana, art deco and
silver cutlery. It is well worth looking out for the stall that sells old
shops signs and tins and for Banana Dance, which specializes in
decorative arts from the Twenties and Thirties and has a good range of
Clarice Cliff china.

Prices are what you'd expect in the now rather chi chi area the
market inhabits, but quality is good.

Upstairs is a very pleasant café, which serves tea, coffee, cakes and
more substantial fare.

• There is also a general street market – operating Mon–Sat
9am–5pm early closing at 1 pm on Wednesdays – which carries a good
range of fruit and vegetables as well as an excellent fish stall.

Northcote Road Antiques Market,
155a Northcote Rd, Battersea, SW11.
0171 228 6850

PETTICOAT LANE   E1
Sun 7am–2pm
Wentworth Street Mon–Fri 7am–2pm

Despite the quaint images the name conjures up, the original
Petticoat Lane, named after clothes dealers in the area in the 1600s,
no longer exists. Petticoat Lane now refers to Middlesex Street and the
surrounding roads, including Wentworth Street and Bell Lane.

In Victorian times horrified Christians drove fire engines through
the market to try to break up the Sunday trading. At various times the
area has been home to Huguenot weavers, Jewish traders, the French,
Spanish and Portuguese. Now the local community is predominantly
Bangladeshi, and work mainly in the rag trade.

The market itself has no particular distinguishing characteristics, and devotes itself primarily to modern fashion with leather goods, particularly bags and shoes, making up a large number of the 850 stalls. Prices are good.

Petticoat Lane Market, Wentworth Street and surrounds, E1.

PORTOBELLO ROAD W11
Sat 6am–5pm antiques
Mon–Fri 8am–5pm, early closing Thur fruit and veg
Fri 8am–3pm general

In 1737, after the battle of 'Puerto Bello' in the Caribbean, when the British, lead by Admiral Vernon, captured that town from the Spanish, a local man renamed his farm 'Puerto Bello' to celebrate the victory. The cart track leading from his farm to the main London road became known as Portobello Farm Lane and eventually became the Portobello Road.

With suitable historic irony, Portobello is now the centre for the Spanish community in London, with a Spanish school, restaurants and delicatessens serving the 12,000-strong first and second generation Spanish population.

A market of some description has been taking place in Portobello since 1870. Weekdays are given over to the usual fruit and veg stalls, but on Saturdays virtually the entire mile-long stretch of the Portobello Road is transformed into a trinket and trophy hunter's paradise. Over 2,000 stalls set up, selling everything from skulls to Seventies suede coats.

The market divides into several distinct sections and you'll need a hefty amount of stamina if you intend to cover the whole market.

Golborne Road

Branching off the Portobello Road at its top end, where the main market begins to fizzle out, Golborne Road is well worth a look for bric-à-brac, second-hand clothes, old tools and back numbers of *Private Eye*. There are also some good and relatively cheap old pine and antique shops. Further along the road is the centre of London's Portuguese community and on Saturday mornings everyone converges on the Lisboa Patisserie at no. 57 for a glass of milky galao coffee and delicious pastries including *bolo de arroz*, *bolo de coco* and *pastel de nata* (custard tart).

The stretch of the market from Golborne Road down to Portobello Green is mainly for bric-à-brac, with old clothes piled high onto stalls; you'll need to rummage. Plenty of second-hand bikes at stall no. 173.

Portobello Green

Stretching under the Westway between Portobello Road and Ladbroke Grove, Portobello Green is home to some of the best second-hand clothes stalls in London. They are always well stocked for the fashion movement of the moment, whether the look is dandy, punk, or A-line miniskirts. There are also a number of young designers selling their own lines, both on the stalls and in the covered arcade. Look out for:

• Catweasle. Unit 21 Portobello Arcade. Catweasle take old clothes and recycle the fabrics into new designs, contrasting textures and colours to create a unique look.

• Cockney Visionaries. Near Portobello Green Fitness Centre. Dave Carroll and his partners grew up with punk and Carroll has dealt in second-hand Seditionaries and Vivienne Westwood originals – now coveted collectors' items which exchange hands for spectacular sums. Cockney Visionaries have now branched out into their own line of punk-inspired clothing, raincoats, jackets, T-shirts, socks and jewellery, frequently bearing the legend 'only anarchists are pretty'. Vastly popular with the Japanese, they keep their Portobello stall because 'it keeps us in touch'.

From Portobello Green down to Colville Terrace is the main general market, with a great variety of quality fruit and veg stalls selling an excellent range of produce, and some especially good fresh fish stalls.

• Look out for the man selling superb, and well-priced, tropical flowers, including heleconia, ginger lilies and Birds of Paradise. He normally stands outside the Anderson O'Day Gallery at 255 Portobello Road, near to the junction with Lancaster Road.

• Mr Christian's. On Saturdays, the table outside Mr Christian's delicatessen at 11 Elgin Crescent is piled high with delicious breads –

honey and walnut, olive, pumpernickel and many others – as well as filling-packed rolls and croissants. Roasted peppers and cheese in ciabatta is delicious.

From Colville Terrace downwards the antiques market begins in earnest and this area is packed with tourists, particularly in spring and summer.

The street stalls along this stretch are particularly good for old luggage, leather and crocodile bags and jewellery.

Along Westbourne Grove and down Portobello Road the area is thick with antiques arcades, selling everything from ostrich eggs to sedan chairs. Worth looking out for are:

• No. 113. Good for bric-à-brac.

• Basement arcade (290 Westbourne Grove). Old advertising tins and memorabilia, a cigarette-card specialist, toy soldiers and other ephemera.

• Red Lion arcade (165–169 Portobello Road). Particularly good for old linens and lace, antique ribbons, buttons, braids and trims. Try The Old Haberdasher (Nos.12 & 13) and also Brenda Linens at stand 30.

• The Good Fairy arcade. Some of the friendliest and nicest dealers are among the 55 stallholders in The Good Fairy arcade. You will find a great selection of silver, from old English hotelware to cutlery, Victoriana, costume and period jewellery.

The Portobello Road Antique Dealers Association can direct you to specialist dealers, and they publish a free brochure about the market. They also run an information booth on market days at the junction of Portobello Road and Westbourne Grove.

Portobello Antique Dealers Association.
0171 371 6960

Portobello Market, Portobello Road, W10.

ROMAN ROAD MARKET   E3
Tue and Thur 8am–2pm Sat 8am–5pm

Roman Road is a typical, vibrant East End market, which really came into its own during the Seventies and was at one point known as the King's Road of the East End.

One of the old charter markets, Roman Road has been running on its present site for at least 100 years and of the 200 or so stalls, over half are devoted to fashion and the rest to household goods and fruit and vegetables.

A recent change has been the digging up of the road and the laying down of Carnaby-Street-style paving. According to one trader, 'the local council thought the market should be a sort of East End Covent Garden'. Certainly the upheaval, together with the recession, has caused problems for the traders and there are those who say the market has never really recovered. However, Roman Road still offers plenty of choice at good prices.

• There is a branch of the Ridley Road bagel bakery and at either end of the road are branches of G. Kelly's noted eel and pie shop', established in 1937.

Roman Road Market, Roman Road, E3.

SHEPHERD'S BUSH MARKET   W12
Mon–Sat 9.30am–5pm early closing Thur.

Running alongside the railway arcade and bounded at either end by the Goldhawk and Uxbridge Roads, Shepherd's Bush is a lively market with a strong West Indian flavour.

There is a good variety of general goods, from clothes to china, watches to washing-up bowls. The West Indian food stalls are among the best and along the side of the market several food shops, like Moon foods, sell salted cod and seasonings.

Look out for:

• Steve Hill (nos. 20–21) selling dasheen, cassava, jelly nuts and numerous varieties of yam – soft, hard, Ghana and coco among them.

• Franco (no. 34) has a good selection of glass, china and pots and pans.

Shepherd's Bush Market, W12.
0181 743 5089

• There's a Car Boot Sale (starts 6am) every Friday, Saturday and Sunday right next to the market in Steptoe's Yard (0171 602 2699).

SPITALFIELDS   E1
Mon–Fri 11am–3pm Sun 9am–3pm

The original Spitalfields fruit and vegetable market began trading in 1682. In 1991 the market was relocated to Leyton and the site earmarked for a Broadgate-style redevelopment. However, the property recession intervened, construction was halted and in 1992 Spitalfields was handed over to Urban Space Management – the company who already run Camden Lock market – on a lease running until 1999.

The result has been the creation of a thriving eclectic market, at its best on Sundays, and based largely around an organic theme. Shops and stalls sell a very good selection of high-quality organic vegetables, fruit and breads, as well as arts and crafts.

It's a particularly good place for a family Sunday out, with dodgems and entertainment available for children, and the Stepping Stones city farm bring in goats rabbits and lambs.

The general feel is very 'right on' (its fathers who are carrying the babies in the slings), but the atmosphere is lively and enjoyable. In the centre is an international food village serving everything from crêpes to couscous.

Shops around the edge include:

• Bogtrotter and Stuffer. Indonesian shirts, Mexican baja tops and other clothing from around the world.

• Eclectics. Velvet and brocade cushions and footstools, fish mirrors, busts and china.

• Where on Earth. Arts and crafts from around the world, particularly Indonesia. Wooden flowers and cacti, tribal dance masks, batik wall hangings.

There is now also a Saturday antiques market and plans afoot include the opening of the Spitalfields Market Opera, and a Bangladeshi festival.

Stalls are available to rent on an ad hoc basis.The shops are open all week.

Spitalfields Market, Brushfield Street, E1.
0171 247 6590

DESIGNER AND CRAFT SHOPS

GABRIEL'S WHARF

The opening of the Waterloo International terminal, the conversion of County Hall into a hotel and a proposed IMAX cinema close to Waterloo Bridge all mean huge changes for London's South Bank. Other development includes the conversion of the famous riverside art deco Oxo Tower into flats and workspaces, due to open in 1995 and proposals have also been invited for the remodelling of the main South Bank buildings.

The renaissance of the area is due largely to the work of the Coin Street Community Builders, a group of local people who are behind the development of the riverside Bernie Spain Gardens and local housing co-op developments.

In the late Eighties Gabriel's Wharf opened as a home for designers 20 workshops on the site. They are unique in that they are open to the public on a daily basis and many will undertake commissions.

There are also several restaurants on the site, including the American-style Studio Six (popular with staff from the next-door LWT building) and The Gourmet Pizza Company both of which have outdoor tables, near the river, in summer.

Some of the current shops include:

• Vivienne Legg. Working at her potter's wheel in the window of her studio at no. 16, Vivienne creates delicate, pastel flower painted bowls, plates and vases in porcelain. Bowls from £17.

• Gattopavone. Brightly coloured handmade children's furniture, Picasso-inspired lamps and handpainted wooden jewellery.

• David Ashton. Jeweller. Works in gold, silver and platinum, specializing in 2-colour gold.

• Shanley & Clark. Lauren Shanley's forte is one-off jackets, dresses, waistcoats, quilts and hats made from opulent recycled fabrics – brocades are a favourite.

There is also a craft market on the site every Friday.

The Coin Street Community Builders will be opening a further development of shops-cum-workshops in July at the Oxo Tower Wharf. A spectacular rooftop restaurant is also included in their plans.

Gabriel's Wharf, 56 Upper Ground, SE1.
0171 620 0544
Oxo Tower Wharf, Barge House Street, SE1.
0171 620 0544

COCKPIT WORKSHOPS

Another group of working designers are located in the
Cockpit Workshops in Clerkenwell. Although the workshops,
home to around 90 craftspeople, are not open to the public on
a daily basis, they do hold several open days each year when
you can watch the designers at work and buy their creations,
including jewellery, textiles, ceramics, woodwork and metalwork.

Cockpit Workshops, Cockpit Yard, Northington Street, WC1.
071 831 6761

• Another crafts centre which is home to designers and holds open
days each year, usually at the end of November, is 401½.
401½ Wandsworth Road, SW8.
0171 622 7261

CAR BOOT SALES

A phenomenon of recent years, car boot sales take place all over the
capital every weekend.
    Originally it was a way for individuals to sell or swap unwanted
household items but, more often than not, it has now become just
another form of market where old and new are sold side by side.
    The biggest are run like military manoeuvres, with hundreds of cars
being marshalled into position and all manner of goods emerge from
the vehicles and are set out on display. The smaller ones tend to
reflect the original premise and on the whole are a better try for the
bargain hunter.
    How to find them:

• Local papers are best for regular listings.

• Some established sites are listed below – but do check first as they
are likely to change without warning.

Over 200 pitches:

Sun 7am. Pickford' s Cottage, Sewardstone Road, Chingford, E4.
0181 529 3922

Sun 8am. Royal Albert Dock (opp. City Airport), Docklands, E16.
0171 474 3449

Sun 6am. Hackney Wick Greyhound Stadium, Waterden Road, E15.

Sun 7am. Lewisham Centre Multi Storey Car Park,
Molesworth Street, Lewisham, E13.
01426 924 201

Sat and Sun 6am. Behind the Blind Beggar Pub, Whitechapel Road, E1.
0171 240 7405

Under 100 pitches:

Sun 9am. Bromyard Leisure Centre, Bromyard Avenue, Acton, W3.
01895 253 087

Sat and Sun 7am. The Old Bus Garage, Harmond Street,
off Chalk Farm Road, Chalk Farm, NW1.
0171 240 7405

Sat 1pm. Ashburnham Community Centre,
Burnaby Street, Lots Road, SW10.
0171 352 3335

Sat and Sun 9am. Park Road, Crouch End, N8.
0171 833 0780

Sat and Sun 7am. Goswell Road (opp Angel station), Islington, N1.
0171 240 7405

On alternate Sundays 8am. Highbury Round House,
71 Ronalds Road, Islington, N5.
0171 359 5916

Sun 9 am. Helen's car boot sale, Kensal Rise School,
Harvest/Chamberlayne Road, NW6.
0181 960 6521

Sun 8 am. Kilburn College, Carlton Vale, Kilburn, NW6.
0171 625 7730

Sun 8am. Burghley Hall Pub, 33 Princes Way, Southfields, SW19.
0181 788 5180

Sat and Sun 7am. Opposite West Hampstead Tube Station,
West Hampstead, NW6.
01923 770 515

JUMBLE SALES

Another great hunting ground for the astute bargain hunter; choose a
relatively affluent area, like Fulham or Chelsea.

Jumble sales are advertized in local libraries, local newspapers and
often in nearby shop windows. Remember to get there the minute
things start and to move quickly; any decent bargains are normally
gone within the first 20 minutes.

• Charity shops are also good for bargains – again, try the more
affluent areas for the best pickings!

AUCTIONEERS

DOWELL LLOYD AUCTIONS

An average 'furniture and miscellaneous' auction at Dowell Lloyd consists of over 600 lots, with an eclectic selection of items on offer. As well as antique and modern furniture, you could pick up, for example, a Louis Vuitton bag, Edwardian commode, penny farthing bicycle, gilt-framed mirrors, prints, jewellery and terracotta urns. Modern goods include video cameras and recorders.

Dowell Lloyd also handle Customs and Excise Goods and items for the Metropolitan police, so cases of sparkling wine and an unclaimed chandelier may also be among the lots. Metropolitan police auctions also include car radios, bicycles, and electrical goods.

The atmosphere is relaxed and making a bid is easy. Bargains are a definite possibility. There are several auctions each month, with viewing the day before. Ring for details.

Dowell Lloyd Auctioneers, Putney Auction Galleries, 118 Putney Bridge Road, SW15.
081 788 7777

• Other London auction houses:

Lots Road Galleries, Lots Road, Chelsea, SW10.
0171 351 7771

Chelsea Auctioneers, 35 New Kings Road, SW6.
0171 384 1927

Grays Auctions Ltd, 34–36 Jamestown Rd, Camden Town, NW1.
0171 284 2026

Academy Auctioneers & Valuers, Northcote House, Northcote Avenue, Ealing, W5.
0181 579 7466

Criterion Auction Rooms, 53–55 Essex Road, Islington, N1.
0171 359 5707

Phillips, 101 New Bond Street, W1.
0171 495 0225

Macgregor Nash and Co, Lodge House, Lodge Lane, N12.
0181 445 9000

ARTS AND ENTERTAINMENT

EATING AND DRINKING

While you could nurse a coffee and dijestif into the small hours in almost any other European capital, until very recently London closed down after 11pm, leaving little choice other than to head for an expensive club or home for hot chocolate.

Our licensing laws are still a little archaic in some areas, but now more and more of London's bars are being granted late-night licences, with Soho's café-bars leading the way. Quaglinos is modelled on the stylish late-night brasseries of Paris and a good range of ethnic restaurants are now joining the Turkish, Lebanese and Chinese eateries which have been alone up until now in keeping London's late birds fed and watered. The late night licences are issued on the condition that the bar owner provides adequate control of his premises – this roughly translates into an admission charge, which is more often than not imposed after 10pm.

Here is a range of places, all of which offer something a little different (See also Eating and Drinking by the River p.220–223 and Canalside p. 225–227). If, however, you are seeking something specific and none of these fit the bill, try calling Restaurant Services 0181 888 8080 who have since 1979 been offering Londoners a free restaurant advisory and booking service. They also offer a research service for the more complex requests.

LATE-NIGHT LONDON

ANDREAS   W1

A friendly, family-run Greek restaurant started in 1960 by Andreas Constantinides and now run by his son Gabriel, Andreas provides good Greek food in comfy surroundings.

Dinner 5.30pm–1am 7 days a week.
Andreas, 22 Charlotte Street, W1.
0171 580 8971

ATLANTIC BAR AND GRILL   W1

Converted from the cavernous basement of the Regent Palace Hotel, the Atlantic is the brainchild of entrepreneur Oliver Peyton, whose previous successes have included the club RAW and bringing the designer drinks Sapporo and Absolut Vodka to London's bars. Of the new venture he says: 'The idea is to eat out and drink out late in London in a club atmosphere without the hassle of getting a club membership' .

  The original art deco interior has been restored and now houses a

200-seat restaurant plus, if you just want a drink, there are 2 late night bars, one devoted to champagne and cocktails.

With a Connaught-trained chef in the kitchen and Dick Bradsell, the former manager of trendy member's club Fred's, in charge of the bar, Atlantic Bar And Grill successfully fills a gap in the late night London market.

Mon–Sat 12noon–3am. Last food orders 2.30am. Open for brunch on Sunday.

Atlantic Bar and Grill, 20 Glasshouse Street, W1.
0171 734 4888

BALANS   W1

One of the newest additions to the thriving Soho café bar scene, Balans is reminiscent of a 1950s coffee bar, recreating that Fifties feeling with tiger-print lamps and primary coloured walls. An open front lets you observe the passing street scene.

The clientele is largely gay in the evenings, and more mixed during the day and at weekends. Food for under a fiver includes dishes like oyster mushroom and cream cheese ravioli and eggs benedict.

Mon–Sat 9am–2am Sun 9am–midnight.

Balans, 60 Old Compton Street, W1.
0171 437 5212

BOARDWALK   W1

Several floors of decor that is best described as 'deep south distressed' include a ground-floor restaurant which serves seafood gumbo, jambalaya and cajun, and an upstairs bar which has a good cocktail list, and where you can just have a drink.

Popular with large groups and there's a disco downstairs.

Mon–Wed 12noon–1am Thur–Fri 12noon–2am Sat 6pm–2am. Closed Sun. Last food orders half an hour before closing.

Boardwalk Restaurant Bar, 18 Greek Street, W1.
0171 287 2051

CAFÉ BOHÈME   W1

Inspired by the all day and night Falstaff café in Belgium, Bohème's wooden floors, swirling ceiling fans, street-side tables and great opening hours, create some Gallic flair on Old Compton Street.

You could roll up here at 8am for *petit dejeuner* and eat and drink your way through to 3am if you so chose. Dishes range from *croque monsieur* to Chateaubriand, with a special shorter menu after midnight.

As this is one of Soho's most popular café bars, there is a complete crush late at night; it is much quieter during the day. There is live jazz between 3pm and 5pm.

Mon–Sat 8am–3am Sun 11am–11pm.

Café Bohème, 13 Old Compton Street, W1.
0171 734 0623

THE EDGE W1

On the other side of Soho Square and slightly away from the main Soho mêlée, The Edge was one of the first designer gay and straight café bars.

Nineties decor means plenty of metalwork and gallery art, while Nineties food includes scallop tartlets and mini croissants with fresh fruits drizzled with honey.

Food is available until 6pm and drinks (including frozen vodka shots – try chilli, coriander or toffee) until 1am.

Mon–Fri 11am–1am Sat 10am–1am Sun 12noon–10.30pm.

The Edge, 11 Soho Square, W1.
0171 439 1313

HAAGEN-DAZS WC2

If you don't feel like a full meal, but could kill for ice cream, the good news is that the Haagen Dazs parlour on Leicester Square stays open until 1am on Friday and Saturday nights.

Mon–Thurs 10am–midnight Fri-Sat 10am-1am.

Haagen-Dazs on the Square, 14 Leicester Square, WC2.
0171 287 9577.

HAMINE W1
A stylish, minimalist fast-turnover Japanese noodle bar on 2 floors. Choose and pay at the front counter and your food is served to you while you watch Japanese satellite TV and leaf through Japanese comics.

Mon–Sat 12noon–2.30am Sun 12noon–midnight.

Hamine, 84 Brewer Street, W1.
0171 439 0785

HODJA NASREDDIN N1

This tiny Turkish restaurant has a tented ceiling and decor which has been described as 'an Aladdin's cave of kitsch'.

Renowned as one of London's best cheap Turkish restaurants, Hodja Nasreddin serves all the usual specialities.

Mon–Fri 12noon–1am Sat–Sun 12noon–3am.

Hodja Nasreddin, 53 Newington Green Road, N1.
0171 226 7757

• Other late-night Turkish restaurants include:

Istanbul Iskembecisi, 9 Stoke Newington Road, N16.
0171 254 7291
11am–5am daily.

Samsun, 34 Stoke Newington Road, N16.
0171 249 0400
11am–2am daily.

JOE ALLEN   WC2

Joe Allen's is still the stars' favourite late night haunt; after the show they pile in for salads, burgers and ribs. As last orders aren't until 12.45am, there's plenty of time to get in some serious celebrity spotting but it gets very busy, so its best to book first.
    Mon–Sat 12noon–12.45am Sun 12noon–11.30pm.

Joe Allen, 13 Exeter Street, WC2.
0171 836 0651

LOS LOCOS   W1/WC2

Loud in most senses of the word, and definitely better for groups than an intimate tete-a-tete, especially once the disco gets going.
    The Mexican menu includes chimichangas, quesadillas and steaks but you can just have a drink if you choose.
    Mon–Sat 5.30pm–3am Sun 3pm–9pm.

Los Locos, 14 Soho Street, W1.
0171 287 0005

Also at 24–26 Russell Street, WC2.
0171 379 0220

MR KONG   WC2

One of the few Chinese restaurants in the area which consistently gets into the Good Food guides, Mr Kong serves imaginative and original dishes such as braised duck web in oyster sauce.
    Daily 12noon–2am.

Mr Kong, 21 Lisle Street, WC2.
0171 437 7341

• Other late-opening Chinese restaurants:

The Lido 41 Gerrard Street, W1.
0171 437 4431
11.30am–4.30am daily.

Mayflower, 68–70 Shaftesbury Avenue, W1.
0171 734 9207.
5pm–4am daily.

New Diamond, 23 Lisle Street, WC2.
0171 437 7221
12noon–3am daily.

Yungs, 23 Wardour Street, W1.
0171 437 4986
12noon–4.15am daily. Licensed until midnight.

THE 'O' BAR   W1

A crowded and lively bar where the main attraction is the pitchers of margaritas, Long Island Iced tea and sangria – guaranteed to make the staidest night out start swinging along.
    The ground floor is light and airy and attractive with a huge mosaic

on the wall, while the downstairs has a more subterranean feel.
Mon–Wed 1pm–1am Thur 1pm–2am
Fri and Sat 1pm–3am.

The 'O' Bar, 83–85 Wardour Street, W1.
0171 437 3490

QUAGLINOS SW1

Sir Terence Conran's stylishly successful emporium. You can book for the full-scale restaurant experience or turn up to the balcony bar where you can just have a late night drink or choose from the shorter and cheaper bar menu.
Mon–Thur, last food orders midnight, last drink 12.50am. Fri–Sat last food orders 1am, last drink 1.50am. Sun last food orders 10pm, last drink 10.50pm. Live jazz in the bar.

Quaglinos, 16 Bury Street, St James's, SW1.
0171 930 6767

RANOUSH W2

For a late-night non-alcoholic pick-me-up, drop into the Ranoush juice bar. One counter serves freshly squeezed juices, like mango, melon or carrot, and the other serves Middle Eastern snacks.
9am–3am daily.

Ranoush, 43 Edgware Road, W2.
0171 723 5929

UP ALL NIGHT SW10.

Full of Fulham clubbers, refuelling on burgers, chargrills, steaks and salads from the lengthy menu.
Mon–Fri 6pm–6am Sat noon–6am. Last food orders 5.30am. Licensed until midnight.

Up All Night, 325 Fulham Road, SW10.
0171 352 1996

• Additional late night extras.

Calamitee's, 103 Heath Street, NW3.	0171 435 2396
Cuba, 11-13 Kensington High Street, W8.	0171 938 4137
Frog & Nightgown, 148 Old Kent Road, SE1.	0171 701 1689
Gin Palace, 205-209 Old Kent Road, SE1.	0171 237 4911
The Gallery, 76 Parry Street, SW8.	0171 820 9857
WKD, 18 Kentish Town Road, NW1.	0171 267 1869

MUSIC, DRINK AND FOOD

AMERICAN BAR AT THE SAVOY WC2

Everything a cocktail bar should be and suitably expensive to match. The piano playing by Mike McKenzie is some of the best in London.
    Mon–Sat 11.30am–3pm 5.30pm–11pm. Sun 12noon–3pm 7pm–10.30pm.

American Bar, Savoy Hotel, The Strand, WC2.
0171 836 4343

BABOON RESTAURANT AND PIANO BAR W1

Modern British cuisine served against a background of piano music from 7pm–11pm Monday through to Saturday. The cocktail bar is suitably sophisticated!
    Mon–Fri 12noon–3am Sat 6pm–11pm.

Baboon Restaurant and Piano Bar, 76 Wigmore Street, W1.
0171 224 2992

BAR MADRID W1

Café-bar-restaurant serving tapas at the bar or a full restaurant menu and drinks until 3am. There is Latin music until midnight when a DJ takes over (admission charge on some nights). They also run salsa and samba classes earlier in the evening.
    Mon–Sat 7pm–3am.

Bar Madrid, 4 Winsley Street, W1.
0171 436 4649

• An upstairs Brazilian tapas bar called Viva Brazil operates on the same premises.

CUBA LIBRE N1

Stylish Cuban restaurant and bar where the extensive menu includes the Havana speciality *Masitas de puerco a la Habanera* (pork marinated in cumin) and *Ropa vieja a la Cubana* (shredded braised beef in a herb sauce). The bar serves Cuban beers and cocktails.
    Live Latin music every Thursday, Friday and Saturday nights.
Sun–Wed Restaurant 12noon–11.30pm Bar 12noon–midnight
Thur–Sat Restaurant 12noon–12.30am Bar 12noon–2am.

Cuba Libre, 72 Upper Street, N1.
0171 354 9998

DOVER STREET WINE BAR W1

Live bands offering jazz, blues, jump jive and swing perform nightly in this basement restaurant. The surroundings are more functional than glamorous, but the food(French and modern European) is good and the prices some of the most reasonable on the dinner/dance circuit.

Dover Street Wine Bar, 8-9 Dover Street, W1.
0171 629 9813

ELYSEE W1

A 5-piece band fronted by Greek singers provide the music in this traditional Greek restaurant. Entertainment also includes belly dancing. Its loud and fun and not a venue for concentrated talk!
  Mon–Fri 12noon–3pm and 7pm–3.30am.

Elysee, 13 Percy Street, W1.
0171 636 4804

KETTNERS W1

Known for its champagne bar, lengthy list of champagne bottles and excellent pizzeria, Kettners also enhances the proceedings with some lively piano music.
  Mon–Sun 11.30am–12midnight.

Kettners, 29 Romilly Street, W1.
0171 734 6112

MAROUSH W2

One of a chain of good Lebanese restaurants, where 3-piece bands play Arabic music and singers and belly dancers help to provide the evenings entertainment. Surroundings are opulent and charges are high.
  Mon–Sun 12noon–2am.

Maroush, 21 Edgware Road, W2.
0171 723 0773

R BAR SW3

Jazz and vocalists perform here but not every evening so if its important you need to check first. Food is described as light 'Anglo Aussie fare' but it is highly recommended.
  Mon–Tues 7.30pm–11.30pm Wed–Sat 7.30pm–12midnight.

R Bar, 4 Sydney Street, SW3.
0171 352 3433

SOUTHAMPTONS 124 WC1

Live bands play jazz and blues early on in the evening and progress to soul and funky later in the evening. Cuisine is modern European and there is also a small dance floor.
  Mon–Fri 12noon–3pm Mon–Sat 7pm–1am Sun 7pm–12midnight.

Southamptons 124, 124 Southampton Row, WC1.
0171 405 1466

VILLA CARLOTTA W1

A 2-piece band provides music on Friday and Saturday nights in this most traditional of Italian restaurants.
  Mon–Thur 12noon–3pm 6pm–11pm Fri–Sat 12noon–3pm 6pm–11.30pm.
Villa Carlotta, 33 Charlotte Street, W1.
0171 636 6011

EATING AND DRINKING

BREAKFAST FROM MIDNIGHT

If you've reached the stage where going home would seem like a cop-out, but you need refuelling, here are some favourite all-night and early morning 'breakfast' haunts.

AMANDINE   SW10

If you fancy a croissant and a cappuccino for breakfast, then the freshest, as well as pain au chocolat and brioche, are available hot from the oven at the Amandine patisserie from 4.30am.

Takeaway or sit in, when you can also opt for a fry-up. 4.30am–7pm daily.

Amandine, 228 Fulham Road, SW10.
0171 376 8801

BAR ITALIA   W1

This famed Italian hang-out, a Soho fixture since 1949, stays open until at least 4am most nights and all night on Saturdays. Loud and lively, with recordings of Italian football matches blaring out from the TV at the back and Rocky Marciano glaring down from the wall, Bar Italia serves what is probably the best cappuccino in town.

Bar Italia, 22 Frith Street, W1.
0171 437 4520

BRICK LANE BEIGEL BAKE   E1

Open 24 hours every day, the Beigel Bake is the favoured haunt of cabbies, clubbers and Brick Lane market traders. Everyone queues for coffee and smoked salmon and cream cheese bagels – at 85p one of the best bagel buys in the capital.(See also Markets, p.133)

Brick Lane Beigel Bake, 159 Brick Lane, E1.
0171 729 0616

CHELSEA BRIDGE SNACK WAGON   SW8

This all-night cabbies' haunt is also particularly popular with bikers, who converge at the bridge from all over London on a Friday night for a burger or hot dog and a very strong cup of tea.

The last Saturday of every month sees The Chelsea Cruise, a convoy of classic Cadillacs, customized creations and more mundane campers and Cortinas, which tours around the area and ends up in Battersea Park, where gleaming chrome is compared, cars bought and sold and envious glances exchanged.

The Cruise has been a fixture since the Forties; no one organizes it – it just happens.

10.30pm–12noon seven days a week.

Chelsea Bridge Snack Wagon, Chelsea Bridge (Battersea side), SW8.

THE COCK TAVERN   EC1

You can bet the bacon doesn't come any fresher than at the Smithfield market hostelries, where porters in white, blood-spattered aprons sit down to consume the cooked version of what they've just spent the past hours lugging about.

Ketchup bottles sit welcomingly on the tables at The Cock and breakfasts can range from a restrained scrambled eggs on toast to the complete, no-holds-barred Cock breakfast involving sausage, egg, bacon, beans, kidneys, liver, black pudding and tomato – and a trip to the cardiologist shortly after! Despite the early hour, the tavern is licensed so workers can wind down with a quick bevy or two.

Open from 5.30am to 10.30am for breakfast. Licensed from 6.30am.

The Cock Tavern, East Poultry Avenue, Smithfield Market, EC1.
0171 248 2918

OLD COMPTON CAFÉ   W1

This is a largely gay café serving sandwiches, snacks, soups and jacket potatoes 24 hours a day. Not licensed.

Old Compton Café, 34 Old Compton Street, W1.
0171 439 330

THE FOX AND ANCHOR   EC1

Night and day collide in the early hours at the Fox and Anchor. Meat porters from Smithfield and nurses from Barts drop in for a big breakfast after their shifts, while pinstripe-clad City dealers stoke up on their way into work.

The breakfast menu ranges from fillet steak to black pudding toasted sandwiches. There is also a vegetarian breakfast and smoked salmon and scrambled egg.

The 200-year-old pub is licensed from 6am.

Mon–Fri 6am–10pm Breakfast 7am–10.30am Sat 8am–12noon Breakfast 8am–10.30am.

The Fox and Anchor, 115 Charterhouse Street, EC1.
0171 253 4838

HARRY'S   W1

Virtually a Soho institution, Harry's has been providing late-night sustenance to clubbers, local workers and night owls for years. You can have anything from a hot chocolate to the 'Sophistication' breakfast of scrambled eggs, smoked salmon, orange juice and tea or coffee.

Mon–Sat 10pm–6am.

Harry's, 19 Kingly Street, W1.
0171 434 0309

THE HOPE TAVERN   EC1

This historic Smithfield tavern is famed for its upstairs oak-panelled Sirloin Restaurant, which serves legendary champagne breakfasts. The Hope is a particular favourite with surgeons and anaesthetists from Bart's hospital, who opt for 10oz of well-hung steak (£9.50). It is advisable to book.

Breakfast Mon–Fri 7.15am–9.30am.

The Hope Tavern, 94 Cowcross Street, EC1.
0171 250 1442

THE MARKET CAFÉ   E1

Opening hours here are the reverse of the norm, with the net-curtained café opening up in the middle of the night at 2am and closing down the following lunchtime.

Breakfasts are served to cabbies and late-night workers and much-praised good home cooking is the order of the day.

Mon–Fri 2am–1.30pm Sat 2am–10am. Closed Sun.

The Market Café, 5 Fournier Street, E1.
0171 247 9470

RIDLEY HOT BAGEL BAKERY   E8

Another 24-hour bagel bakery, where gefilte fish and latkes are also available as well as doughnuts and other sweet things.

Ridley Hot Bagel Bakery, 13–15 Ridley Road, E8.
0171 241 1047

SIMPSONS   WC2

For the first 160 years of its life the Simpsons restaurant only opened for breakfast once – to oblige Henry Kissinger – but since the beginning of 1994 it has started to open every day.

For a special occasion breakfast it is unbeatable. The full works, cooked to perfection, including S-shaped Simpson's croissants, costs £8.50. Dress smart for this one.

Breakfast from 7am.

Simpsons, 100 Strand, WC2.
0171 836 9112

TEA BREAK

Afternoon tea conjures up a particularly British image, but in London you can drink the brew in French Salons de Thé and Hungarian or Russian tea houses as well as more conventionally English venues. As the liquid itself is usually just the sideliner to the main event, namely cake, it's good to know that patisserie is becoming ever more popular in the capital. The choice of places to sample something scrumptious grows ever wider, and most of the new patisseries are putting in at least a few chairs and tables to satisfy on-the-spot cake cravings.

Here are some tea-time favourites:

THE CRITERION   W1

With a gold mosaic ceiling that's definitely worth craning your neck for, and marble walls inlaid with semiprecious stones, the neo-Byzantine interior of The Criterion remains as impressively excessive as it must have been when it first opened in 1874.

The Criterion has seen many changes during its 120-year history, operating variously as a cafeteria, and a 1960s 'grill and griddle' (during which time the marble was covered with rather less aesthetically pleasing formica), before being restored and reopened as a brasserie in 1984. Shut once again in 1990 for the redevelopment of the surrounding Criterion site, it finally reopened as, simply, The Criterion in 1992.

Afternoon tea is served 7 days a week. You can choose the set afternoon tea blowout – sandwiches, scones, cakes and profiteroles for £7.50 – or rein yourself in with toasted teacakes. They also serve Sunday brunch.

Mon–Sat 12noon–11.30pm Sun 12noon–5.30pm.

The Criterion, 224 Piccadilly, W1.
0171 925 0909

THE GALLERY TEAROOMS   SW11

Tasselled table lamps, floor-length tablecloths and tapestries on the pink-painted walls all give the tearooms a camp and cosy parlour feel. The biggest aspidistra in the world would be perfectly at home here.

The real draw are the cakes: carrot, coffee, apricot, raspberry cheesecake, and pear and apple strudel. Beautifully decorated whole chocolate cakes are perfect for a birthday tea. Monster milk shakes, toasties and speciality teas also tempt the varied clientele and their Sunday brunch menu includes eggs benedict and kedgeree.

As you feel you're in your great aunt's front room, it can be difficult to remember to pay before you leave.

At night the Tearooms metamorphoses into a restaurant serving, rather incongruously given the decor, Mediterranean and Californian food.

Mon–Sun 11am–7pm Sunday brunch 11am–2pm. Wine bar 11am–midnight. Restaurant 7pm–midnight.

The Gallery Tearooms, 103 Lavender Hill, SW11.
0171 350 2564

LOUIS   NW3

Louis was opened in 1960 by Louis Permayer, who came to Britain after the 1956 Hungarian uprising.

The patisserie remains charmingly old fashioned with wood panelling and waitresses gliding though green curtains. Delicious pastries, cheesecakes and Hungarian delicacies.

Daily 9.30am–6pm.

Louis Patisserie, 32 Heath Street, NW3.
0171 435 9908

THE ORIGINAL MAIDS OF HONOUR   Kew

Almost opposite Kew Gardens, the Maids of Honour tearoom is famous for its eponymous cakes. A confection of puff pastry with a sweet, cheesecake-like centre, maids of honour originated in

Richmond and apparently were given their name by Henry VIII when he found Anne Boleyn and other Maids of Honour eating them.

In the mid-1800s the recipe passed into the hands of the Newens family who have passed its secret down the generations.

The tearoom's interior is very traditional – dark wood tables, chintzy curtains and china figurines – and everything is home-made in the bakery at the back, including the vegetable pasties, veal and ham, and chicken pies.

Set tea includes a pot of tea, scones and a cream cake or Maid of Honour for £4.15, but a pot of tea on its own is a pretty outrageous £1.75.

Maids of Honour is popular with American tourists visiting Kew Gardens. There is a takeaway bakery at the front of the shop.

Mon 9.30am–1pm Tues–Sat 9.30am–6pm. Closed Sundays. Morning coffee, lunches and teas.

The Original Maids of Honour,
288 Kew Road, Kew Gardens, Surrey. TW9 3DU.
0181 940 2752

MAISON BERTAUX   W1

Actress Michele Wade waitressed on and off at Maison Bertaux for 14 years before buying the 100-year-old business in 1988.

The vaguely tatty ambience, formica tables, mismatched china, subdued Edith Piaf songs and old wall heaters, give Maison Bertaux a far more genuine French feel than many of the more chi-chi French-imitators that have come along since.

There are a few tables downstairs and a bigger room upstairs, which sometimes plays host to theatrical performances.

The high-class patisserie includes both fruit and chocolate eclairs, savoury tarts and chocolate gateaux; everything is baked on the premises by patissier Michael Young. The croissants are often pronounced by fans to be the best in London.

9am–8pm daily.

Maison Bertaux, 28 Greek Street, W1.
0171 437 6007

MAISON SAGNE   W1

Opened in 1921 by an immigrant Swiss pastry lover, Sagne's is famous for its classical-mural-painted walls and chandeliers. For years it was the favourite haunt of Marylebone *grand dames* of a certain age who slipped in elegantly for a lunchtime omelette and éclair, served by white-uniformed waiters.

Nothing stays the same forever though, and in 1993 Maison Sagne was bought by Patisserie Valerie who are endeavouring to retain the genteel ambience, while extending the opening hours. They also have plans to create more space with a new conservatory. Maison Sagne serves the same stunning patisserie as the other Valerie branches, plus light meals.

Mon–Sat 8am–6pm Sun 10am–5.30pm.

Maison Sagne, 105 Marylebone High Street, W1.
0171 935 6240

PATISSERIE VALERIE *Soho* W1/SW3/WC2

One of Soho's landmarks; beatniks, hobos, art students, the stylish and poseurs have all sipped their tea, cappuccino and hot chocolate at Pat Vals.

The original Patisserie was opened by Madame Valerie, a Belgian, in 1926 and is now owned by 3 Italian brothers, Enzo, Victor and Robert Scalzo. The cake display in the window is a mouthwatering delight: perfectly glazed fruit tarts nestle up to plump éclairs and gateaux decorated with elaborate scrolls of chocolate.

Long, shared, constantly crowded wooden tables make exchanging confidences difficult, so concentrate on the cakes instead. At breakfast there are baskets of freshly baked croissants on the tables.

In 1992, the Scalzo brothers opened a second branch of Patisserie Valerie on the Brompton Road. This branch is licensed and slightly ritzier, with brass lamps and a Knightsbridge clientele. It also serves light meals.
Mon–Fri 8am–8pm Sat 8am–7pm Sun 10am–5.30pm.

Patisserie Valerie, 44 Old Compton Street, W1.
0171 437 3466

215 Brompton Road, SW3.
0171 823 9971
Mon–Fri 7.30am–7.30pm
Sat 7.30am–7pm Sun 9am–7pm.

8 Russell Street, WC2.
0171 240 0064
Mon–Sat 7.30am–11.00pm Sun 9am–6pm.

STRAVINSKY'S RUSSIAN TEA HOUSE *rather out of our way* SW6

Tzars may be thin on the ground in Fulham, but Russophiles should make for Stravinsky's. Owner David Fanailou comes from Azerbaijan and wanted to create an authentic Russian tea house featuring the specialities of his homeland.

Decorated in relaxing eau de nil, with wood-panelled flooring and well-spaced tables (the one in the alcove between the lower and upper floors is particularly attractive), the tea house offers a range of Russian specialities, cooked by David and his mother. Included are Georgian meatballs, kotletki, Baku borsch, sweet or regular stuffed cabbage and beef and okra stew, all at about £3.50.

The sevruga caviar comes from Azerbaijan and cakes include chocolate gogolov, poppyseed and beetroot, and raisin.

Among the 24 types of tea are Russian Caravan and their own house blend. All are served in the traditional Russian way using glass cups and tea warmers. Opera plays gently in the background.
Daily 10am–9pm.

Stravinsky's Russian Tea House, 6 Fulham High Street, SW6.
0171 371 0001

TEATIME

Clapham's famous tea house has been serving sustaining teas and cakes to Sunday Common-strollers for years.

Soothing green walls, pink tablecloths and Lloyd Loom chairs provide the backdrop to large portions of lemon cake, pecan pie, mocha cake and Teatime's own-recipe chocolate cake.

Breakfast choices include kedgeree, and smoked salmon with scrambled egg. Sandwiches are also available. On Thursday, Friday and Saturday evenings they are open for bistro-style cooking.

Mon–Sun 10am–6pm.

Teatime, 21 The Pavement, SW4.
0171 622 4944

WALDORF

The Waldorf Hotel offer an excellent tea in its beautiful Palm Court reception room Monday to Friday inclusive. On Saturdays and Sundays the set tea becomes a tea dance and for around £21 per person you can dance to a 5-piece band and enjoy finger sandwiches, scones and pastries in between the sets. Tea dances are very popular so it is advisable to book.

3pm–6pm daily.

Waldorf Hotel, Aldwych, WC2.
0171 836 2400

• Also:

Primrose Patisserie, 136 Regents Park Road, NW1.
0171 722 7348

The Regent, 222 Marylebone Road, NW1.
0171 631 8000

The Tea House, 45 Fitzalan Road, N3.
0181 349 0690

EATING AL FRESCO

Although there never seem to be enough summer days when the weather allows the fantasy of sitting outdoors, bathed in sunlight, sipping wine and eating good food, there are restaurateurs with the courage to create gardens, terraces, patios and tiny outdoor spaces to fulfil our summer dreams.

CAFÉ GROVE

Perched above the quirky Wong Singh Jones shop, Café Grove has a large open air terrace from which you can look down on the virtually non-stop entertainment the Portobello Road provides.

The café provides good pasta and vegetarian dishes with a busy but relaxed atmosphere.

Mon–Fri 9.30am–5pm Sat 9am–6pm Sun 11am–5pm.

Café Grove, 253a Portobello Road, W11.
0171 243 1094

DAPHNE *Near Camden Town*

NW1

In ancient Greek mythology Daphne was the daughter of the river God Peneus. She resisted the attentions of Apollo and was turned into a laurel tree by the earth Goddess Gaea.

Her namesake restaurant is one of the best Greek Cypriot eateries in north London; regulars come for the good food and relaxed and friendly service.

The menu ventures beyond the Greek standards; it includes starters like spanakopita (fresh spinach with feta cheese in filo pastry) and features plenty of fish dishes, such as xifias (charcoal-grilled cubes of marinated swordfish). There are also daily specials and the meze is particularly popular.

On the top floor is a pretty, trellised roof terrace which seats about 24 people. *1260 A4*

Lunch 12noon–3pm Dinner 6pm–midnight.

Daphne, 83 Bayham Street, NW1.
0171 267 7322

DAPHNE'S *Chelsea*

SW3

Danish-born Mogens Tholstrup has cleverly turned Daphne's into the fave rave of the smart set.

A big attraction is the light and airy garden room, which has a sliding glass roof for summer dining.

Despite the glitz, the food – mostly Mediterranean in style – is actually quite reasonably priced for what feels like something above the run-of-the-mill night out.

Lunch Mon–Sat 12noon–3pm Sun 11am–4pm. Dinner daily 7pm–11pm.

Daphne's, 112 Draycott Avenue, SW3.
0171 589 4257

LA FAMIGLIA *Chelsea*

SW10

Enduringly popular, especially with publishing and magazine folk, La Famiglia has a beautiful garden – ideal for sipping a glass of chilled chianti while tucking into a plate of pasta and imagining yourself in Tuscany.

Be warned: the garden is very popular in good weather and although it's pretty essential to book, you can't reserve an outside table – it's first come first served.

La Famiglia, 7 Langton Street, SW10.
0171 351 0761

FREDERICKS *Camden*

N1

A long-term Islington favourite, Fredericks is perfect for a romantic summer lunch or dinner, with a conservatory at the back and beyond that an outdoor patio. The French food has been highly praised and there are set menus to help keep the cost in line.

Mon–Sat Lunch 12noon–2.30pm Dinner 6pm–11.30pm.

Fredericks, Camden Passage, N1.
0171 359 2888

THE GATE W6

Despite the unlikely location, just off the Hammersmith one-way system and behind the old Hammersmith Odeon, The Gate is a real find. The award-winning vegetarian menu features imaginative dishes, and even the most hardened meat eater won't feel they're missing out.

Downstairs from the main restaurant is a sheltered courtyard with a few outdoor tables.

Lunch Tues–Fri 12noon–3pm Dinner Mon–Sat 6pm–10.45pm.

The Gate, 51 Queen Caroline Street, W6.
0181 748 6932

GLAISTERS SW10

This restaurant has a large sunken garden area, full of plants and statuary and cleverly protected from the vagaries of the weather by a retractable sunroof.

The menu features a varied selection of bistro-style dishes, with burgers, cracked crab salad and salmon fishcakes (see also p.170).

Glaisters, 4 Hollywood Road, SW10.
0171 352 0352

THE OPERA TERRACE RESTAURANT WC2

A perfect site for a restaurant, perched above the Piazza and looking down on the action below. The terrace can seat up to 45 people and is a real suntrap.

The pan-European menu offers such summery temptations as chilled melon soup and frosted vodka gazpacho, with main courses including smoked salmon ravioli and roasted vegetable couscous. The intention is to be flexible, so for a light pre-theatre supper you could choose 2 starters rather than a starter and main course. Starters average £3.50, main courses £7.50.

Inside, the restaurant has recently been refurbished in peacock colours with murals to reflect the opera theme.

There is also a café bar area which also has some outside seating and could be the place to stop for a mid-shopping cappuccino.

Opera Terrace Restaurant, 35 East Terrace, Covent Garden Piazza, WC2.
0171 379 0666

SECRET GARDEN, FRANKLINS ANTIQUE MARKET SE5

From the front, Franklin's rickety exterior, facing the Camberwell Road, gives no hint of the delights within. Step through the door, however, and you're in a treasure trove crammed with huge mirrors, old busts, prints and numerous beds from brass to French maple, all covered in a reassuring layer of dust.

Through all this you suddenly stumble on the cosy restaurant, with tables squeezed into alcoves and prints covering every wall. And out the back is the final and best surprise – a walled garden, crammed, in a higgeldy-piggeldy fashion, with statuary and old tables and chairs.

Food is very well priced, with dishes like pork and cider cassserole and bulgur wheat and lentil pilaf at about £3.00.

There is a roast lunch on Sundays and children are welcome.

Mon–Sat 10am–4pm Sun 1pm–5pm.

The Secret Garden, Franklin's Antique Market,
161 Camberwell Road, SE5.
0171 703 8089

• A few more to choose from:

Bellini, 47 Kensington Court, W8.
0171 937 5520

Chapter 11, 47 Hollywood Road, SW10.
0171 351 1683

La Mancha, 32 Putney Hight Street, SW15.
0181 780 1022

San Marino, 26 Sussex Place, W2.
0171 723 8395

Studio Six, 56 Upper Ground, SE1.
0171 928 6243

Taberna Etrusca, 9–11 Bow Churchyard, EC4.
0171 248 5552

CHILD-FRIENDLY RESTAURANTS

Even if the restaurant is friendly, the other customers quite
often won't be, and McDonalds again may not seem ideal.
  Usually it's the Italian, Greek, Turkish and other ethnic
restaurants in London that manage to make kids genuinely
welcome, but there are other restaurants who make a big effort to be
child friendly. After all, today's tiny tot is tomorrow's American
Express gold card holder!

DEALS   **W6/SW10/W1**

The newest branch of Viscount Linley's Deals chain opened in
Hammersmith in early 1994. Part of the new Hammersmith shopping
development, the building dates from 1709 and was once a post office,
but is now converted to feature limed wood panelling and stripped
wood floors.
  Sunday lunchtimes are geared towards families with a free magician
to entertain and face painting on offer for £2.50. There are plenty of
high chairs, children's cutlery and a special kids' menu, which
features baby bangers and burgers, though the west London infants
here would probably be equally adept with the smoked chicken salad.
  Young, friendly staff are good with kids and any excitable fathers.

Deals, Bradmore House, Queen Caroline Street, W6.
0181 563 1001

Also at:
Chelsea Harbour, SW10.
0171 795 1001

14–16 Foubert' s Place, W1.
0171 287 1001

THE DEPOT   SW14

A hugely popular riverside restaurant, the Depot is packed with
families on Sunday lunchtimes. Children's portions and high chairs
are available; the brasserie-style menu includes fish and pasta dishes
(see also p.222).

The Depot, Tideway Yard, Mortlake High Street, SW14.
0181 878 9462

GLAISTERS   SW10

If the thought of a child-free Sunday lunch seems deeply appealing,
then Chelsea restaurant Glaisters may offer the solution. While
parents eat in peace and tranquillity at the restaurant, children are
taken care of by qualified staff at the extremely popular Nipper
Snippers crèche next door. A sandwich lunch is laid on for them and
entertainment includes painting and video games and tons of toys.

The restaurant has a large garden room, with a retractable roof for
sunny summer days and the Sunday menu offers a roast as well as a
wide variety of other dishes from bruschetta to bangers and mash (see
also p.168).

Glaisters, 4 Hollywood Road, SW10.
0171 352 0352

Nipper Snippers, 8 Hollywood Road, SW10.
071 351 2329

THE INEBRIATED NEWT   SW11

A well-established Battersea favourite, The Inebriated Newt has a
special children's menu, including a roast on Sundays, at £4.95.
Crayons on the tables and plenty of decorations for special days like
Halloween all provide entertainment.

Bistro-style food includes burgers, salads and pasta and the staff get
full marks for child-friendliness; as one grateful mum put it: 'They
were totally unfazed by a large family turning up at 3.30pm and asking
for lunch and were very good with the kids.'

The Inebriated Newt, 172 Northcote Road, SW11.
0171 223 1637

MARINE ICES   NW3

For kids, big and little, nothing can quite beat the lure of ice cream
and at Marine Ices they do it better than anywhere else.

The Italian Mansi family have been in the ice cream business since
the turn of the century and their white, ocean-liner-like gelataria has
been a familiar landmark on Haverstock Hill since 1930.

Brothers Aldo and Anacleto have been joined by their sons Dante,
Gaetano and Gino in the business which also supplies around 1500
restaurants across the capital.

The selection of sundaes and sorbets, coppas and cassatas is
unrivalled anywhere in London. There are 18 irresistible ice cream
flavours include marsala, stracciatella and tiramisu. Sundaes come
exactly as you want them to, piled into tall glasses with long silver

spoons. Ice cream £1.15 per scoop, knickerbocker glory £3.30 eat in.

A favourite half-term and school holiday haunt, as is the nextdoor pasta and pizza restaurant.

Mon–Sat 10.45am–10.30pm.

Marine Ices, Haverstock Hill, NW3.
0171 485 3132

PLANET HOLLYWOOD   W1

Already publicized to within an inch of its life, Planet Hollywood hardly needs any more attention. Suffice to say that portions are huge, the memorabilia good fun, and you can't go far wrong with the menu, which is mostly geared towards burgers, pizzas and salads.

No advance bookings.

Planet Hollywood, junction of Coventry and Rupert Street, W1.
0171 287 1000

P.J.'s GRILL   WC2

Saturday and Sunday lunchtimes are particularly aimed at families, with lots of laid-on entertainment provided by Uncle P.J.'s Fun Club in a specially set-aside play area.

There is also a special children's menu featuring some imaginative ideas. For parents the American menu includes clam chowder, Caesar salad, chargrilled steaks and chicken dishes.

P.J.'s Grill, 30 Wellington Street, Covent Garden, WC2.
0171 240 7529

SMOLLENSKY'S BALLOON   W1/WC2

Sunday lunchtimes at Smollensky's provide a non-stop stream of small-person fun and entertainment: table-side magic, a clown, face-painting, Nintendo and cartoons as well as a post-lunch Punch and Judy show.

The children's menu (£3.99) features 10 choices, from burgers and bangers to ravioli and vegeburgers and a choice of 7 puddings. There are even kiddies' cocktails, like the Ghostbuster and the manager's favourite, the Incredible Hulk.

Smollensky's Balloon, 1 Dover Street, W1.
0171 491 1199

Smollensky's on The Strand, 105 Strand, WC2.
0171 497 2101

• Other good places for kids:

Banners, 21 Park Road, N8.
0181 348 2930

Chicago Pizza Pie Factory, 17 Hanover Square, W1.
0171 629 2552

Chuen Cheng Ku, 17 Wardour Street, W1.
0171 437 3433

Rock Island Diner, Plaza Centre, London Pavilion, W1.
0171 287 5500

Shilli Beers, Carpenter Mews, North Road, N7.
0171 700 1858

Sticky Fingers, 1a Phillimore Gardens, W8.
0171 938 5338

Uncle Ian's Deli Diner, 8–10 Monkville Parade, Finchley Road, NW11.
0181 458 3493

BUDGET EATS

London has many showpiece restaurants, but also a great selection of places where you can eat good, interesting food for about a tenner a head. A number of these aren't licensed, but you can take your own wine and pay a small amount for corkage.

Many of the restaurants below lead dual lives, operating as fairly standard cafés during the day, then transforming by night to serve a completely different style of cuisine.

Don't forget that many of these restaurants prefer cash and won't accept credit cards – best to check first.

ADAMS CAFÉ   W12

A greasy spoon café by day that becomes a Tunisian restaurant by night, serving spicy meatballs, couscous, chargrilled lamb and other specialities. Tunisian pastries complete the meal.

Adam's Café, 77 Askew Road, W12.
0181 743 0572

BEDLINGTON CAFÉ   W4

The first and most successful of the current huge crop of café-by-day-Thai-by-night restaurants. The Bedlington has a firm following in Chiswick and far beyond for its jungle curries and other dishes. Booking is advisable. Not licensed, so take your own.

Bedlington Café, 24 Fauconberg Road, W4.
0181 994 1965

BRAHMS   SW1/SW11/NW6

Despite the unprepossessing exterior, which makes it look like a Seventies disco pub, Brahms is a tribute to Peter Ilic's ability to offer good food at extremely reasonable prices. The starters, such as steamed mussels, are under £2, main courses are under £4.00 and desserts about £1. All Ilic's restaurants serve the same menu and economies of scale are reflected in the prices.

Brahms, 147 Lupus Street, SW1.
0171 834 9075

- Other Peter Ilic restaurants:

Cote a Cote, 74 Battersea Bridge Road, SW11.
0171 738 0198

The Fish in a Tie, 105 Falcon Road, SW11.
0171 924 1913

The Little Bay, 224 Belsize Road, NW6.
0171 372 4699

CHUEN CHENG KU   W1

Chinese restaurants usually offer a good range of dishes at affordable prices and Chuen Ken Kuen is no exception! It does in addition, however, serve varied and very reasonably priced dim sum between 12 noon and 5pm.

There are over 30 different dishes to choose from the trolleys that are wheeled past the tables in this huge restaurant. The various noodle soups are particularly comforting on cold winter days as are the steamed dumplings! Lack of expertise in the names of the different dishes is unimportant as pointing is quite sufficient, and the staff are very helpful.

Chuen Cheng Ku, 17 Wardour Street, W1.
0171 437 3433

THE DOME   W8

The leader in a chain of French-style brasseries recently opened all over London by the owners of the Pelican Café in St Martin's Lane.

The restaurant offers a daily set meal of 3 courses for around £5 alongside snacks and more substantial meals. The set menu changes daily and ingredients used tend towards the seasonal, cooked simply. The portions are generous and the standard of food in relation to the price is excellent.

The Dome, 35a Kensington High Street, W8.
0171 937 6655

JIGSAW   W12

Owned by the same people as Adams Café, Jigsaw is performing a similar service for French food and has quickly gained a reputation for simple, delicious, well-priced dinners, with a set menu at £8.50.

Jigsaw, 74 Askew Road, W12.
0181 743 8002

LUBA'S BISTRO   SW3

A sudden Russian boom has hit London with several new East European additions to London's eating scene.

None of this is likely to faze Luba's, which has been serving up huge servings of borscht, blinis and beef stroganoff in Knightsbridge for many years.

The decor is dark, Russian staff are friendly, but the restaurant is unlicensed so take your own booze.

Luba's Bistro, 6 Yeoman's Row, SW3.
0171 589 2950

OSMANI   NW1

Couscous is the speciality at this cosy north-African restaurant. Other main courses included chicken tagine and starters are a selection of salads including the familiar tabouleh or less well-known chachouka. Puddings are French-influenced.

Osmani, 46 Inverness Street, NW1.
0171 267 4682

PIZZERIA CASTELLO   SE1

An oasis in the dining desert of south-east London, Pizzeria Castello draws pizza lovers from all over south London and beyond. Pizzas are thin-crusted, garlicy and delicious and include the house speciality, the Castelana.

Pizzeria Castello, 20 Walworth Road, SE1.
0171 703 2556

SHAMPAN   E1

Shampan is one of the most authentic of Brick Lane's Bangladeshi-owned restaurants, offering traditional dishes from the Sylhet region. A good selection of fish dishes includes slices of Arr, served with a sweet onion flavour sauce. There is also a fish thali.

Smartish decor makes it a favourite with well-heeled local Bangladeshi businessmen, Brick Lane locals and a few strays from the City.

Shampan, 79 Brick Lane, E1.
0171 247 2505

SMOKEY JOE'S DINER   SW18

Among the menu highlights at this Jamaican diner and take-away are peppered prawns and jerk chicken or pork, all served with rice and peas. Not licensed.

Smokey Joe's Diner, 131 Wandsworth High Street, SW18.
0181 871 1785

STAR CAFÉ   W1

With its reliable and affordable home cooking, the Star provides an oasis of comfort food for Soho media lunchers weary of fancier fare. The day starts with big breakfasts, and lunches include roasts, pies and liver and bacon, as well as pasta, salads and sandwiches, with crumbles and steamed puds to follow.

The Star Café, 22b Great Chapel Street, W1.
0171 437 8778

TOKYO DINER   W1

If you like Japanese food but are normally thwarted by the outrageous prices, try the Tokyo Diner where the Bento boxes, sushi and sashimi are probably the best-priced in town.

The British proprietor is a fluent Japanese speaker. Note that tipping is not permitted and credit cards are not accepted.

Daily noon–midnight.

Tokyo Diner, 2 Newport Place, W1.
0171 287 8777

EVENT RESTAURANTS

For something a little out of the ordinary try a night out at one of the following:

ANEMOS   W1

This is not the place to go for a quiet evening *à deux!* Loud both in decor and music Anemos offers suitably matching entertainment – Greek dancing, belly dancing, disco dancing and if it's not too crowded, plate smashing.

Mon–Sat 12noon–3pm 6.30pm–11.45pm.

Anemos, Charlotte Street, W1.
0171 636 2289

• Similar venues are:

Appollonia, 17a Percy Street, W1.
0171 636 4140

Maple's, 56 Maple Street, W1.
0171 580 4819

BEACH BLANKET BABYLON   W11

The bar, which is generally packed with the trendsetters of Notting Hill, has a Romanesque feel and is dominated by a giant lion's head with flames roaring from its mouth! The dungeon-like restaurant is entered via a wooden gangplank supported by creaky but mercifully thick chains!

Bench tables are well spaced in the nooks and crannies. More fun than romantic!

Beach Blanket Babylon, Ledbury Road, W11.
0171 229 2907

BLUE ELEPHANT   SW6

If you like authentic Thai cuisine and a distinctly tropical backdrop, the Blue Elephant is for you. Streams, bridges and a wealth of greenery help to create an authentic jungle in which to savour some of the best Thai cooking in London.

Sun–Fri 12noon–2.30pm Mon–Sat 7pm–12.30am Sun 7pm–10.30pm.

The Blue Elephant, 4 Fulham Broadway, SW6.
0171 385 6595

BRICK LANE MUSIC HALL E1

Actually not naff or touristy, the Brick Lane is a proper old music hall, where after a typical dinner of boiled beef and carrots you can hear traditional entertainment, with a bill that often includes London favourites such as Barbara Windsor. Practise those London lyrics ready for a singsong.

Shows Wed–Sat. Dinner plus show about £20.

Brick Lane Music Hall, 152 Brick Lane, E1.
0171 377 9797

CAFÉ ROYAL GRILL ROOM W1

The Café Royal Grill Room has to be one of the most lovely dining rooms in London and with the current Michelin star rating it is starting to offer a cuisine and wine list to match. Both modern and traditional cooking are on offer and the romantic setting allows you to dress up and make the evening a special occasion!

Alternatively the Green Room provides an all-inclusive dinner and cabaret from Tuesday to Saturday starting at 8pm.

Café Royal Grill Room, 68 Regent Street, W1.
0171 437 9090

CONCORDIA NOTTE W2

A large dungeon where live bands provide nightly music with support from Vincent Zara, the well-known cabaret artist. Weekends are best if you like a good crowd, but the food is good and the atmosphere fun.
Mon–Sat 8.20pm–2am.

Concordia Notte, 29–31 Craven Road, W2.
0171 723 3725

• Also try Talk of London, Parker Street, Drury Lane, WC2.
0171 224 9000

COSTA DORADA W1

A traditional Spanish restaurant which offers 2 flamenco floor shows a night: Monday to Thursday at 9pm and 11.30pm and on Fridays and Saturdays 10pm and 12.30pm. It seats 250 and offers a dance floor, so if Spanish music is your passion Costa Dorado has quite a bit to offer!
Mon–Sat 7.30pm–3am.

Costa Dorada, 47–55 Hanway Street, W1.
0171 636 7139

GRACELANDS PALACE SE15

This is the venue for a Chinese meal, followed by a show featuring London's finest Chinese Elvis, Paul Chan, who has a cult following.

Gracelands Palace, 883 Old Kent Road, SE15.
0171 639 3961

• For a floating Elvis show try 'Elvis – the cruiser diner', which croons and gyrates its way from Charing Cross pier to the Thames Barrier and back. Dinner is served on board and the hour-long Elvis show is performed by Steve Halliday, who has been given the seal of approval by the offical UK Elvis fan club. Details: 0171 237 5134.

JUST AROUND THE CORNER   NW2

Whether this is an event restaurant or one to test your powers of judgement and honesty is debatable, but it certainly offers an evening with a difference. Having been presented with a price- free menu specializing in French cuisine and chosen and eaten your preferred dishes, you are invited to pay whatever you feel the meal was worth. No guide lines are offered but as the restaurant has been running for many years it would seem that estimates are fair and appreciative! It gets pretty busy, especially at weekends, so booking is advisable.

Just Around the Corner, 446 Finchley Road, NW2.
0171 431 3300

MATSURI ST JAMES   SW1

This is one of those Japanese restaurants where you can witness the amazingly theatrical display of the teppan-yaki chefs wielding the razor sharp knives at your table while they prepare your food. They also offer a dedicated sushi bar with over 20 different types of fresh seafood.
   If you are feeling both wealthy and very hungry there is a special 10-course menu on offer!

Matsuri St James, 15 Bury Street, SW1.
0171 839 1101

• Also try: Benihana, 77 Kings Road, SW3
0171 376 7799

TERRAZZA EST   EC4

Dine on Italian food whilst being serenaded with well-known operatic arias. The tenor, soprano and pianist will also take requests but it is probably wisest to bring the music with you if it's one of the less well-known arias!
   Singers Mon–Fri 7.30–11pm.

Terrazza Est, 109 Fleet Street, EC4.
0171 353 2680

TIROLER HUT   W2

Decorated in typical chalet style, with the full Austrian works: yodelling, lederhosen, and accordians to accompany your schnitzel.
   Set-price menus start from around £15.00 include entertainment.

Tiroler Hut, 27 Westbourne Grove, W2.
0171 727 3981

TRADITIONAL TREATS

Fish and Chips
THE SEASHELL   NW1

Famous for 20 years, The Seashell is a connoisseur's fish and chip shop.
There are few fish and chip takeaways serving salmon, dover or lemon
sole or halibut wrapped up in newsprint along with the more plebeian
piscatory. Plaice here means not just 'plaice and chips', but a choice of
middle plaice, plaice fillet or plaice on the bone.

The owners declare their continued success lies in using the freshest
fish and best-quality groundnut oil.

The classy green-tiled exterior is decorated with window boxes and
next door is the sit down (more expensive) restaurant where your fish is
fried, grilled or poached to order.

Seashell of Lisson Grove, 33–35 Lisson Grove, NW1.
0171 723 8703

UPPER STREET FISH SHOP   N1

Another up-market takeaway featuring a broader than usual choice of
fish. The red-and-white checked tableclothed restaurant is also
extremely popular; it's not licensed, but you can bring your own wine.

Upper Street Fish Shop, 324 Upper Street, N1.
0171 359 1401

• A few more to choose from:

Geales, 2 Farmer Street, W8.	0171 727 7969
Grahames, 38 Poland Street, W1.	0171 437 3788
Nautilus, 29 Fortune Green Road, NW6.	0171 435 2532
Rock & Soul Plaice, 47 Endell Street, WC2.	0171 836 3785
SeaFresh, 80–81 Wilton Road, SW1.	0171 828 0747

Pie and Mash
F. COOKE & SONS   E8/N1

The Cooke family have been involved with pie and mash since 1862 and
the Dalston shop was opened in 1910. Today the business (frequently
mentioned in food guides) is run by Fred and Chris Cooke, great-
grandsons of the original founder.

The brothers have maintained the much-admired original decor, with
its stained-glass skylights, mirrored walls and marble-topped tables.

Pie and mash is a family business, and Fred and Chris's wives, Brenda
and Elaine, work in the shop. The family's cousins are the Pooles, who
run M. Manze on Tower Bridge Road next to Bermondsey Market.

The pies are made to a family recipe and served with the infamous
liquor (parsley sauce). Two tons of live eels are kept in tanks at the back

F. Cooke and Sons, 41 Kingsland High Street, E8.
0171 254 9322

Also: 150 Hoxton Street, N1.
0171 729 7718

- Other London pie and mash shops include:

A. Cooks, 48 Goldhawk Rd, W12.	0181 743 7630
R. Cooke, 84 The Cut, SE1.	0171 928 5931
G.F. Kelly, 526 & 600 Roman Road, E3.	0181 980 3165
M. Manze, 87 Tower Bridge Road, SE1.	0171 407 2985
and 105 Peckham High Street, SE15.	0171 277 6181

PUB CULTURE

There are around 7,500 pubs in London, and they make up a vital part of the capital's social life. In many cases they have something extra to offer, whether it be great music, outstanding food, its own bit of greenery or a quirky style. Here are just a few to illustrate the diversity of London's drinking life.

THE ALMA   SW18

The Alma is a great Youngs pub serving excellent, French-influenced food at pub prices. Particularly popular for its Sunday lunches.

The Alma, 499 York Road, SW18.
0181 870 2537

THE BELL   N1

The highlight of the week at this friendly gay pub is The Cactus Club, a yee-hah night of country-and-western dancing, on Mondays and Fridays.

The Bell, 257–259 Pentonville Road, N1.
0171 837 5617

BIDDY MULLIGAN'S   NW6

This is a traditional Irish pub with a mainly Irish clientele and live Irish music, with occasional forays into country and western 7 nights a week.

Biddy Mulligan's, 205 Kilburn High Road, NW6.
0171 624 2066

THE BLACKFRIAR   EC4

Built on the site of a former monastery, the Blackfriar is a stunning example of an Arts and Crafts style pub. The monastic theme is set by numerous bronze reliefs of chubby friars, and the 'side chapel', an amusing dome-ceilinged riot of marble and mosaic, is particularly worth a look.

Copper lettering spells out the sobering exhortations 'Haste is Slow', 'Finery is Foolery', and 'Wisdom is Rare', sentiments which are largely lost on the mainly City clientele.

The Blackfriar, 147 Queen Victoria Street, EC4.
0171 236 5650

DOVE E8

The Dove scores points on every count – as a friendly local, for its good imaginative food and for a welcoming atmosphere.

The location, in Broadway market, is not the most attractive, but all the other elements make it worth a visit.

Dove, 25–27 Broadway Market, E8.
0171 275 7617

THE EAGLE EC1

This was the first of the new-style London pubs, where the interiors have been opened out and spruced up to accommodate sofas and create a relaxed, clubby atmosphere. The creative food is an important attraction.

The Eagle is a particularly popular with journalists from the *Guardian*, whose offices are nearby.

Food is cooked in an area behind the bar and includes ingredients like salt cod. There is an art gallery upstairs.

The Eagle, 159 Farringdon Road, EC1.
0171 837 1353

• For a similar style see also:

The Peasant, 240 St. John Street, EC1.
0171 336 7726

The Engineer, 65 Gloucester Avenue, NW1.
0171 722 0950

THE FRENCH HOUSE W1

This pub was once the York Minster, but became 'The French' during the war when it was the unofficial headquarters of the Free French, with de Gaulle among the regulars.

After the war it became a favourite writers' haunt with a post-war Soho set that included Dylan Thomas, Francis Bacon and Brendan Behan. The clientele still tends towards the creative and the eccentric. The upstairs dining room serves award-winning meals.

The French House, 49 Dean Street, W1.
0171 437 2477

THE GEORGE INN SE1

Rebuilt after the Southwark fire of 1676, this is London's only surviving coaching inn, and it is now owned by the National Trust.

Open galleries look down on a large and pretty cobbled courtyard with plenty of picnic tables. A beer Festival with up to 14 real ales is held on the third Monday of every month and farm cider and mulled wine is served in winter. The coaching inn is mentioned by Charles Dickens in *Little Dorrit*.

The George Inn, 77 Borough High Street, SE1.
0171 407 2056

HEN AND CHICKENS N1

One of London's theatre pubs, the Hen and Chickens puts on a broad range of work, with new writing alongside works from established playwrights like Jim Cartwright. Mondays feature London Theatresports who improvise plays and sketches from audience suggestions. It is always crowded and has live music on Monday, Thursday, Friday and Saturday.

Hen and Chickens, 109 St Paul's Road, Highbury Corner, N1.
0171 704 2001

• Other theatre pubs:

The Bush, Shepherds Bush Green, W12.
0181 743 3388

Kings Head, 115 Upper Street, N1.
0171 226 1916

Man In the Moon, 392 Kings Road, SW3.
0171 351 2876

The Old Red Lion, 418 St John's Street, EC1.
0171 837 7816

THE HOLLYBUSH NW3

A pretty pub tucked up a narrow Hampstead street. The interior is dark and cosy with a number of different low-ceilinged rooms, including a 4–seater snug, ideal for intimate tête-à-têtes. Open fires in winter.

The Holly Bush, 22 Holly Mount, NW3.
0171 435 2892

O'HANLONS EC1

John O'Hanlon runs this most Irish of Irish pubs and he has imported his mother to do the cooking! Lots of excellent Irish fare and real Irish soda bread are on offer to soak up the draught Guinness!

O'Hanlons, 8 Tysoe Street, EC1.
0171 837 4112

ROYAL VAUXHALL TAVERN SE11

This is London's most famous drag pub, with entertainment every night.

372 Kennington Lane, SE11.
0171 582 0833

- Other good drag pubs:

Black Cap, 171 Camden High Street, NW1.
0171 485 1742

Two Brewers, 114 Clapham High Street, SW4.
0171 622 3621

STATION TAVERN W1

The Station Tavern is a very popular blues pub with a reputation for high-quality music. Bands play 7 nights a week.

Station Tavern, 41 Bramley Road, W10.
0171 727 4053

- Other good music pubs:

Amersham Arms, 388 New Cross Road, SE14.
0181 692 2047

   Variety, from Irish jam session to indie bands.

Bulls Head, 373 Lonsdale Road, Barnes, SW13.
0181 876 5241

   Jazz.

The Swan, 215 Clapham Road, Stockwell, SW9.
0171 978 9778

   New bands, particularly Irish.

Trolley Stop, 28 Stamford Road, N1.
0171 241 0581

   Live music every evening, usually soul, jazz or R 'n' B.

THE SUN WC1

This pub carries the largest selection of real ales in London – anything between 10 and 16 different brews on handpump from all over the country, they are regularly rotated from a much wider choice housed in the cellar. Walls list all the beers stocked and their strengths.

The Sun, 63 Lamb's Conduit Street, WC1.
0171 405 8278

THE WINDMILL SW4

This lovely old Victorian Inn on the edge of Clapham Common has something for everyone. Monday night is opera night, when the conservatory offers young rising stars a chance to show their skills. Friday night offers a good range of cabaret and on Sunday nights it's jazz. The Courtyard is lovely for summer lunches, and the food available is well above average.

The Windmill, Clapham Common South Side, SW4.
0181 673 4578

MUSIC

The choice of music available in the capital is usually so good that the difficulty is often not where to go but what you cannot afford to miss!

London is world famous for the quality and quantity of its classical and contemporary music scene and whether you like classical, jazz, rock, folk or country, as long as you know where to look you will find the choice large and varied. Venues range from huge concert arenas to small rooms at the back of pubs.

Daily newspapers (including Saturdays) – *The Times, Guardian, Daily Telegraph* and *Independent* – carry substantial listings, as do the *Sunday Times, Observer, Sunday Telegraph and Independent on Sunday*. They also advertise special offers either through club membership or priority booking opportunities, essential for the really popular concerts and performances. It is also worth checking if an individual venue, or orchestra, has a mailing list for concert or theatre promotions, as extremely good discounts are often available if the tickets purchased are part of a seasonal subscription.

Weekly magazines offer the widest coverage – *Time Out* and *Whats On* carry the full range – or you can consult the specialist magazines.

• Youth and Music offer discounts of up to 60 per cent for Arts events across the country to anyone aged between 14 and 30.
For a Stage Pass application form call Youth & Music (0171 379 6722).

CLASSICAL CONCERTS

London plays host to 4 major orchestras but it is also seen as a major venue for the cream of the foreign orchestras (the London review is still all important), so the choice of classical music in the capital is excellent.

For the very best in orchestral performances you cannot do better than visit the Royal Festival Hall or the Barbican. The Royal Festival Hall is the more adventurous in its programming unless the London Symphony Orchestra is playing. The Barbican tends towards middle-of-the-road programming and very well established artists.

For recitals the first to try are the Wigmore Hall and St Johns, Smith Square, but these are just the tip of the iceberg.

If, on the other hand, you wish to play in an orchestra or sing in a choir, write to the secretary of a local music group – your library should carry a list and many of the groups welcome new members. Libraries also carry a professional register of music teachers if your talents need a little improvement!

Here are just some of the special highlights on offer in the Capital:

LUNCHTIME MUSIC

It is now very possible to take in a concert while you eat your sandwiches in the main arts centres such as the Royal Festival Hall and the Barbican. In Westminster they have even begun a series of lunchtime concerts in some of the libraries. They last for approximately 50 minutes and, more often than not, they are free or limited to a donation of your choice.

St Johns, Smith Square   SW1

Possibly one of the most famous lunchtime venues for concerts is St John's Smith Square, where for the last 25 years the performances have been broadcast live on Radio 3 at 1pm on Mondays. Unlike most lunchtime concerts tickets are a hefty £6, but the choice and quality of performance is excellent.

There are also evening concerts and look out for the series of Christmas Concerts by Candlelight in December.

St John's, Smith Square, SW1.
0171 222 1061

St Anne and Agnes   EC1

Another excellent venue is the Church of St Anne and St Agnes, which was rebuilt by Christopher Wren after the Great Fire of London. This church is part of the Lutheran Church in Great Britain and stands in the mainstream of Christian denomination.

Lunchtime concerts are held every Monday and Friday. Bring your own sandwiches, and coffee is served.

The musical programme is inextricably linked to the church's diary and in any month you will find the music on offer will more than likely include works by Schubert, Chopin, Telemann, Dandrieu, Bizet, Corelli, Hammerschmidt, Mozart and Quantz. The vespers on Sunday evening at 7pm include Bach Vespers, Jazz Vespers and Choral Mass.

There is no admission charge for the lunchtime concerts but there is a post-performance collection.

Church of St Anne and St Agnes, Gresham Street, EC2.
0171 606 4986

Other regular lunchtime venues:

The Royal Festival Hall. Daily.
The South Bank, SE1.

Southwark Cathedral. Mondays and Tuesdays.
London Bridge Street, SE1.

St Martin-in-the-Fields Church. Mondays, Tuesdays and Fridays.
Trafalgar Square, WC2.

St Georges, Hanover Square, W1. Thursdays.

St James, Piccadilly, SW1. Thursdays.

• For details of lunchtime concerts in libraries contact the Arts Officers on 0171 798 2498

• For details of the full range of lunchtime concerts in the City call the City Information Service at St Paul's Churchyard, EC4. 0171 606 3030.

FESTIVALS

London is good for Festivals! In the Events section (see p.235) we cover the Spitalfields Festival, Soho Jazz Festival, London Jazz Festival, Notting Hill Carnival, Greenwich Festival, Fleadh, the City of London Festival and the Proms. Various societies, such as the London Bach Society, run the London Bach Festival but most of these are well advertised in the various venues in which they appear.

London Bach Festival (01883 717372).

OPEN AIR CONCERTS

Concerts of light orchestral music are a feature of summer weekend evenings in London. Programming starts to become available in May, with the concerts usually scheduled for the end of July and through August.

As a general rule it is worth checking any park for a bandstand and if one is present you can be sure that some sort of musical programme is available through the summer months.

The Royal Parks, which include Hyde, St James and Regents, all have outside concerts and publish a booklet (available from mid-May) which lists all the concerts and indeed other events happening throughout the summer season. Their season runs from the end of May through till the beginning of September and tends to be scheduled for Friday, Saturday and Sunday evenings. Historically the musical programme has been limited to military and band music, but this is now changing and a far wider programme is being instigated.

The evening concerts are usually scheduled for the end of July through August and probably the best known are the Kenwood Concerts (see the Events section p.246) but evening concerts can also be found at Alexandra Park, Crystal Palace Bowl, Holland Park and Marble Hill House.

Details of lunchtime open air concerts in the City are available from the City Information Service (0171 606 3030) but usual venues are Broadgate, Finsbury Circus Gardens, Paternoster Square and St Paul's steps.

Alexandra Park. Sundays in August.
0181 883 7173

Marble Hill House. Sundays in August.
0181 892 5115

Regents Park. Mailing list available.
0171 486 7905

CHURCH MUSIC

The London churches are awash with excellent music and there is no doubt that you will be able to find whatever combination of music you are seeking.

Organ recitals are to be found at:

St Bride's, Fleet Street, EC4. Wednesday

St Paul's Cathedral, EC4. Friday

Southwark Cathedral, SE1. Monday

For details of above-average choirs and Christmas carols see page 95.

COFFEE CONCERTS

A pleasant way to spend a Sunday morning is to wander along to the Wigmore Hall where they hold concerts at 11.30 am.

Concerts last about an hour and cost £7, but they are extremely well attended, so it is best to book beforehand.

The Barbican also has foyer music in the afternoons and at lunchtime but not every day, so if you are planning to make a special visit check first.

Wigmore Hall, 36 Wigmore Street, W1.
0171 935 2141

Barbican Centre, Silk Street, EC2.
0171 638 4141

• All the major music colleges tend to hold daytime and evening student concerts. They do advertise in the press but it is probably better to call the colleges direct.

• The British Music Information Centre, which specializes in twentieth-century music, regularly give free evening concerts.

The British Music Information Centre, 10 Stratford Place, W1.
0171 499 8567

• National Music Day has been set up to 'celebrate all types of music from massed steel bands, brass bands, rock, classical and youth orchestras,' and to encourage more people to become involved. It always takes place the last week of June and the office co-ordinating the events can be contacted on 0171 491 0044.

CONCERT HALLS

Barbican Hall Silk Street, EC2.	0171 638 8891
Central Hall Storeys Gate, SW1.	0171 222 8010
Conway Hall Red Lion Square, WC1.	0171 242 8032

Purcell Room Belvedere Road, SE1.	0171 928 3002
Queen Elizabeth Hall Belvedere Road, SE1.	0171 928 3002
Royal Albert Hall Kensington Gore, SW7.	0171 589 8212
Royal College of Music Prince Consort Road, SW7.	0171 589 3643
Royal Festival Hall Belvedere Road, SE1.	0171 928 3002
St John's Smith Square, SW1.	0171 222 1061
Wigmore Hall 36 Wigmore Street, W.1.(closed July and August)	0171 935 2141

CONTEMPORARY MUSIC VENUES

The contemporary music scene changes every day and looking in the national papers, listings or specialist press is going to give you the widest picture of what is available that night or in the coming weeks. But there are some venues which specialize in a particular type of music and might be worth contacting for forthcoming events:

African

Africa Centre 38 King Street, WC2.	0171 836 1973

Latin American

Bass Clef 35 Coronet Street, N1.	0171 729 2476

Blues

The Arena 167 Drury Lane, WC2	0171 430 0565
Blues Bar 20 Kingly Street, W1	0171 287 0541
Station Bar 41 Bramley Road, W10.	0171 727 4053

Folk and Country

Cecil Sharp House Regents Park Road, NW1.	0171 485 2206
Halfway House 142 The Broadway, West Ealing, W13.	0181 567 0236

Hare and Hounds 181 Upper Street, N1.	0171 226 2992
Mean Fiddler 24 Harlesden High Street, NW10.	0181 965 2487
Weavers 98 Newington Green Road, N1.	0171 226 6911

Irish

National Ballroom 234 Kilburn High Road, NW6.	0171 328 3141
Scruffy Murphys 15 Denman Street, W1.	0171 437 1540
The Swan 215 Clapham Road, SW9.	0171 274 1526

New, Indie and Rock Bands

Academy Brixton 211 Stockwell Road, SW9.	0171 924 9999
Alexandra Palace Wood Green, W12.	0171 240 7200
Astoria 157 Charing Cross Road, WC2.	0171 434 0403
Borderline Orange Yard, W1.	0171 734 2095
Earls Court Exhibition Centre Warwick Road, SW5.	0171 385 1200
Equinox Leicester Square, W1	0171 437 1446
Fairfield Hall Park Lane, Croydon.	0181 688 9291
The Forum 9–17 Highgate Road, NW5.	0171 284 2200
The Grand St Johns Hill, SW11.	0171 738 9000
Labbatt's Appollo Queen Caroline Street, W6.	0181 741 4868
London Arena Limeharbour, E14	0171 538 8880
Marquee 105 Charing Cross Road, WC2.	0171 437 6603
Powerhaus 1 Liverpool Road, N1.	0171 837 3218
The Rock Garden The Piazza, Covent Garden, WC2.	0171 836 4052

Royal Albert Hall	0171 589 8212
Kensington Gore, SW7.	
Shepherd's Bush Empire	0181 740 7474
Shepherd's Bush Green, W12.	
Underworld	0171 482 1932
174 Camden High Street, NW1.	
Union Chapel	0171 226 1686
Compton Avenue, N1.	
Venue	0181 692 4077
21 Clifton Rise, SE14.	
Wembley Arena	0181 900 1234
Empire Way, Wembley, Middlesex.	

OPEN AIR ROCK CONCERTS

Wembley Stadium	0181 900 1234
Empire Way, Wembley, Middlesex.	

PERFORMANCE

THEATRE

Theatre continues to be one of London's great triumphs with a range of productions from pub theatre through to the main West End stages to satisfy most tastes.

Don't forget:

• Buying directly from the Box Office saves booking fees and agency commissions.

• Reduced seat prices are available through theatre clubs, many of which are run by national newspapers, or try The Theatregoers Club of Great Britain, 56 St Martin's Lane, WC2 (0171 836 7517).

• Early-in-the-week bookings offer you a wider choice of seats and quite often, in the non-West-End theatres, good ticket-price reductions.

• The Society of West End Theatre's half-price ticket booth in Leicester Square offers half-price tickets (cash only) on the day of the performance for many theatre shows. Tickets are restricted to 4 per person and the queues tend to be long!

• The National Theatre sell a number of tickets on the day, even for the hit shows.

• Artsline (0171 388 2227) – a free advice and information service for disabled people to arts and entertainment in London. Free monthly arts listing magazine available.

• *London Theatreviews* carries the most comprehensive news and reviews of productions both in and out of London. The monthly magazine is available on an annual subscription of £60 from Blanche Marvin, 21a St. John's Wood High Street, NW8 7NG.

• When time is limited and a booking fee is a worthwhile investment for an efficient and knowledgeable service, West End Booking (0181 424 2066) provides the sort of customer care that justifies the additional booking charge.

• If you've always wanted a chance to see what goes on behind the iron curtain, Stage by Stage run backstage theatre tours (0171 328 7558).

• Dress Circle has one of the most comprehensive ranges of show recordings, posters, souvenirs, videos, books, music and merchandise.

Dress Circle, 57-59 Monmouth Street, Upper St Martin' s Lane, WC2. 0171 240 2227

WEST END THEATRES

ADELPHI THEATRE The Strand, WC2.	0171 836 7611
ALBERY THEATRE St Martins Lane, WC2.	0171 867 1115 c.c. 0171 867 1111
ALDWYCH THEATRE The Aldwych, WC2.	0171 836 6404
AMBASSADORS THEATRE West Street, WC2.	0171 836 6111 c.c. 0171 836 1171
APOLLO THEATRE Shaftesbury Avenue, W1.	0171 494 5070
APOLLO VICTORIA THEATRE Wilton Road, SW1.	0171 630 6262
ARTS THEATRE CLUB Newport Street, W1.	0171 836 2132
BARBICAN THEATRE Silk St, EC2.	0171 638 8891
BLOOMSBURY THEATRE 15 Gordon Street, WC1.	0171 388 8822
CAMBRIDGE THEATRE Earlham Street, WC2.	0171 494 5080
COLISEUM St Martin's Lane, WC2.	0171 836 3161 c.c. 0171 240 5258
COMEDY THEATRE Panton Street, SW1.	0171 867 1045
CRITERION THEATRE Piccadilly Circus, W1.	0171 839 4488
DOMINION THEATRE Tottenham Court Road, W1.	0171 580 9562 c.c. 0171 580 8845
DONMAR WAREHOUSE THEATRE Earlham St, WC2.	0171 867 1150 c.c. 0171 867 1111

DRURY LANE THEATRE Catherine Street, WC2.	0171 494 5060
DUCHESS THEATRE Catherine Street, WC2.	0171 494 5075
DUKE OF YORKS THEATRE St Martin's Lane, WC2.	0171 836 5122
FORTUNE THEATRE Russell Street, WC2.	0171 836 2238
GARRICK THEATRE Charing Cross Road, WC2.	0171 494 5085
GIELGUD THEATRE (GLOBE) Shaftesbury Avenue, W1.	0171 494 5065
HAYMARKET THEATRE Haymarket, SW1.	0171 930 8800
HER MAJESTY'S THEATRE Haymarket, SW1.	0171 494 5400
ISLAND THEATRE (see Royalty Theatre)	
LONDON PALLADIUM Argyll Street, W1.	0171 494 5020
LYRIC THEATRE Shaftesbury Avenue, W1.	0171 494 5045
MERMAID THEATRE Puddle Dock, EC4.	0171 410 0000
NATIONAL THEATRE South Bank, SE1.	0171 928 2252
NEW LONDON THEATRE Drury Lane, WC2	0171 405 0072 c.c. 0171 404 4079
OLD VIC Waterloo Road, SE1.	0171 928 7616
OPEN AIR THEATRE Regents Park, NW1.	0171 935 5884
PALACE THEATRE Cambridge Circus, W1.	0171 434 0909
PHOENIX THEATRE Charing Cross Road, WC2.	0171 867 1044 c.c. 0171 867 1111
PICCADILLY THEATRE Denman Street, W1.	0171 867 1118 c.c. 0171 867 1111
PLAYERS THEATRE Villiers Street, WC2.	0171 839 1134
PLAYHOUSE THEATRE Northumberland Avenue, WC2.	0171 839 4401
PRINCE EDWARD THEATRE Old Compton Street, W1.	0171 734 8951

PRINCE OF WALES THEATRE Coventry Street, W.1.	0171 839 5987 c.c. 0171 839 5972
QUEENS THEATRE Shaftesbury Avenue, W.1.	0171 494 5040
ROYAL COURT THEATRE Sloane Square, SW1.	0171 730 1745 c.c. 0171 836 2428 (Upstairs) 0171 730 2554
ROYAL OPERA HOUSE Bow Street, WC2.	0171 240 1066 c.c. 0171 240 1911
ROYALTY THEATRE (ISLAND THEATRE) Portugal Street, WC2.	0171 494 5090
SAVOY THEATRE The Strand, WC2.	0171 836 8888
SHAFTESBURY THEATRE Shaftesbury Avenue, WC2.	0171 379 5399
ST MARTIN'S THEATRE West Street, WC2.	0171 836 1443
STRAND THEATRE Aldwych, WC2.	0171 930 8800 c.c. 0171 344 4444
VAUDEVILLE THEATRE The Strand, WC2.	0171 836 9987 c.c. 0171 344 4444
VICTORIA PALACE Victoria Street, SW1.	0171 834 1317
WESTMINSTER THEATRE Palace Street, SW1.	0171 834 0283
WHITEHALL THEATRE Whitehall, SW1.	0171 867 1119 c.c. 0171 867 1111
WYNDHAMS THEATRE Charing Cross Road, WC2.	0171 867 1116 c.c. 0171 867 1111

'THE BEST OF THE REST'

ALMEIDA Almeida St, N1.	0171 359 4404
BATTERSEA ARTS CLUB Lavender Hill, SW11.	0171 223 2223
THE BUSH Shepherds Bush Green, W12.	0181 743 3388
THE COCHRANE Southampton Row, WC1.	0171 242 7040
THE COCKPIT Gateforth Street, NW8.	0171 402 5081
DRILL HALL Chenies Street, WC1.	0171 637 8270

THE GATE Pembridge Road, W11.	0171 229 0706
GREENWICH THEATRE Crooms Hill, SE10.	0181 858 7755
HACKNEY EMPIRE Mare Street, E8.	0181 985 2424
HAMPSTEAD THEATRE Avenue Road, NW3.	0171 722 9301
ICA The Mall, SW1.	0171 930 3647
KING'S HEAD 115 Upper Street, N1.	0171 226 1916
LYRIC HAMMERSMITH King Street, W6.	0181 741 2311 (Studio) 0181 741 8701
OLD RED LION St Johns Street, N1.	0171 837 7816
ORANGE TREE Clarence Street, Richmond.	0181 940 3633
RIVERSIDE STUDIOS Crisp Road, W6.	0181 741 2255 c.c. 0181 563 0331
RICHMOND THEATRE The Green, Richmond, Surrey.	0181 940 0088
SADLERS WELLS THEATRE Rosebery Avenue, EC1.	0171 278 8916
THEATRE ROYAL STRATFORD EAST Gerry Raffles Square, E15.	0181 534 0319
TRICYCLE THEATRE Kilburn High Road, NW6.	0171 328 1000
WIMBLEDON THEATRE The Broadway, SW19.	0181 540 0362
YOUNG VIC The Cut, SE1.	0171 928 6363 c.c. 0171 344 4444

• Smaller venues and pub theatres abound – check *Time Out* for-up-to date listings:

• Lunchtime theatre can be found at the King's Head
Theatre most weeks.

• Touring Theatre Companies to watch out for:

Cheek by Jowl	0171 793 0153
Paines Plough	0171 240 4533
Shared Experience	0171 434 9248
Theatre de Complicite	0171 700 0233
Trestle Theatre Company	0181 441 0349

OPERA

Opera has never been so popular! Historically its appeal was rather limited to the wealthy but over the last 10 years a new recording by one of the big opera stars, Domingo, Pavarotti, TeKanawa or Carreras is as likely to be found in the top 10 pop charts as it is the classical ones.

It is now standard to have public television relays of the famous operatic events and the video and record sales are huge. As it is for classical musicians and orchestras, London is an all important venue for opera singers and we are fortunate in the range and calibre of performers London's opera houses command.

COLISEUM THEATRE   WC2

London's largest (2,354 seats), and for many its most beautiful, theatre has been home to the English National Opera since 1968.

The English National's repertoire is extensive and accessible .– performances are in English. Considered to be the least stuffy of opera venues, it welcomes patrons of all ages and runs various workshops for children. Check with the Box Office for ticket discount deals.

The London Coliseum, St Martin's Lane, WC2.
0171 836 3161 (box office)
0171 836 7666 (recorded Information)

ROYAL OPERA HOUSE   WC2

The current building is the third edition of the Royal Opera House, the previous 2 having been burnt to the ground. Home to the Royal Opera and Royal Ballet, it has to be London's most controversial opera house with a reputation for attracting the major international opera performers. The programming comes in for a lot of discussion – mostly negative! – for being too esoteric or uninteresting, as do the high ticket prices.

Foreign language performances are translated in sub-titles over the proscenium.

Royal Opera House, Covent Garden, WC2.
0171 240 1066

• The Barbican Centre programme also includes some opera.

Barbican Centre, Silk Street, EC2.
0171 638 8891

• Almeida Theatre runs an Opera Festival in July.

Almeida Theatre, Almeida Street, N1.
0171 359 4404

• See The Windmill (page 182) for Pub Opera.

• Both the Royal Opera House and The Coliseum have shops offering a specialist range of current recordings, books and videos.

FILM

All the national newspapers carry a film listing but the most comprehensive and detailed guide to cinemas throughout London has to be that provided by *Time Out*.

WEST END

For 'West End' First Runs, Leicester Square probably offers the best choice, but any of the big chains (MGM and Odeon) show the very latest films on release. A lot of the cinemas now offer a booking service but that invariably carries an additional charge. Cinemas include:

Empire, Leicester Square, WC2.	0171 437 1234
MGM, Trocadero, WC2.	0171 434 0031
Odeon, Leicester Square, WC2.	01426 915683
Odeon West End, Leicester Square, WC2.	01426 915574

MIDNIGHT MOVIES

The Leicester Square cinemas usually offer a late-night movie on Friday and Saturday evenings as does the Gate at Notting Hill ('Late at the Gate'), the Odeon (Kensington) and MGM's Trocadero screens. Cinemas include:

MGM Trocadero, Trocadero, WC2.	0171 434 0031
Odeon Kensington, Kensington High Street, W8.	01426 914666
Gate Cinema, Notting Hill Gate, W11.	0171 727 4043

REPERTORY

For less commercial showings check out the National Film Theatre which offers a good selection and is the key venue to the London Film Festival (See Events section, page 248).

National Film Theatre, South Bank, SE1.
0171 928 3232

- Some of the rest:

Electric Cinema, 191 Portobello Road, W11.	0171 792 2020
Everyman, Hollybush Vale, NW3.	0171 435 1525
ICA Cinematheque, Nash House, The Mall, SW1.	0171 930 3647
Phoenix, 52 High Road, N2.	0181 444 6789
Rio, 107 Kingsland High Street, E8.	0171 249 2722
Riverside Studios, Crisp Road, W6.	0181 748 3354

- The Cinema Bookshop provides the most comprehensive range of film books but the National Film Theatre Bookshop is also excellent.

The Cinema Bookshop, 13 Great Russell Street, WC1.
0171 637 0296

National Film Theatre Bookshop, South Bank, SE1.
0171 928 3232

DANCE

There is no shortage of dance in London, whether it is one of the famous ballet companies or a troupe specializing in contemporary dance. Listings magazines provide the greatest detail on the programme available but national newspapers also carry information on the key events.

Dance Umbrella (see Events section, page 241) is the most exciting showcase for new dance and premieres the best and most creative work of young choreographers from around the world.

The main dance venues include:

THE LONDON COLISEUM

A summer home for the English National Ballet and a first choice venue for visiting dance companies such as the Bolshoi and Kirov Ballets and the Dance Theatre of Harlem.

The London Coliseum, St. Martins Lane, WC2.
0171 240 5258

THE PLACE

Home to the London Contemporary Dance School, this is probably the most exciting dance venue in London. An intimate space with a seating capacity of 300 which doubles up as a classroom by day.

The Place, 17 Dukes Road, WC1.
0171 380 1268

THE ROYAL OPERA HOUSE

The Royal Ballet (the resident company) are definitely the quality end of dance programming and performances tend to be expensive and popular. The Royal Opera House's ticket policy includes 50 standing-room tickets sold on the day.

Riverside Studios, Crisp Road, W6.   0181 748 3354.
Sadlers Wells Theatre, Rosebery Avenue, EC1.   0171 278 8916.
South Bank Centre, Belvedere Road, SE1.   0171 928 8800.

• For one of the best ranges of books on dance try:
Dance Books, 9 Cecil Court, WC2.
0171 836 2314

POETRY

There are over 50 poetry groups and workshops in and around London. The groups usually invite published poets to read from their works and meet for general poetry appreciation whilst workshops are specifically there to discuss the work of members. The Poetry Society is at the heart of this resurgence of interest in poetry and are able to offer you a list of active groups and workshops and venues.

Poetry International is the biggest poetry festival in England and takes place every 2 years for a week at the South Bank Centre.

One of the new vogues hitting London's poetry world is Poetry Slam, where the audience either boo or cheer the programme depending on its quality.

The Poetry Society, 22 Betterton Street, WC1.
0171 240 4810

The Poetry Library, Level 5, Royal Festival Hall, SE1.
0171 921 0943

The Poetry Book Society, Book House, 45 East Hill, SW18.
0181 870 8403

• *Time Out* offer the only comprehensive listing for Poetry Events in London.

CLUBS

COMEDY CLUBS

Alternative comedy in London has thrived. Throughout the 1980s clubs sprang up all over London, with stand-ups targeting Mrs Thatcher, yuppies and many other Eighties phenomena ripe for ribbing.

In the Nineties the comedy boom continues. The word 'alternative' has all but vanished and stand-up is now more often referred to as 'new comedy' and in certain moments of hysteria as 'the new rock and roll'. There are over 50 comedy clubs or nights around the capital, with new nights and venues still opening up regularly.

As William Cook, comedy critic for the *Guardian* says: 'There's this myth that alternative comedy is a guy in ripped jeans in a bleak pub in Lewisham, trying to overthrow the state. In fact comedy clubs now are very user-friendly, with a huge range of venues providing somewhere to drink, eat, smoke and answer back. Comedy is attracting the kind of audiences who in the Sixties would have been going to the Royal Court.'

Nothing can compare with the buzz of a live performance and here are 12 favourite chuckle spots.

APPLES AND SNAKES   WC2

Strictly speaking a poetry venue, where you can catch such verse masters as John Cooper Clark, John Hegley and Benjamin Zephaniah.
Performances on Friday nights.

Apples and Snakes, Covent Garden Community Centre, 46 Earlham Street, WC2.
0171 639 9656

BALHAM BANANA   SW12

This is a friendly intimate venue where the local audience are discerning comedy aficionados and the performers determined not to disappoint.
Shows Fri, Sat, Sun.

Banana Cabaret, The Bedford, 77 Bedford Hill, SW12.
0181 673 8904

CANAL CAFE

A lovely venue in a canalside pub in the middle of Little Venice which serves up good food and comedy. The main feature is Newsrevue (Thur–Sun) which has been going for years; Rory Bremner and Rob Newman both rose to stardom via its ranks. The cast is constantly changing and the quality of the show depends on who is around at the time.

Canal Cafe Theatre, The Bridge House, Delamere Terrace, W2.
0171 289 6054/6056

THE COMEDY CAFE

Reminiscent of a Hamburg bierkeller, the atmosphere at the Comedy Cafe is rough and ready and the food, served at the tables, is good. On Wednesday night they have an Open Mike night when, among the newcomers, you're likely to see 1 or 2 big names who use the venue to try out new material.
   Shows Tues–Sat.

The Comedy Café, 66 Rivington Street, EC2.
0171 739 5706

COMEDY IN TATTERS

There is nothing particularly different about the club, but the venue, on board an old paddle steamer, certainly is. It's friendly and comfy and you can take a stroll around the decks between acts.
   Sundays only.

Comedy in Tatters, Tattershall Castle Paddle Steamer, Victoria Embankment, WC2.
0171 733 7795

THE COMEDY STORE

The unofficial National Theatre of new comedy where Dawn French, Jennifer Saunders and Ben Elton cut their comedy teeth and Alexei Sayle was the first compere. It also spawned the Channel 4 series *Whose Line is it Anyway*, based on the Comedy Store Players improvisation evenings.
   In 1993, The Comedy Store moved from Leicester Square to its current 400-seater venue in Piccadilly. Some say it is scarcely alternative now, but it still has the biggest queues, and still pulls in the biggest names.
   Tues–Sun. Late night shows Fri and Sat.

The Comedy Store, 1 Oxendon Street, SW1.
0426 914433 (information)
0171 344 4444 (bookings)

COSMIC COMEDY CLUB

The old rock venue, London Globe, has now been refurbished and turned into a glitzy space with nightly comedy acts. Check out their special events programme and if you think you have an eye for emerging new talent – Try Out Nights are every Tuesday.

Cosmic Comedy Club, 177 Fulham Palace Road, W6.
0171 381 2006

JONGLEURS   SW11

Jongleurs' Battersea location made it particularly popular
with Sloaney stripe-shirted types in the mid-Eighties, when a
heckler's response to a routine about an overdraft was most
likely to be 'what's an overdraft?'

It is still hugely popular, spawning a younger branch in
Camden, and a big-name line-up is guaranteed. Lenny Henry
tries out his new material here.

Shows Fri and Sat nights. Booking advisable. Late bar and food.

Jongleurs, The Cornet, 49 Lavender Gardens, SW11.
0171 924 2766

JONGLEURS CAMDEN   NW1

The canalside warehouse was specially converted for Jongleurs from
the old Dingwalls, making it the first purpose-built comedy club.
Clientele comprises plenty of black-poloneck-clad Camden dwellers.

Shows Fri and Sat nights.

Jongleurs Camden Lock, Dingwalls Building, Middle Yard,
Camden Lock, NW1.
0171 924 2766

THE PARIS STUDIO   SW1

Historic site where *Round The Horn, Hancock's Half Hour, The Navy
Lark, The Goon Show* and other legendary comedy classics have all
been recorded.

A radio comedy recording is far less painful than the TV equivalent;
you don't have to sit through all the retakes or worry about whether
you've been caught in the audience reaction shots.

You need to contact the BBC ticket unit for tickets to the most
popular shows, but otherwise just turn up on the night for an
evening's free comic entertainment.

Paris Studio, Lower Regent Street, SW1.
0171 765 5807/4276

RED ROSE CABARET   N7

In many ways this club is the best of both worlds, combining some of
the better qualities of the upmarket clubs with a slightly rough and
ready, gutsy feel, making it a particular favourite with many
performers. Great line-ups. Food available.

Shows Fri and Sat nights.

Red Rose Club, 129 Seven Sisters Road, N7.
0171 281 3051

UP THE CREEK   SE10

Owned and run by anarchic comic Malcolm Hardee, Up The Creek is
the successor to his previous venue The Tunnel Club. Its exotic
clientele is interesting and often pretty rowdy. Malcolm Hardee also
pulls in performers from the northern club circuit, with the
occasional spectacular success. Charlie Chuck started off here.

Shows Fri, Sat and Sun. Food available.

Up The Creek, 302 Creek Road, SE10.
0181 858 4581

• You could also try Cupboard, a monthly cabaret-club-come-talent-show which defies description! Many of the acts are amateur, nearly all of them bizarre and with a casual vetting procedure the quality of performance is haphazard.

Rheingold Club, Sedley Place, 361 Oxford Street, W1.
0171 272 8862

JAZZ CLUBS

Jazz is currently big music news in the capital. An increasing number of restaurants and bars are laying on mealtime jazz, from Café Boheme in Old Compton Street (see Late Night section, p.154), which has free jazz every afternoon between 3pm and 5pm, to Sir Terence Conran's Quaglino's (see p.157). There is even a jazz brunch at the Victoria and Albert Museum on Sundays.

Jazz pubs include the famous Bull's Head in Barnes (373 Lonsdale Road, SW13), one of the first of London's regular jazz venues and still one of the best.

London also plays host to 3 different annual jazz music festivals: the London Jazz Festival, the Soho Jazz Festival and the Capital Radio Jazz Parade (see Events section).

Here is a selection of some of the capital's jazz venues.

100 CLUB   W1

Another Soho landmark, where just about every form of music has played over the years. The roll call of 100 Club artists ranges from The Who and the Rolling Stones in the Sixties to the Sex Pistols and The Clash in the Seventies.

The musical menue remains eclectic, with the emphasis now on jazz, jive, R 'n' B and swing.

Mon–Wed 7.30pm–midnight Thur 7.30pm–1am Fri 7.30pm–1am. Sun 7.30pm–11.30pm. Admission normally around £5.

100 Club, 100 Oxford Street, W1.
0171 636 0933

606 CLUB   SW10

The 606, run by Steve Rubie for the last 14 years is everything you would hope for in a classic jazz club. The music ranges from traditional jazz to contemporary, with an emphasis on modern jazz trios and quartets. There is a singers' night on Sundays.

The clientele covers a broad age range and jazz aficionados and novices can feel equally comfortable. Most people go to have dinner as well as listen to the music and the food is good. Licensing restrictions mean that non-members can only drink alcohol if they also eat.

The music charge is reasonable compared to many clubs. Once you've visited you'll definitely want to return.

Admission normally around £4. Mon–Sat 8.30pm–2.30am.
Sun 8.30pm–11.30pm.

606 Club, 90 Lots Road, SW10.
0171 352 5953

JAZZ CAFÉ   NW1

Popular, trendy venue where the music spans Latin, soul, African
and hip hop as well as jazz.

The best views can be had from the upstairs balcony restaurant.
Downstairs you'll need to arrive early for a good seat. If you eat as well
there is a minimum £10 charge, plus up to £12 for admission, which
can start to make for an expensive night out.

A diverse selection of artists including Cassandra Wilson, Courtney
Pine, Astrud Gilberto and the Brodsky Quartet have all played here. At
the weekends there are popular club nights, Sunday lunchtime jam
sessions, and comedy nights on Sunday evenings.

Sun–Thur 7pm–midnight Fri and Sat 7pm–2am.

Jazz Café, 5 Parkway, NW1.
0171 916 6000

PIZZA ON THE PARK   W1

Peter Boizot's Pizza on the Park is famed for its jazz, frequently
attracting big international names, and its cabaret seasons – a
musical form currently making a big comeback in the capital. Here
the entrance fee is about £15 and you can either book a table to eat or
just come for the music.

Peter Boizot also owns the Pizza Express in Dean Street, which
features jazz on the menu in the basement. There is a house band and
the music cover charge, depending on who is playing, is between
£3.50 and £10 on top of your meal.

Pizza on The Park, 11 Knightsbridge, Hyde Park Corner, W1.
0171 235 5550
Daily 8pm–midnight.

Pizza Express, 10 Dean Street, W1.
0171 437 9595
Daily 11.30am–midnight.

RONNIE SCOTT'S   W1

Steeped in history, Ronnie Scott's legendary club has been running for
35 years, firstly in Gerrard Street and since 1965 in Frith Street.

The list of those who have played there reads like a Who's Who of
jazz: Sonny Rollins, Chet Baker, Blossom Dearie, George Melly, John
Dankworth and Georgie Fame, to name a few. Ronnie Scott's is also
popular with record companies as a venue to showcase new bands.

The club covers 3 floors, with the main room, a first-floor disco and
a quieter downstairs bar. The food is fairly standard – or you can just
feed on the atmosphere.

Mon–Sat 8.30pm–3am.

Ronnie Scott's, 47 Frith Street, W1.
0171 439 0747

Dubbing itself 'The Home of British Jazz', the Vortex is a cosy, friendly upstairs venue above the bookshop of the same name in Stoke Newington.

The club has been running since 1986 and the music policy covers the jazz spectrum, from avant-garde to mainstream.

Mon–Sat 11am–midnight Sun 12noon–10.30pm.

The Vortex, 139–141 Stoke Newington Church Street, N16.
071 254 6516.

Where else can you go if you want to push up the odds of meeting someone? Ideas vary from joining a dance class (Le Roc – a jive, lindyhop, jitterbug cross-breed – is a current hot London favourite) to the more usual notions of taking up a sport. The sports and health clubs are fast becoming the new meeting grounds of the Nineties (see pp.61–76).

DANCE CLASSES

Dance classes are the new capital craze. Not the waltz or foxtrot, but a new wave of fast-moving, sexy styles like ceroc.

This new breed of dance classes don't take place in draughty church halls, but in style-setting nightclub venues with around 250 people attending each class. The emphasis is on having fun but plenty of romances seem to thrive along with the jive.

The other growth area is sexy Latin dances, with salsa and tango sweeping the clubs alongside the current vogue for Latin American music.

Many clubs and bars organize salsa, samba and tango classes, including Bar Madrid and Bar Rhumba. See listings magazines for details.

CEROC

Ceroc is a French jive, which first evolved when American GIs were posted to France during the war. The man responsible for the British ceroc boom is James Cronin, who began organizing classes in 1989 and has since taught around 20,000 Londoners.

The dance is a mix of gallic jive, jitterbug and rock and roll with easy to learn moves that have been described as 3-dimensional flirting.

Everyone changes partners frequently, so you don't need to take one with you, and most of those taking part are in the 25-35 age range. After the class the freestyle section gives you the chance to ask or be asked. Classes take place throughout the week at a variety of London clubs including SW1, The Gardens and Turnmills. Admission is around £4.50. Call the ceroc information line on 0181 742 9148 for details of forthcoming ceroc nights.

THE LONDON SCHOOL OF CAPOEIRA

Capoeira was first developed by slaves in Brazil and is best described as a blend of acrobatic dance and martial art, accompanied by strong African rhythms. It was capoeira that evolved into break-dancing after it was introduced into New York in the 1960s.

The London School of Capoeira runs a variety of classes for adults and children. There is a free demonstration every Friday night between 8.30pm and 9.30pm.

The London School of Capoeira, Aberdeen Court, 22 Highbury Grove, N5.
0171 354 2084

FLAMENCO

The Portobello area of London has a strong Spanish community and culture. Every weekend Nuria and Conchita's Escuela de Baile takes over the Kensal community centre to run flamenco classes.

All levels of Spanish dancing are taught, using live guitar music and, where appropriate, a flamenco singer to give pupils a sense of the flamenco 'compas' or rhythms. Those taking part range in age from 5 to 65.

Kensal Community Centre, Kensal Road, W10.   0181 960 2637

- For other dance classes and teachers:

Flamenco: Zandra Escudero   0171 727 8801

Classical: Anna Du Boisson   0171 629 6183

Contemporary: Bill Louther   0171 629 6183

Jazz: Sheila Sangster   0181 341 4713

Rock and Roll: Kav Kavanagh   0181 859 3055

NIGHT CLUBS

'All clubbing life is here,' says Andy Pemberton, Club Editor for the British bible of dance music, *Mixmag*.'The London club scene is very healthy at present and the spectrum is very broad, from hard house and techno at Final Frontier to kitsch disco tunes and party games at Smashing.'

The club scene changes faster than *Eastenders* plot lines and there is a huge range of one-nighters appearing and disappearing and new venues springing up all the time.

Although we're still not a 24-hour city, many of London's clubs are fast heading that way since all-night clubbing was legalized in 1990.

Here are some of the hardy annual venues and nights, whose longevity proves their quality, plus some of the best of the new arrivals. Now it's the DJ who matters more than the venue and some of the hottest names to look out for include Andy Weatherall, Smokin' Joe, Norman Jay, Darren Emerson, Danny Rampling and Gilles Peterson. See *Time Out* and other listings magazines for comprehensive details.

BAR RHUMBA   W1

A bar and club with a strong Latin flavour, Bar Rhumba offers salsa and tropical rhythms early in the evening, giving way to a mixture of sounds later on.

On Monday nights Gilles Peterson hosts 'That's How It Is', a top-

rated jam session, where artists like Bjork and Urban Species have all played unannounced.
   Mon–Sun 5pm–3am.

Bar Rhumba, 36 Shaftesbury Avenue, W1.
0171 287 2715

FANTASY ASHTRAY   EC1

A Holborn haunt which offers raucous punk, funk and hip hop from 11pm to 6am on Friday nights. Fashion victims abound!
   Fridays 11pm–6am.

Fantasy Ashtray, The Leisure Lounge, 121 Holborn, EC1.
0171 242 1345

THE GARDENING CLUB   WC2

This Covent Garden venue boasts a great range of one-nighters. Wednesday's Betty Ford Clinic is popular with DJ's and promoters on their night off. Club for Life on Saturdays is another big favourite.
   Located in 4 low-ceilinged cellar rooms, this venue creates an intimate atmosphere. The music is mostly house.
   Sun–Thur 10pm–3am Fri–Sat 11pm–6am.

The Gardening Club, 4 The Piazza, WC2.
0171 497 3153

ICENI   W1

Situated over 3 glamorous floors, Iceni is as much a lifestyle place as a club. Mixing house, garage, rap, swing and Latin sounds, it also offers you the opportunity to sit around and chat, get a cappuccino, or watch films.
   The most popular night is Flipside on Saturdays, which features funky music, a jam session, board games, and a chill-out area complete with tarot card reader.
   Wed, Fri, Sat 10pm–3am.

Iceni, 11 White Horse Street, W1.
0171 495 5333

THE LEISURE LOUNGE   EC1

This is one of the new breed of clubs whose stylish interiors are set to do justice to the crowd they attract. Like United Kingdom – which has the same promoter, Sean McClusky – the Leisure Lounge is a converted former snooker hall, now boasting 2 dance floors, several bars and an evolving photographic exhibition.
   Offers raucous punk, funk and hip hop for fashion victims with lots of fun fur and blue hair!

The Leisure Lounge, 121 Holborn, EC1.
0171 242 1345

MAMBO INN   SW9

Friendly, funky and worldly wise, The Mambo Inn features funk, rap and world music with a little lambada and merengue thrown in.

204

There are 2 levels: a basement bar and a snack bar. The Mambo Inn is justifiably popular and the very reasonable entrance fee is an added bonus.

Fri 10pm–2am Sat 10pm–2am.

The Mambo Inn, Loughborough Hotel,
39 Loughborough Road, SW9.
0171 737 2943

THE MINISTRY OF SOUND   SE1

The Ministry of Sound has managed to establish itself as London's leading night spot for the young and the beautiful, and is officially acknowledged to have the best sound system in London, if not the entire country. Fridays and Saturdays are packed with house-loving clubbers and the music is mixed by some of the world's best DJs.

Successful spin-offs include a Ministry clothing store in Covent Garden and their own record label. Perfect if you like your music mostly house: the sound of the New York underground is at The Ministry of Sound.

Friday midnight–8am and Saturday midnight–10am.

The Ministry of Sound, 103 Gaunt Street, SE1.
0171 378 6528

SUBTERANIA   W10

A long-established club, located under the looming Westway in Portobello. It is purpose built, with stylish decor, a good range of music and some live performance.

Mon–Thur 8pm–2am Fri–Sat 10pm–3am.

Subterania, 12 Acklam Road, W10.
0181 960 4590

TURNMILLS   EC1

If you're after a marathon night out, then head for Turnmills, the first club in the UK to be awarded a 24-hour club licence. Clubbers who have already put in a long night's work elsewhere appear here at 3am on Sunday mornings for Trade, a gay-mixed extravaganza for die-hard hedonists. Breakfast is served from 6am.

FF on Sunday nights is for the gay crowd.

Mon–Thur 7pm–4am Fri 7pm–11pm midnight–7am Sat 7pm–3am 3.30am–10am Sun 9pm–5am.

Turnmills, 63 Clerkenwell Road, EC1.
0171 250 3409
0891 516666 (information line)

TWILIGHT ZONE   SW8

After a hard night's clubbing go along to the Twilight Zone which opens its doors, on Saturday and Sundays, at 5am to welcome you. There you can chill out with soft soul and funk records till noon. Food is available and even board games are on offer.

Twilight Zone, Tearooms des Artistes, 697 Wandsworth Road, SW8.
0171 652 6526

With 3 rooms, all equally frenetic, United Kingdom has quickly established itself as one of south London's hottest venues. The music is house, techno, trance and acid, and the purple room provides a retreat with sofas and space to chill out.

Final Frontier on Fridays is currently the most popular night, with an incomparable DJ line-up playing Euro-techno, trance and acid.

Friday 10pm–6am Sat 10pm–6am. Free buses run between the venue and Trafalgar Square.

United Kingdom, 105a Buckhold Road, SW18.
0181 877 0110

• Also worth checking out:

Billion Dollar Babes, RAW, 112a Great Russell St, WC1.
0171 637 3375

The Cross, Goods Yard Way, Kings Cross, N1.
0171 837 0828

Velvet Underground, 143 Charing Cross Road, W1.
0171 439 4655

VISUAL

MUSEUMS AND HOUSES

There are well over 70 museums in London. Alongside the major showpieces are many smaller museums and collections, each reflecting particular aspects of the capital's history and life and helping to illuminate London's past.

• Check out the London White Card, which provides discounted admission to London's major charging museums and galleries.

DENNIS SEVERS' HOUSE   E1

American Dennis Severs has magically recreated eighteenth- and nineteenth-century London in his Spitalfields house, which was built in 1724.

Each room is decorated to evoke a style of the periods between 1685 and 1919, from the reign of Queen Anne to that of Queen Victoria. It may be a time warp, but it is no museum piece – details such as still-smouldering candles, a steaming cup of tea and tipped-over wine glasses give the impression of rooms only recently left, 'like a land-based Marie Celeste,' as one visitor put it.

For the past 15 years Dennis Severs has conducted tours of the house 3 times a week, vividly recreating, in his distinctive and memorable style, the life of several generations of an imaginary family, from their arrival in the house as Huguenot silk weavers at the start of the eighteenth century.

Each performance lasts for nearly 3 hours, and the intention is for visitors to use their imagination, not their intellect, to participate in the history of the house.

Performances 3 times a week. £30 per person. Ring for details. The house is also open to view on the first Sunday of each month, entry £5.

Dennis Severs House, 18 Folgate Street, E1.
0171 247 4013

FULHAM PALACE SW6

In a list of London's palaces, Buckingham, Kensington and Hampton Court roll easily from the tongue, Lambeth may also come to mind, but Fulham Palace somehow sounds highly unlikely. However, in the grounds of Bishops Park is Fulham's palace, the summer retreat of over 100 Bishops of London from the eleventh century until 1973.

The palace has been called London's best-kept secret and is well worth seeking out. Among its attractions are a Tudor courtyard, with a fountain and diamond-patterned redbrick walls and an elegant Georgian east front.

The rooms of the palace are gradually being restored. So far 2 of them, Bishop Howley's Dining Room and the Porteus Library house the museum. Several other rooms can be viewed on the Sunday tours. Fundraising plans are underway to continue the restoration.

The gardens, once enclosed by the longest moat in England, are a peaceful retreat. Bishop Grindal sent grapes from the palace vine to Elizabeth I, and Bishop Compton grew the first magnolias in Europe.

Museum open: Mar–Oct, Wed–Sun 2pm–5pm. Nov–Feb, Thur–Sun 1pm–4pm. Grounds open daily. Tours of the open rooms usually every second Sunday, but ring to check. Admission about £1.

Fulham Palace, Bishops Avenue, SW6.
0171 736 3233

THE GEFFRYE MUSEUM E2

The Geffrye museum is housed in a row of former almshouses, built in 1715 from a legacy bequeathed by the Master of the Ironmongers company and one-time Lord Mayor of London, Sir Robert Geffrye. In 1910 the Ironmongers Company decided to buy land in a less-populated part of the capital and the London County Council bought the almshouses. After consultation the Council decided to turn them into a furniture museum, reflecting the history of the Shoreditch area as a centre for the furniture and cabinet-making industries, the products of which were once sold in huge warehouses on Curtain Road.

Furniture still forms the basis of the museum, which is now divided into room sets recreating the style and design of interiors from 1600 to the 1950s, from an oak-panelled Stuart room to a 1930s deco lounge.

There is a reading room stocked with books on the decorative arts and design magazines, and in the grounds is a walled herb garden.

The museum also runs occasional courses connected with furniture, for example Victorian DIY, concentrating on restoring original Victorian features.

Tues–Sat 10am–5pm Sun 2pm–5pm. Cafe. Admission free.

The Geffrye Museum, Kingsland Road, E2.
0171 739 9893

LINLEY SAMBOURNE HOUSE   W8

A Victorian time capsule, this Kensington terraced house was originally owned by Linley Sambourne, chief political cartoonist for *Punch* magazine, who lived there between 1874 and 1910.

The house remained in family ownership until 1980, when it was presented to the Victorian Society.

The interior has been perfectly preserved, and gives an atmospheric idea of a Bohemian Victorian home, furnished in the 'artistic' style, with original wallpaper and carpets by William Morris and rooms packed with Victorian prints and possessions.

Mar–Oct Wed 10am–4pm Sun 2–5pm. Admission £3.

Linley Sambourne House, 18 Stafford Terrace, W8.
0181 994 1019

• The Victorian Society hold lectures and events for members.
The Victorian Society, 1 Priory Gardens, W4.
0181 994 1019

LONDON CANAL MUSEUM   N1

London is also a city of lost rivers and streams. Rivers like the Hol Bourne and the Kil Bourne once flowed in the capital, along with streams such as the Neckinger and the Tygris. Now they have dried up or flow underground – a tributary of the old Ty Bourne can still be seen in the basement of Gray's Antique Market. (see Markets section, p.139).

The London Canal Museum traces the history of the Regent's Canal from its days as a trade and transport waterway to today's more leisurely pursuits.

The building is a former ice warehouse built in the 1850s for Carlo Gatti, an ice-cream manufacturer. In the days before refrigeration, ice was a difficult commodity which had to be collected in winter from rivers, lakes and ponds and stored in deep wells.

Gatti began to import huge quantities of ice from Norway, which were carried on the Regent's Canal from the dock at Limehouse to the warehouse and its two 40-foot deep wells. One of these has now been excavated and is on show to the public.

The museum organizes a regular series of lectures on London's canals and waterways, and exhibitions change regularly.

Every day (except Mon) 10am–4.30pm. Adults £2.50, children £1.25.

London Canal Museum, 12–13 New Wharf Road, King's Cross, N1.
0171 713 0836

LONDON TRANSPORT MUSEUM   WC2

During a major re-fit a couple of years ago the London Transport Museum was substantially improved and now gives a detailed and fascinating insight into the evolution of the world's oldest and most famous transport system.

Colourful displays of trams, tube trains, London buses, maps, and posters illustrate the history of London transport with good hands-on exhibits including being able to simulate driving a London bus or tube train.

The museum also runs a series of exhibitions in their 2 galleries, many of which draw on extensive poster, film and photo collections – the recent one on Sporting London was excellent.

Daily 10am–6pm.

London Transport Museum, Covent Garden, WC2.
0171 379 6344 (24-hour information)

THE MUSEUM OF LONDON   EC2

To put the history of the capital in context, a visit to the Museum of London is essential. Tracing the history of London from Roman times to the present day, it manages to be both informative and entertaining and is packed with fascinating artefacts. There are also regularly changing major exhibitions related to London life.

Tues–Sat 10am–6pm Sun 12noon–6pm.

The Museum of London, 150 London Wall, EC2.
0171 600 3699

SUTTON HOUSE   E9

A chequered history has seen sixteenth-century Sutton House used as a nobleman's home, a school, a union headquarters and a squat. Finally, just as the National Trust, its owners since 1935, were planning to sell it off for development into flats, pressure brought to bear by local people forced them to change their mind. A restoration programme costing £2 million began and the house, the oldest domestic dwelling in the East End, opened to the public in 1993.

Sutton House was originally built by Ralph Sadleir, Cromwell's right-hand man, in 1535. During its time as a girls' school in the seventeenth century, the lascivious Samuel Pepys was particularly keen on trips to Hackney: 'that which we went chiefly to see was the young ladies of the schools, whereof there is a great store, very pretty.'

Part of the task of restoration involved reclaiming the fabulous seventeenth-century linenfold oak panelling. After the squatters were evicted, thieves had ripped it out and sold it, but an architectural salvage dealer recognized it and it was eventually restored.

The National Trust's rather obtrusive style of restoration means that almost the first thing you come across is the Trust's shop, but the house is well worth a visit. Its mixed history adds to the allure, and one of the squatters' wall murals remains in an upper room, putting the sixteenth and twentieth centuries side by side. Sutton House also hosts a series of concerts on Sunday evenings. Ask to be put on their mailing list.

Wed–Sun 11.30am–5.30pm. Admission £1.50.

Sutton House, 2–4 Homerton High Street, E9.
0181 986 2264

Some of the rest:

• The Bank of England Museum, housed in the Bank of England.

Bank of England, Threadneedle Street, EC2.
0171 601 4889

• Bramah Tea and Coffee Museum, details the impact both trades had on the Port of London. Run by ex-tea planter, taster and collector Edward Bramah.

Bramah Tea and Coffee Museum, Butlers Wharf, SE1.
0171 378 0222

• Museum of the Moving Image, detailing the ever-changing story of film, television and video.

Museum of the Moving Image, South Bank, SE1.
0171 401 2636

• Clink Prison Museum, one of the first women prisons, which include an armoury and a history of prostitution.

Clink Prison Museum, I Clink Street, SE1.
0171 603 4535

• Kew Bridge Steam Museum, features a unique collection of working steam engines.

Kew Bridge Steam Museum, Green Dragon Lane, Brentford, M'sex.
0181 568 4757

• Pollock's Toy Museum, a real must for those wanting to recapture childhood memories.

Pollock's Toy Museum, 1 Scala Street, W1.
0171 636 3452

• In September last year the Department of National Heritage, in conjunction with the architectural organization Open House, held the first London Open House Day. This provides the opportunity for members of the public to see buildings of architectural significance and interest to which they do not normally have access. It was a great success and the plan is to hold it again on 16 September 1995.
    Open House also organize architecturally related events in and around London.

Open House, West Hill, House, 6 Swains Lane, N6 6QU.
0181 341 1371

ART GALLERIES

London's art galleries contain some of the richest collections in the world and the fact that many are free to enter makes the consumption of culture ever more enjoyable! Even if you do have to pay an entrance fee it is usually not that high and as with museums it is well worth checking out what 'deals' are available.
    Current exhibitions are well represented in the broadsheets and the listing magazines.

• One of the best selection of art books in London can be found at the Long Acre branch of Dillons.
0171 836 1359

A selection of London Galleries with free admission:

• Chisenhale Gallery. An enormous space with an emphasis on contemporary innovative work.

Chisenhale Gallery, 64–84 Chisenhale Road, E3.
0181 981 4518

Iveagh Bequest. A collection of eighteenth-century paintings including Rembrandt and Gainsborough.

Iveagh Bequest, Kenwood House, Hampstead Lane, NW3.
0181 348 1286

• Leighton House Museum. A collection of pre-Raphaelite and High Victorian works of art.

Leighton House Museum, 2 Holland Park, W14.
0171 602 3316

• National Gallery. Works from all the major schools of art and arguably one of the most comprehensive collections of Western European art.

National Gallery, Trafalgar Square, WC2.
0171 839 3321

• National Portrait Gallery. Founded in 1856 especially to collect pictures of important political figures. Portraits include the only known one of William Shakespeare.

National Portrait Gallery, 2 St. Martin's Place, W2.
0171 306 0055

• Saatchi Collection. Represents the contemporary art scene and for anyone interested in current artists should not be missed.

Saatchi Collection, Boundary Road, NW8.
0171 624 8299

• Serpentine Gallery. Known for its excellent exhibitions, beautiful surroundings and Sunday afternoon lectures.

Serpentine Gallery, Kensington Gardens, Hyde Park, W2.
0171 402 6075

• Tate Gallery. Probably one of the most airy and peaceful galleries in London, the Tate is the museum of British Art and holder of the national collection of international contemporary paintings. It also houses the Turner Collection.

Tate Gallery, Millbank, SW1.
0171 821 1313

• Wallace Collection. An excellent collection of eighteenth-century French paintings housed in exquisite surroundings!
Wallace Collection,Hertford House, Manchester Square, W1.
0171 935 0687

- Whitechapel Gallery. An innovative gallery known for its mix of contemporary exhibitions. Whitechapel Open is the only major show of East London artists.

Whitechapel Gallery, Whitechapel High Street, E1.
0171 377 0107

SOCIAL

The singles market is now big business in London, and dating agencies catering for all tastes have opened up. You can expand your social circle by shelling out £500 for an in-depth profile or join a more casual group. Blind-date parties, common-interest groups and even an agency supplying escorts, just to escort, are doing well.

As Jeremy Wright who runs The Picture Dating Agency says: 'There is still a stigma attached to joining a dating agency but it's getting less and less. London is such an unfriendly place and you can't just strike up a conversation with someone on the bus. For most people it is just lack of opportunity that stops them meeting others.' Almost all the agencies declare their members to be busy, working professionals who don't get enough time to meet new people.

The old-fashioned image of the marriage bureau is fading fast and with the new telephone, picture and video dating services you at least get the chance to hear the voice or see the face of a potential date before deciding to go ahead, shortening the odds against a nightmare night out.

Approach it all with a sense of humour and a deep breath, and be certain the service is offering what you want before handing over any large sums of money. If you reply to an ad in a newspaper or magazine, make sure you take sensible precautions to protect your safety.

For introduction agencies there is a members' organization called the Association of British Introduction Agencies who will send you a list of their members (0171 937 2800).

Big-city isolation can happen to anyone and here are a range of clubs which can help you solve it.

AMERICAN SINGLES

Described by co-ordinator Tammy Burton as 'a loosely knit social group, not a dating agency', American Singles is designed to help single Americans living in London to meet up on a casual basis. It is also open to other nationalities, though a fascination with President Clinton and the state of the baseball league might be a help.

The group meets up for various events – brunch, cocktails, or dinner – and has close links with other American groups in London. Most of those who go along range in age between their late twenties and late forties. There is no membership fee, but details of the events are published in a bi-monthly newsletter. Subscription for a year costs £20.

American Singles
0171 243 3044

CINELINK

Cinelink has been running for 3 years. They have around 150 film buff members, who meet up to see the latest movie releases and go for a meal or a drink afterwards. They also arrange a theatre visit each month and usually a visit to an exhibition as well.

This is not an agency, but most of the members are single people in the 25 to 45 age range and the possibility of romance is never ruled out. Membership costs £45 for 6 months, £80 for a year.

Cinelink
0181 800 4822

CONSORTS FOR CONNOISSEURS

Consorts for Connoisseurs is emphatically not an agency and there is a complete ban on the word 'escort' and all its attendant connotations. Deborah Campbell describes her company as 'a walking-out service'.

Deborah, a former sales and marketing manager, and a single mother with a 4-year-old child, had the idea for this service when she couldn't find anyone to take her to an important awards dinner. 'I actually ended up not going and I thought, "Stuff this, there must be somewhere you can go to sort this out", but there wasn't.'

Now she has 30 male and female walkers, aged between 22 and 73 on her books, chosen from over 400 applicants for their confidence, charm, good conversation and presentability. They are guaranteed not to let you down, whether you need a partner for the company dinner dance, or any other important event. A lot of her business comes from people on a short working visit to London, who would like someone to accompany them to the opera, dinner or an exhibition. Most of the consorts have a specialist area, for example the arts, wine, or music.

Strictly professional, consorts arrive with a chauffeur and any misunderstandings are dealt with firmly but graciously. One female consort, offered £1,000 to return to a client's hotel room, told him it would not be possible, but that she should be delighted to accept the money as a gratuity.

The service isn't cheap: a consort and a chauffeured limousine for the evening will set you back £200.

Consorts for Connoisseurs
0171 945 6050

DINNER DATES

Hilly Marshall started Dinner Dates 6 years ago. 'I'd always been an amateur matchmaker and I thought there was a gap in the market that I could fill,' she says.

Dinner Dates holds dinner parties at upmarket restaurants around the capital, including Claridges and The Roof Gardens. Each dinner is for 16 men and 16 women and begins with a drinks party. At dinner there is a seating plan, worked out on the basis of the questionnaires that each member has filled in. After the main course the men are moved round.

The next day everyone is rung up to see if they would like to be put in contact with any of the other diners, provided the other party agrees. Apparently nearly everyone does!

Dinner dates claims 6,000 members around the Capital, each of whom pays a one-off membership of £60, entitling them to attend as many dinner parties as they wish, each of which costs £55. The age range is between 20 and 70 but the dinner parties are made up of people of a similar age.

Dinner Dates 0181 741 1252

• Dinner party groups have become extremely popular.
Some others include:

Meet 'n' Eat   0171 629 5534
Circles   0181 426 9168

DOUBLE SIX CLUB   W1

This is not an agency but a club which, every Tuesday night, invites you to literally play the night away at Wilde's in the depth of Chinatown. Choose your favourite board game from a games menu which runs from Kerplunk to Buckeroo, Operation or Mastermind and play away to the sound of background ambient music. At the Double Six Club, playing board games is more than a trivial pursuit.
    Tues 7pm-3am.

Double Six at Wilde's, 13 Gerrard Street, W1.
0171 494 1060

EBONY DATING SERVICE

Ebony Dating Service's members are mainly of Afro-Caribbean origin, but membership is not restricted to any ethnic group.
    Clients fill in a questionnaire and are then matched up with prospective dates via a computer.
    Members can choose whether to have their phone number passed on or to communicate first by letter through the office.
    The annual fee is £65, which includes 3 lists of potential introductions, after which the fee for a further list is £7.

Ebony Dating Service
0181 840 8635

NATURAL ATTRACTION   WC2

Natural Attraction is the brainchild of American Kim Franklin, who first came across the idea of video dating as a single woman living in LA, where it is hugely popular and hugely expensive.
    Not being able to afford the $2,000 required to join, she forgot the idea until several years later when, having married and moved to London, she was looking to start up a business.
    Run from a 4-storey listed building in Covent Garden, Natural Attraction is set up to feel like a club. New members fill out a questionnaire and are then interviewed on video. They can then view other members' tapes over a cup of coffee before deciding who they would like to meet. Members can select an unlimited number of potential dates during their membership. There is also a monthly drinks party and other social events. The age range is 25 to 60.

Membership £390 for a year, £100 to renew. Six-month membership also available.

Natural Attraction, 17 Maiden Lane, WC2.
0171 379 6697

THE PICTURE DATING AGENCY   WC2

Jeremy Wright and Saphel Rose set up The Picture Dating Agency 4 years ago. Having had experience of dating agencies themselves, they felt they could do better.

They have over 2,000 members, aged from 18 to 70, but concentrated in the 28 to 40 age group, with a fairly even split between the sexes. Each member fills in a comprehensive questionnaire and supplies a colour photograph.

Gold service members can look through the pictures and personality profiles to decide who they might like to meet. For standard service the agency will match questionnaires and then select and send you the pictures and personality profiles of 5 potential dates.

Gold service is around £130 for a year and standard service £60, plus £5 for each further set of 5 names. They also hold parties every few weeks in London wine bars where members can also bring their unattached friends.

The Picture Dating Agency, 29 Villiers Street, WC2.
0171 839 8884
0181 297 1424

SIGNIFICANT OTHERS

Significant Others is an agency for non-scene lesbians and gays who would like to meet a partner.

Set up by Mary Balfour, who also runs the long-time succesful heterosexual agency Drawing Down The Moon, it aims to offer a personal service, with specially recruited staff.

After an initial telephone interview, potential clients have a face-to-face meeting, fill out a questionnaire and supply a photograph. Once accepted onto the agencies books, they can look through the files of other clients and select anyone they might like to meet. Those selected are contacted and then have the choice of accepting an introduction.

Those for whom confidentiality is of paramount importance can choose to have a confidential file which is not seen by other members.

A year's membership costs around £425.

Significant Others
0171 938 4400

• Some of the others:

Classical Partners. Aims to bring together classical music lovers.
0181 903 0211

Mothermatch. An agency for single mums.
0181 340 5616

Vegetarian Matchmakers.
0181 348 5229

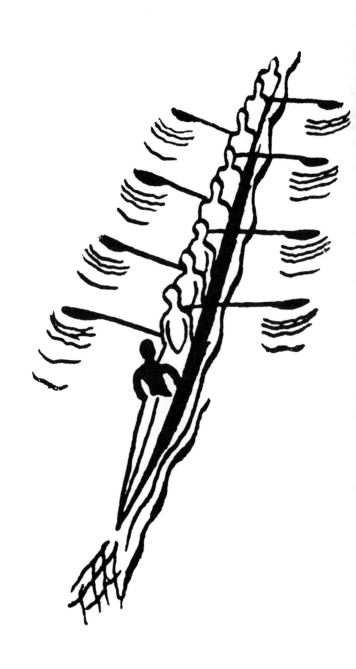

LONDON CALM

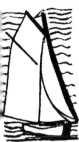

THE RIVER THAMES

London was the first capital city in the world to experience the industrial revolution and its unrivalled importance as London's main channel of transport was captured on canvas by many famous artists, including Turner and Canaletto.

With the emergence of other methods of transport the need for the extensive network of docks declined as did the river's day-to-day importance, leading to years of neglect and pollution.

Changes are at last afoot and the Thames is finally being accorded some much-needed attention. A recent Government study looked at ways of opening the river to Londoners, of expanding freight and passenger transport, of improving the design of buildings bordering the water, and examining the possibility of a network of 'green routes' for walkers and cyclists by the river.

The most ambitious plan is for a 210-mile river walk from the source at Kemble in Gloucestershire to the Thames Barrier at Woolwich. It is due for completion in the summer 1996.

Other plans include a new River Thames Centre as part of the converted Oxo Wharf development on the South Bank. This is to feature exhibitions and educational programmes looking at the history and ecology of the river; there is also a proposed development at Deptford Creek for a marina with hotels and homes, with sufficiently deep moorings to allow cruise liners to dock.

The banks of the River Thames pay tribute to its past glories and hopefully all these plans and schemes will come to fruition and a large part of London life will once again revolve around the river.

• For the perfect riverside browse visit the book fair held daily in front of the National Film Theatre on the South Bank. Organized by a group of independent booksellers, stalls start to go up around midday and close late afternoon depending on the weather.

BOAT TRAVEL

River trips are divided into 'downriver' from Westminster Pier to Tower Bridge, Greenwich and the Thames Barrier and 'upriver' from Kew to Richmond and Hampton Court. The downriver timetable runs throughout the year but sailing times are far less regular from November through to March. Upriver trips are nearly all limited to the summer months, i.e. Easter to the end of September.

For details of the various trips available call the London Tourist Board's river trips information line (01839 123432). Otherwise just turn up at the landing stage and buy a ticket!

• Thames Commuter Services have taken over the old Riverbus service, which runs between Festival Pier and London Bridge City Pier and on to Canary Wharf between 7.30am and 9.30am and 4.45pm and 7.30pm. For further details contact the Thames Passenger Service Federation (0171 231 7122).

BOAT HIRE

A number of river boats can be hired out for large parties or smaller occasions. Contact the companies for details of boats, menus and the entertainment they can offer.

For river trips

• Bateaux London offer lunch, afternoon tea and dinner cruises (not Monday nights) throughout the year.
0171 925 2215

• Catamaran Cruises have 6 boats whose capacity range from 150 to 300 people. They also run Sunday lunchtime and evening cruises during the summer.
0171 987 1185

• The Elizabethan Paddle Steamer (Replica of an 1890s Mississippi steamer) has capacity for up to 180 people.
0181 780 1562

• *M.Y. Aberdonia* is a classic 48-foot motor yacht moored at Chelsea Harbour Marina and available for cocktail parties with a maximum of 15 and dinner parties for as few as 6. They also run river day trips.
0171 351 9192

• Tidal Cruises' range of boats available for private hire cover parties from 130 to 250 people. 0171 928 9009.

• Turks' range of boats for private hire cover from 40 to 150 people.
0181 546 2434

• Westminster run evening cruises between Richmond and Teddington but this is a summer service only.
0171 930 4721

Permanently moored

HERONS REST DUTCH BARGE   E19

A floating restaurant where you can either book a table for 2 or hire privately.

Herons Rest Dutch Bar, Marsh Wall, Harbour Exchange, E19.
0171 537 2595

R.S. HISPANIOLA   WC2

A floating restaurant and bar with private hire facilities.

R.S. Hispaniola, opposite Embankment Tube, WC2.
0171 839 3011

REGALIA   EC4

A floating restaurant which also offers dinner and dance on
Friday and Saturday evenings (book first). Private hire
facilities are available.

Regalia, 23 Swan Pier, Swan Lane, London Bridge, EC4.
0171 623 1805

• The boats and barges named in the Eating by The River
section (p.220–223) are also frequently available for hire, as
are those on the Regent's Canal. For further information
contact the individual companies.

BOAT SPORTS

The river plays host to lots of events and activities which are
covered in the Watersports section (p.82–83) but here are a
couple of the more unusual ones.

DRAGON BOAT RACING

Dragon boat racing on the Thames – involving 40-foot vessels adorned
with dragon's head and tail – is very colourful and exciting. Dragon
boats have been around for over 2000 years in the South China Sea
and came to the banks of the Thames in the early Eighties. A 20-
strong crew row to the rhythmic sound of a drummer and in 1989 a
Kingston crew won a bronze model at the Hong Kong International
Races; now there are teams in Shadwell, Docklands, Kingston and
Richmond.

British Dragon Boat Racing Association
0171 930 2296

THE GREAT RIVER RACE

This is the River Thames' London Marathon on Water! Held annually
the Great River Race for traditional boats covers a 22-mile course
from Richmond (Ham House) to the Isle of Dogs. With around 200
boats of every size, shape and type this is the most wonderful spectator
sport. Competitors from all over the world take part competing in 20
different classes to become the United Kingdom Traditional Boat
Champions.
  The date changes each year but 1995's race will take place on 23
September, starting in Richmond at 2.15pm

The Great River Race Organisation, MB Aries, Thames Marina,
Portsmouth Road, Thames Ditton, Surrey. KT6 5QD.
0181 398 9057

• The London Docklands Development Corporation run an events
listing service on activities in and around the Docklands, many of
which are river related.

The London Dockland Development Corporation, 191 Marsh Wall, E14.
0171 512 8451

EATING AND DRINKING BY THE RIVER

From East to West

THE CUTTY SARK   SE10

An attractive Georgian pub looking across the wide sweep of the river
to the Isle of Dogs.   Plenty of outside seats or perch on the wall to
gaze into the waters below. Its location, slightly away from the main
Greenwich drag, stops it getting too overcrowded.

A favourite with comics performing at the local Up the Creek club
and actors from Greenwich Theatre. Bar food available.

The Cutty Sark, Belfast Quay, Lassell Street, SE10.
0181 858 3146

• Also:

The Yacht, Crane Street, SE10.
0181 858 0175

THE GRAPES   E14

Dickens mentioned this sixteenth-century pub in *Our Mutual Friend*
and Rex Whistler used it to inspire some of his most beautiful
paintings, but it was also from this pub that watermen are reputed to
have rowed out with drunks, drowned them and then sold their
salvaged bodies to the anatomists!

A glass-roofed back balcony provides a sheltered view of the river as
does the upstairs restaurant. The food, which is predominantly fish, is
excellent.

The Grapes, 76 Narrow Street, E14.
01711 987 4396

PROSPECT OF WHITBY   E1

The oldest and still the most evocative of London's riverside pubs, the
Prospect of Whitby dates from 1520 and was once known as the Devil's
Tavern because of its associations with thieves and smugglers.

The small timbered balcony at the back has superb views across the
river and from the small flight of steps – the Pelican Stairs – at the
side of the pub, it is easy to imagine contraband being loaded and
unloaded.

Famous on the tourist trail, the pub is best avoided at the height of
the season and is most enjoyable at quiet times and in winter. Bar
food is available and there is also an upstairs restaurant.

Prospect of Whitby, 57 Wapping Wall, E1.
0171 481 1095

THE MAYFLOWER   SE16

This dark and cosy seventeenth-century pub named after the boat in
which the Pilgrim Fathers set sail for America in 1620 recently
became the film company local when A Fish Called Wanda was filmed
nearby. It is also the only pub in London allowed to sell American
postage stamps.

A jetty overlooks the river and bar food is available.

The Mayflower, 117 Rotherhithe Street, SE16.
0171 237 4088

ST KATHERINE'S HAVEN E1

For coffee and a perfect view of the marina, St Katherine's Haven is worth a visit.

St Katherine's Haven, Maritime Centre Street,
52 St Katherine's Way, E1.
0171 481 8350

THE ANGEL SE16

Judge Jeffries once watched the hangings at Execution dock on the opposite bank from the pillared balcony of The Angel and trap doors in the floor of this fifteenth-century pub were used by pirates!

The Angel is owned by Forte's, and pub food is available in the downstairs bar, while upstairs the restaurant serves modern British cuisine. A table by the window at sunset, with a magnificent view of Tower Bridge, is perfect for a romantic dinner.

Again it is popular with tourists and so is best enjoyed out of season.

The Angel, 101 Bermondsey Wall, SE16.
0171 237 3608

• Also:

The Founders Arms, 52 Hopton Street, SE1.

Old Thameside, Clink Street, SE1.

• see Hidden London (page 230).

THE ANCHOR, BANKSIDE SE1

Once the haunt of smugglers, pirates and pressgangers, with bearbaiting laid on for entertainment, the Anchor was certainly the place for a raucous night out. In 1666 customers watched the Great Fire of London reflected in the waters of the Thames and in the eighteenth century, Dr Johnson and his associate Boswell were among the regulars.

The present timbered building is around 170 years old and the large riverside terrace has good views across to St Pauls and Southwark Bridge.

It has 5 bars, a minstrels' gallery, an eighteenth-century dining room and a new riverside terrace as well as a barbecue and a beer garden.

The Anchor, 35 Park Street, SE1.
0171 407 1577

• The Globe. Close to The Anchor is the site of Shakespeare's Globe Theatre, whose restoration actor/director Sam Wanamaker made his life's work until his death in late 1993. The theatre is due to re-open in 1995.

The Globe Museum, 1 Bear Gardens, Bankside, SE1.
0171 928 6342

THE BATTERSEA BARGE BISTRO   SW8

Not very easy to find, but well worth the hunt, the barge, named
Maria, is discreetly moored on the river between Chelsea and Vauxhall
bridges. Close by is the Covent Garden flower market at Nine Elms.

Originally built in Holland in 1931, *Maria* has a fascinating history,
which includes carrying grain in France, being requisitioned by the
Germans and a spell of retirement in Lymington, before her
reincarnation as a restaurant 7 years ago.

Reasonably priced bistro food includes avocado and tomato salsa
with main courses such as beef stroganoff or fish casserole. *Maria* can
also be hired for private parties.

Battersea Barge Bistro, Nine Elms Lane, SW8.
0171 498 0004

THAI ON THE RIVER   SW10

Opened in March 1994, this restaurant is located in a former flour
mill, and the original hopper can still be seen in the middle.

It has good views over the sweep of the river towards Battersea and
St Mary's church where William Blake was married and where Turner
(who in later life lived nearby in Cheyne Walk) came to paint the river.
The church apparently also holds a record for the most marriages
performed in one day.

An extensive menu of northern Thai dishes includes green and red
curries and pad phet taleh – stir-fried mixed seafood with Thai herbs,
lime leaves, lemon grass and oyster sauce. Prices reflect the Chelsea
Wharf location.

Thai on the River, 15 Lots Road, Chelsea Wharf, SW10.
0171 351 1151

THE SHIP   SW18

Known locally for its excellent annual firework display, The Ship has a
large riverside terrace which really comes into its own in the summer.
Partly cobbled and on 2 levels, it has picnic tables set out among
hanging baskets and flowerbeds. Inside the main bar is light and airy
and the food is excellent.

The Ship, 41 Jews Row, SW18.
0181 870 9667

THE DEPOT   SW14

Right on the bend of the river at Mortlake, The Depot has one of the
best river views in London, stretching away in either direction towards
Chiswick and Barnes Bridges.

Stripped pine tables and a relaxed atmosphere make it a great place
for a romantic dinner or a laid-back Sunday lunch.

The reasonably priced brasserie-style menu includes salmon crêpes,
spaghetti with marinated beef and prawn stir-fry. Also open in the
morning and afternoon for tea and coffee.

The Depot, Tideway Yard, Mortlake High Street, SW14.
0181 878 9462

- Also: Duke's Head, 8 Lower Richmond Road, SW15.
0181 788 2552

THE DOVE

The Dove has plenty of literary associations: Graham Greene and Ernest Hemingway apparently drank here and the poet James Thomson composed *Rule Britannia* in an upstairs room. John Thaw is a more recent regular.

The oak-beamed seventeenth-century inn, tucked away down a quiet lane, has an open fire and cosy corners for winter as well as a riverside terrace and upstairs balcony area for summer.

Food is standard pub grub at lunchtime, with Thai food available in the evening.

A particular favourite on Boat Race day with excellent views – get there early to benefit.

The Dove, 19 Upper Mall, W6.
0181 748 5405

- Just along the way at no. 26 Upper Mall, is Kelmscott House, once home to Sir Francis Ronalds, inventor of the electric telegraph, but better known as the London home of William Morris. The main house is private, but in the basement the William Morris society have organized an exhibition of original Morris prints and other artefacts. Open Thur and Sat, 2pm–5pm. Free. There is also a William Morris Gallery at his childhood home in Walthamstow.

- Also close by is one of London's 2 remaining independent brewers, Fullers (the other is Youngs in Wandsworth). Ale has been brewed on this site since 1845 and there are tours of the brewery several times a week. Write for details; they are booked up months in advance. Beer, a minimum of 14 pints, can also be bought direct from the brewery.

Griffin Brewery, Chiswick Lane South, W4.
0181 994 3691

CANALSIDE

While it is difficult to plan any lengthy river walk along the Thames without having to return frequently to the roads, London's canal towpaths can offer a virtually continuous walkway and a chance to glimpse the capital from a very different, and peaceful, perspective. It is now possible to walk some 40 miles along the towpaths from East to West London.

The most famous of London's canals, the Regent's Canal was designed by John Nash and joined the Grand Junction, later the Grand Union, at Paddington with the Thames at Limehouse. Completed in 1820, the 8.5 mile stretch of canal provided the capital with a link to the expanding manufacturing district of the Midlands.

At Little Venice, also known as Browning's Island (after the Victorian poet Robert Browning who lived in nearby Warwick Crescent), the

Paddington arm of the Grand Union Canal heads off to Southall, a distance of 13 miles, where it joins up with the main section of the Grand Union Canal.

Since the canals ceased to be important commercial waterways, stretches have become very run down and neglected. However, various initiatives over the past decade, both by canalside London boroughs and other groups, have done much to improve the waterways and progress continues. The Hammersmith and Fulham Amenity Trust is currently working on the section of the Paddington arm of the Grand Union Canal that crosses the borough close to Kensal Green cemetery. Improvements have included building a mini nature reserve, cleaning up graffiti, installing seating and bird and bat boxes for wildlife.

A major – and far more commercially based – initiative is one developer's current proposal to turn the neglected Paddington Basin into a complex of waterside offices, shops and flats – a sort of mini-docklands in W2.

• The London Tourist Board and British Waterways have jointly produced a new guide (£1.25) to the canal called *Explore London's Canals*. The 34-page leaflet contains 6 walks and includes historic highlights, local attractions and nearby pubs.

London Tourist Board, 26 Grosvenor Gardens, SW1.
0171 730 3450

London Canals Office, Little Venice, W2.
0171 286 6101

CANAL TRIPS

Weather plays a major role in canal trips so if it is not a blazingly hot summer day it might be worth a phone call first.

Trips take place daily during the summer, with increased scheduling during holiday time but in the winter months they tend to operate at weekends only. Single and return tickets are available on all trips.

Private hire is also available.

JASON'S TRIP   W9

Jason's Trip have been running canal narrowboat trips, along the Regent's Canal between Little Venice and Camden Lock since 1951. Lunches and teas are available on board and the journey takes about 45 minutes. Return tickets are under £5.

Jason's Trip, opposite no. 60 Blomfield Road, W9.
0171 286 3428

THE LONDON WATERBUS   W9

The London Waterbus runs boats from Little Venice to Camden Lock via London Zoo and back. Ticket prices include admission to the Zoo, or not, as you choose. The landing stage at Camden Lock is the West Yard.

The London Waterbus Company, Warwick Avenue, W9.
0171 482 2550

JENNY WREN CRUISES

Jenny Wren Cruises runs gaily painted narrowboats from their restaurant at 250 Camden High Street. The trip takes in London Zoo, Regents Park up to little Venice and back. They also run the My Fair Lady restaurant which offers lunch and dinner cruises (see below for details).

Jenny Wren Cruises, 250 Camden High Street, N1.
0171 485 4433

EATING AND DRINKING CANALSIDE

There are a number of boats offering lunch and dinner cruises on the Regent's Canal, but one of the most romantic is probably Alaphia's.

ALAPHIA'S   W10

A traditional narrowboat cruising the Regent's Canal serving gourmet lunches and dinners.

Alaphia Bidwell describes her food as modern British with a strong Italian influence, specializing in seasonal risottos and soups like chilled wild-nettle bisque.

On Sundays there is a breakfast cruise, complete with fresh fruit, Rossmore oysters and the Sunday papers.

Tues–Sat lunch and dinner cruises and a late-evening supper cruise. Sunday breakfast cruise, afternoon Mad Hatter's tea party and also a High Tea cruise. All about £16.50 excluding wine etc. Booking essential.

Alaphia's, 63 St. Helens Gardens, W10.
0181 964 5033

FENG SHANG   NW1

The Feng Shang can be found nestling at the side of the Cumberland Basin, housed in an authentic Chinese boat. Good Chinese food is served from quite formal dining rooms which stretch over 2 floors. Not normally famed for their friendly and attentive service this particular Chinese restaurant is a shining example!

Feng Shang, Cumberland Basin, Prince Albert Road, Regents Park, NW1.
0171 485 8137/0216

MY FAIR LADY   N1

My Fair Lady serves a traditional Sunday roast lunch whilst you enjoy a 2 and a half hour cruise on the canal. The meal is cooked on board and there's no choice of menu (other than a vegetarian dish) but with a seating capacity of 82 this popular lunch gets pretty booked up.

Also on offer are evening cruises, although their frequency rather depends on the bookings received. Unlike Sunday lunch there is a multiple-choice menu and the cruise lasts about 3 hours. The route takes in London Zoo, Regents Park, Maida Hill Tunnel and Browning's Island at Little Venice before returning to Camden Lock.

My Fair Lady Cruises, 250 Camden High Street, N1.
0171 485 4433

- Other combined cruise-and-eat venues include:

The Floating Boater	0171 724 8740
Lace Plate	0171 286 3428
Lady Rose of Regents	0181 788 2669

CAFÉ LAVILLE   W9

Perched on the bridge at the point where the Regent's Canal is crossed by the less than lovely Edgware Road, Café Laville has a small, pretty, open back terrace where you can sip iced coffee and gaze down on the canal boats gliding silently past and into the Maida Hill tunnel below.

This is a particularly good destination on a Sunday, when breakfast is served all day, and includes eggs benedict, smoked salmon and scrambled egg. Pasta dishes, bangers and mash are also available (all at around £5) as are sandwiches and cakes. The hot chocolate is particularly good.

In winter a plastic canopy covers the terrace.

Café Laville, 453 Edgware Road, W9.
0171 706 2620

CANAL BRASSERIE   W10

The Canal Brasserie is set in the Canalot production studios, once a bookcase factory but now home to a large number of small independent television, film and radio production companies, who probably do much of their creative thinking over the Italian-style food in the brasserie.

At the back the conservatory overlooks the Paddington arm of the Grand Union Canal.

Canal Brasserie, Canalot Production Studios, 222 Kensal Road, W10.
0181 960 2732

LE STUDIO CAFÉ   N1

Set within the Holborn studios complex, close to Islington, Le Studio is the canteen for the film-makers, photographers and pop promo video folk using the studios, but is also open to the public.

It faces directly on to the Regent's Canal with huge glass doors opening straight to the water in summer, and there is also a barge to sit on outside. The café is light and airy with plenty of rattan tables and chairs and lots of good-looking people with mobile phones.

Service is friendly and the 2 or 3 lunchtime specials cooked to order. A great place for a relaxing lunch or summer evening drink. Mon–Fri 8am–10pm.

Le Studio Café (in Holborn studios), 49 Eagle Wharf Road, N1.
0171 490 4900

WATERSIDE INN   N1

A new building which has been refurbished to look old! The outside terrace overlooks Battlebridge Basin and on sunny days more often than not a barbecue is sizzling. Inside there are lots of dimly lit alcoves. Folk or jazz music is quite often on the menu, as is good home-made food. The Sunday roast is much admired!

The Waterside Inn, 82 York Way, N1.
0171 837 7118

WATERSIDE RESTAURANT   NW1

Part of the Restaurant Group which offers the My Fair Lady cruising restaurant, the Waterside Restaurant overlooks the Canal and provides a bistro-type menu.

The Waterside Restaurant, 250 Camden High Street, NW1.
0171 485 4433

• Another venue is:
The Paddington Stop, 54 Formosa Street, W9.
0171 286 6776

GREEN SCENE

PARKS AND GARDENS

Thomas de Quincey called the parks 'the lungs of London' and there are over 80 within a 10-mile radius of the centre of the capital.

As well as parks, there are over 2,000 other pockets of green sanctuary tucked away in the capital. One of the best ways to find them is to look for small spaces of green on the A to Z, like the tiny garden and children's playground at the top of Violet Hill in St John's Wood, or the All Hallows garden next to the church in Idol Lane in the City. Other favourites include the Rembrandt Gardens at Little Venice or The Victoria Tower Gardens at Millbank.

• The London Transport Guide to Outdoor London, *Out and About in London,* is available from all good bookshops, priced at £8.99.

The following are particularly worth noting:

THE CHELSEA PHYSIC GARDEN   SW3

The current vogue for natural medicine and herbs makes the Chelsea Physic Garden of particular interest. Founded in 1673 by the Worshipful Company of Apothecaries, the 4-acre garden is still a major centre for botanical research.

The medicinal and herb gardens include an ethnobotanical 'Garden of World Medicine', a perfumery border, a water garden and a rock garden made from Icelandic lava, as well as 5,000 trees, shrubs and rare plants from all over the world.

Seeds sent from the garden to Georgia in the eighteenth century established cotton as the major crop of that region. The garden also features the largest olive tree in Britain.

Apr–Oct, Wed 2pm–5pm Sun 2pm–6pm and every day during the Chelsea Flower Show. Admission £2.50. Garden tea room.

Chelsea Physic Garden, 66 Royal Hospital Road, SW3.
0171 352 5646

THE TRADESCANT GARDEN   SE1

The two John Tradescants, father and son, were seventeenth-century naturalists and gardeners to Charles I. They travelled extensively in Europe and America, bringing back to Britain many of the flowers, shrubs and trees that subsequently became established across the country.

They are buried in the church of St Mary at Lambeth, where part of the churchyard has been designed as a replica of a seventeenth-century garden, containing only plants of the period.

Inside the church is the Museum of Garden History, which looks at the history of gardening and cultivation.

The Museum also organizes various one-day courses and lectures on subjects such as 'Creating A Herb Garden' or 'The Scented Garden' as well as occasional walks on 'Hidden Gardens of the City of London'.

March–Dec, Mon–Fri 11am–3pm Sun 10.30am–5pm. Admission free.

Museum of Garden History and The Tradescant Garden, Lambeth Palace Road, SE1.
0171 261 1891

LONDON GARDENS

Part of the National Gardens Scheme, London Gardens offers the chance to glimpse some of the capital's most attractive private gardens, from award-winning tiny town gardens crowded with roses, to a sub-tropical garden in Leytonstone that features gingers, bananas and bamboos.

All of them open on 1 or 2 afternoons during the summer, usually charging a £1 fee. Quite a few also lay on teas and have plants and produce for sale.

Among the gardens that are part of the scheme are the grounds of Lambeth Palace and some of the private garden squares.

A booklet listing the 100 or so gardens that open, with dates and times, is available from libraries and garden centres, or send a self-addressed envelope to London Gardens, Moleshill House, Fairmile, Cobham, Surrey KT11 1BG.

• Garden Day Tours have been running for 5 years and are increasing their 2 days a week to 3 for visiting gardens both in and out of London. The day starts at 8.30am outside the Embankment Underground station, and takes in 3 gardens, ending around 6.30pm. April–October only.

Garden Day Tours, 62 Redington Road, NW3.
0171 431 2758

• Bostall Heath, SE2 – provides 163 acres of heath and woodland, and the heathers make a lovely sight.

• Holland Park, W11 includes 28 acres of lovely woodland – it's quite difficult to remember you are still in the heart of London as you stroll through them.

Other interesting gardens:

Bunhill Fields, City Road, EC1. Originally a graveyard (William Blake,

John Bunyan and Daniel Defoe's are all buried here) this is a lovely peaceful garden.

Victoria Tower Gardens, Millbank, SW1. This quiet riverside garden looks across the Thames.

Queen Mary's Rose Garden, Regents Park, WI. Probably one of the best examples of the genre in London.

The Sunken Gardens, Kensington Garden, W8. These gardens are wonderfully peaceful and secluded.

ECOLOGY

In 1987 there were only 2 recognized ecology sites in London, at Ruislip and Perryvale Wood. Now 54 sites stretch across the capital, providing secluded and undisturbed areas where nature and wildlife can flourish.

Included among them are the 177-acre Oxleas Wood in south-east London and Camley Street Natural Park in Kings Cross.

Many of the sites are open to the public, managed by groups like the London Wildlife Trust.

LONDON WILDLIFE TRUST   N1

The trust aims to increase awareness of the variety of wildlife in the capital. It manages sites all across London, some of which are staffed and open to the public. It also runs various campaigns and has volunteer programmes.

For further details contact London Wildlife Trust, 80 York Way, N1.
0171 278 6612

• One of the Trust's sites is the Camley Street Natural Park in Kings Cross which covers 2 acres and is bordered by the Regent's Canal. The site was originally wasteland but now has a large pond, a wildlife garden and a bird hide, attracting frogs, newts, toads and butterflies.
  Mon–Fri 9am–5pm Sat–Sun 11am–5pm.

Camley Street Natural Park, 12 Camley Street, NW1.
0171 833 2311

LONDON ECOLOGY CENTRE   WC2

London's green centre provides a comprehensive walk-in information service for the public on environmental matters and staff can answer queries or provide information on any green subject.

The centre has a good selection of literature, runs exhibitions, and houses the first energy savers' shop in London, which stocks green technology goods. There is also a nature shop, vegetarian café and gallery.
  Mon–Sat 10am–6pm.

London Ecology Centre, Shelton Street, WC2.
0171 379 4324

ALLOTMENTS

Once they were the preserve of pensioners, but now a new breed of London allotment holders are taking on plots and growing cardoons and courgettes alongside the more traditional carrots and cabbages.

In some areas the allotments have a thriving social scene, with shed-warming parties and other celebrations a regular fixture.

Allotments are amazingly cheap to rent, normally around £12 per annum. Some boroughs, like Camden and Hackney, have a waiting list, but in others you may be able to start toiling on the soil almost immediately. Systems vary, but most boroughs will give you the number of your local allotment association and you should apply to them for a plot.

HIDDEN LONDON

If you have the energy, one of the best ways to discover London is by walking! The most comprehensive walk, the last section of which was opened by the Queen last year, is the Silver Jubilee Walkway. Covering a length of 12 miles, it circles the centre of London from Lambeth Bridge in the west to Tower Bridge in the east with a branch through Bloomsbury to Euston Station and a loop via the Barbican from St Paul's Cathedral to the Bank of England. The opening of the last section, the Queen's Walk, enables one to walk continuously alongside the river from Lambeth Bridge to Southwark Bridge and, ultimately, as far as Tower Bridge.

The route is marked by 400 aluminium discs and at various stopping points Silver Jubilee Panoramas (stainless steel engravings with explanations of all the key buildings currently in view) help to give a potted history.

Excellent maps of the walkway can be obtained (free of charge) from the London Tourist information desk.

For the more pub-orientated, the stretch of the Thames from Hammersmith to Chiswick is one of the most attractive riverside walks, and waterside pubs include The Blue Anchor and The Old Ship. At Strand on the Green, by Kew Bridge, the riverside Georgian houses (past residents include Nancy Mitford and Dylan Thomas) are very pretty. An interesting point to note is the tiny doors which demonstrate the frequency of flooding prior to the construction of the Thames Barrier. There are 3 pubs within yards of each other on this stretch of the river: the seventeenth-century Bulls Head, the fifteenth-century City Barge, where the Lord Mayor's barge used to moor, and the Bell and Crown, once a famous landing spot for smugglers. From all 3 pubs you can look across to Oliver's Island, where Cromwell is reputed to have hidden from the Cavalier army during the Civil War.

The Ramblers Association also produce a booklet, *The Thames Walk*, which lists 5 London walks, all based round the river and its surrounds.

Much more themed are the guided walks which, if you don't mind being mistaken for a tourist, can provide a substantial amount of additional facts about London.

One of the oldest established companies is The Original London Walks. Their walks cover all the tourist essentials, like Jack The Ripper and Sherlock Holmes, but the range is vast, including Balham and Streatham in the Golden Age, a T.S. Eliot Wasteland walk and a Bloomsbury walk.

Among the guides are several freemen of the City of London, professors, actors and an elephant keeper.

Historical Tours' walks include Legal London, The City in The Blitz and Shakespeare's Playgrounds, while Citisights of London work in association with the Museum of London to provide a series of walks concerning the history and archeology of London. Streets of London also cover the history of London, including an excellent one on Dicken's London.

In most cases the walks start from tube stations, last for a couple of hours and cost around £4. Call or see listings magazines such as *Time Out* for details.

- Guided-walk organisers include:

City Walks	0171 700 6931
Citisights of London	0181 806 4325
Historical Tours Walks	0181 668 4019
The London Ghost Walk	0171 256 8973
The Original London Walks.	071 624 3978
Streets of London	0181 346 9255

- For further information contact:

The Rambler's Association, 1/5 Wandsworth Road, London SW8 2XX. 0171 582 6878

London Ramblers
0171 370 5814

LONDON CALENDAR

The City's annual calendar is peppered with such a large number of festivals, shows and historical traditions that barely a week goes by when you can't enhance your cultural education or take in a bit of innovative entertainment.

The major occasions include the Lord Mayor's Show, the Proms, Wimbledon, the London to Brighton rally, the Royal Academy Summer Exhibition, the Boat Race, Chelsea Flower Show and Notting Hill Carnival, but these are just the tip of the iceberg! There are quite a few local festivals being established and lots of much smaller-scale events that are just fun or celebrate one of London's many old customs.

For up-to-the-minute listings *Time Out* and the *Evening Standard* provide excellent coverage, or the London Tourist Board operates a comprehensive range of recorded information services, updated daily and giving the latest on London events.

The major exhibition and conference centres are also listed in this section as they too provide London with an additional wealth of events.

It is worth double checking times and venues listed as they are always subject to change.

DIARY

JANUARY
New Year's Day Celebrations
International Boat Show
London Contemporary Art Fair
London Mime Festival
Chinatown New Years Festival
   (January/February)

FEBRUARY
The International Performance
Motor Show

MARCH
Daily Mail Ideal Home
   Exhibition
London Classic Motor Show
London Fashion Week
London International Book Fair
Spitalfields Pancake Day Race

APRIL
Blackheath Kite Festival
Chaucer Festival
Easter Show – Battersea
London Harness Horse Parade
London Marathon
Oxford and Cambridge Boat Race
Rugby League Cup Final
Tower of London Church Parade
   (also in June/December)

MAY
Beating the Bounds
Chelsea Flower Show
Covent Garden Festival
FA Cup Final
Festival for Mind, Body & Soul
London Jazz Festival
May Fayre and Puppet Festival
Regents Park Open Air Theatre
   season (and June/July/Aug/Sept)

JUNE

Beating Retreat
The Fleadh
Founders Day
Graduate Fashion Week
  (see London Fashion Week)
Greenwich Festival
Grosvenor House Art and
  Antiques Fair
London to Brighton Bicycle Ride
London International Festival of
  Theatre (June/July)
Royal Academy Summer
  Exhibition (July/August)
Spitalfields Festival
Trooping of the Colour
Wimbledon (June/July)

JULY

Capital Radio Jazz Parade
Cart Marking
City of London Festival
Dogett's Coat & Badge Race
Hampton Court Palace Flower
  Show
Kenwood Lakeside Open Air
  Concerts (August)
London Strollathon
Richmond Festival
Royal Tournament
The Proms (and
  August/September)

AUGUST

Great British Beer Festival
Notting Hill Carnival
Summer in the City
Teddy Bears' Picnic

SEPTEMBER

Chinatown Mid-Autumn Festival
Christ's Hospital March
Covent Garden Market Festival
  of Theatre
Election of the Lord Mayor of
  London
Horseman's Sunday
Last Night of the Proms
Soho Jazz Festival

OCTOBER

Chelsea Crafts Fair
Dance Umbrella
  (October/November)
Her Majesty's Judges & Queen's
  Counsels Annual Breakfast
Horse of the Year Show
London Fashion Week
Pearly Kings and Queens Harvest
  Festival
Quit-Rent Ceremony

NOVEMBER

Admission of the Lord Mayor
  Elect
Christmas Street Lights
  (Covent Garden, Oxford,
  Regent, & Bond Streets)
Guy Fawkes Night
London Festival of Fashion
  (see London Fashion Week)
London Film Festival
London's Grand Christmas
  Parade
Lord Mayor's Procession & Show
London to Brighton Veteran
  Car Run
Remembrance Sunday

DECEMBER

Carol Services
Christmas Tree Lights (Trafalgar
  Square & Covent Garden)
New Year Celebrations
Tower of London Church
  Parades
Watchnight Service

EVENTS AND FESTIVALS

ADMISSION OF THE LORD MAYOR ELECT EC2
November

A completely silent ceremony, lasting about 20 minutes, celebrating the new Lord Mayor of London taking office. The retiring Lord Mayor hands over the insignia to the new Lord Mayor in the Guildhall on the Friday before the Lord Mayor's Show (the second Friday in November).

The Guildhall seats about 200 and you can apply for free tickets (a maximum of 6 per person) by writing or phoning.

The Keepers Office, Guildhall, Gresham Street, EC2.
0171 606 3030

BATTERSEA EASTER SHOW SW11
Easter Sunday

Although the annual Battersea show no longer takes the form of a traditional Easter Parade, the organizers have tried to keep it a London event for all the family.

Attractions range from marching-band displays to kite-flying, laser clay-pigeon shooting, arts and crafts stalls and children's competitions. There is also a traditional funfair. NB Wandsworth Borough Council issue the license and the organizers who have run the show for the last 3 years are not planning to continue. This should not affect the event but check with Wandsworth Borough Council for further details 0181 871 6000.

Battersea Park, Queenstown Road, SW11.
0181 871 7530

BEATING THE BOUNDS EC3
May

The boundaries of the parishes of London were once proclaimed by a special Ascension Day ceremony. In 1980 it was revived and now the pupils of St Dunstans College along with Masters of the Livery Companies and various City VIPs form a procession, carrying willow wands to beat the boundary marks from All Hallows around the Tower of London.

Members of the public can join the procession which starts at about 4pm (although the boat trip to beat the boundary in the middle of the Thames is for a selected few) and continues till around 4.30. The Lord Mayor usually attends the 5.30 service.

All-Hallows-by-the-Tower to St Dunstans, Idol Lane, EC3.
0171 488 4772

BEATING THE RETREAT SW1
June

In view of the military nature of this occasion it is quite suprising to learn that 'The Retreat' does in fact refer to the setting of the sun!

To an audience of nearly 6,000 people, and members of the Royal

Family, the massed bands of the Household Division provide a rousing military display and lots of big band music in Horseguards Parade.

The parade starts at 9pm and usually lasts about one and a half hours.

Ticket prices range from £5.00 to £10.00 and can be purchased in advance or there are usually some available on the day.

Horseguards Parade, Horseguards Rd, SW1.
Military Exchange for tickets and Information.
0171 930 2271

BLACKHEATH KITE FESTIVAL   SE3
Easter Sunday and Monday

Hundreds of fanatical kite flyers make their way to Blackheath every Easter for the annual kite festival.

Kite flying has changed dramatically since the festival first began over 15 years ago. Sophisticated modern kites include 2- and 4-line stunt kites, flown by individuals and stunt kite teams with names like Airkraft and Team XS, who wear matching uniforms to complete the visual extravaganza.

The 2-day festival starts at 10am and finishes about 5pm.

Blackheath Kite Festival, Blackheath, SE3.
0171 836 1666

• London's specialist kite shops:

High As A Kite, 153 Stoke Newington Church Street, N16.
0171 275 8799.

The Kite Store, 48 Neal Street, WC2.
0171 836 1666

Kite Corner, 657 Watford Way, NW7.
0181 959 0619

THE OXFORD AND CAMBRIDGE BOAT RACE
April

It may feature Oxford and Cambridge but the Boat Race really belongs to London!

The first race took place in 1829 and Cambridge currently lead Oxford by 71 victories to 68, not including a dead heat in 1877.

The crews embark on Putney Embankment and the race starts just above Putney Bridge, where the best views are from the top of the bridge. Other good vantage points include Fulham Park and Dukes Meadows.

Pubs with good views along the course include:

• The Star and Garter, Putney, right by the start line.

• The Dove and The Blue Anchor at Hammersmith.

• The Bull's Head, Waterman's Arms and White Hart at Barnes, for the final stages.

• The Ship Inn, Mortlake, right by the finishing line.

The Boat Race.
0171 379 3234

CAPITAL RADIO JAZZ PARADE   SE1
July

Now in its 12th year, the Jazz Parade is a week-long celebration of jazz which takes place every July at the Royal Festival Hall. Some of the greatest names in jazz have performed as part of the parade over the years, including Sarah Vaughan, Ella Fitzgerald, Miles Davies, Fats Domino, Dizzy Gillespie, Ray Charles and B.B. King.

Capital Radio Jazz Parade
0171 608 6080

Royal Festival Hall, Belvedere Rd, SE1.
0171 928 3002

CART MARKING   EC2
July

Cart Marking stems from an Act of Common Council in the 1830s whereby any member of the Worshipful Company of Cars could bring his vehicle along to be marked by the City Corporation. The side of the cart was branded, using a red-hot iron, with the Coat of Arms of the City of London and a letter of the alphabet to mark the year. This enabled the vehicles to stand or ply for hire in the City.

Individual members of the Worshipful Company of Cars can still bring their vehicles along to be branded by the Master and the Lord Mayor in the yard of the Guildhall. A hardwood square is fixed to the side of the vehicle and branded with a red-hot iron in exactly the same way. It's a colourful occasion with full ceremonial dress and there are usually between 35 and 40 vehicles, ranging from superb vintage specimens to petrol tankers and tractor units. It starts at 11am and lasts about an hour.

Guildhall, Gresham St, EC2.
0171 489 8287

CHAUCER FESTIVAL   SE1
April

Costumed pilgrims start to assemble around 12noon outside Southwark Cathedral. There then follows in the Cathedral a Commemoration Service of period music and readings from Chaucer's work.

After the service the costumed cavalcade proceeds from the Cathedral to Tower Bridge and back again. There are plans to extend the day's celebrations by holding a medieval fayre in the gardens of the Tower.

If you don't have your own personal pilgrim outfit – the Chaucer Society does hire them out!

Southwark Cathedral, London Bridge, SE1.
0171 407 3708

Chaucer Society.
01227 470379

CHELSEA CRAFTS FAIR   SW3
October

The aim of the Chelsea Crafts Fair is 'to provide a showcase for quality new work'. With more than 200 contemporary crafts designers exhibiting over the 2 weeks of the fair, it seems justified in its claim to be Europe's finest craft fair.

The range of crafts on offer includes ceramics, furniture, jewellery, textiles and fashion. Designers are selected for the quality and originality of their work by a judging panel set up by the Crafts Council, which took over the running of the fair in 1987.

The best thing about the fair is the chance to pick up a unique design, whether it is a lamp or a piece of jewellery, and to be certain you won't be seeing the same thing in the high street the following week. Prices range from a few pounds into the hundreds.

Tues–Sat 10am–8pm Sun 10am–6pm.

Chelsea Old Town Hall, King's Road, SW3.
0171 278 7700

CHELSEA FLOWER SHOW   SW3
May

The Chelsea Flower Show began in 1888 in the Temple Gardens on the Embankment and moved to the grounds of the Royal Hospital in 1913. Run by the Royal Horticultural Society, the show attracts 170,000 visitors each year.

There are over 700 exhibitors and the highlights are always the display gardens. Other attractions include the various celebrities who roll up to have roses named after them.

The Tuesday and Wednesday of the show are reserved for RHS members only and the public are admitted on the Thursday and Friday. There are 3 admission sessions on the Thursday and just 1 session on the Friday.

On Friday at 5pm all the plants and flowers go on sale, turning the show into a giant horticultural jumble sale where it is possible to pick up some spectacular bargains.

All tickets must be purchased in advance. Thursday admission sessions 8am–8pm 3.30pm–8pm 12 5.30pm–8pm Friday admission session 8am–5pm.

Royal Hospital Grounds, Chelsea, SW3.
0171 828 1744

CHINATOWN MID-AUTUMN FESTIVAL   WC1
September

This festival is similar to, but smaller than, the Chinese New Year. Colourful lanterns of every size and shape are made by and for children, and there's plenty of entertainment and stalls. A stage is set up in Gerrard Street and dragons dance about outside Chinese restaurants and shops. Much of the food on sale is made specially for this festival.

Chinese Community Centre, Gerrard Street and Newport Place, WC1.
0171 439 3822

CHINESE NEW YEAR'S FESTIVAL
Late January/early February

After the bombing of the original Chinatown in Limehouse (Ming Street, Canton Street and Mandarin Street still exist) it moved to the Gerrard Street area of Soho, where around 4,000 Chinese and Vietnamese now live and work.

Chinatown's New Year celebrations take place on the Sunday closest to the lunar New Year, either late in January or in early February.

For the Chinese it is a time to clear debts and to visit old friends. Houses are swept in a particular motion and new clothes worn to signify a fresh start. Children are given gifts of red envelopes called Hung Bao which contain 'lucky money' to bring them future prosperity.

Chinatown's streets are hung with decorations, food stalls line the pavements and people greet each other with the Cantonese New Year saying"Gung hei faat choi' – wishing you prosperity.

The highlight of the day are the traditional lion dances, when performers concealed in magnificent papier-mâché costumes parade the streets to scare away evil spirits and bring good luck.

Festivities normally begin around 11.30am and finish about 6pm. The lion dances start at about 1pm, continuing through the early afternoon, firstly on the stage in Leicester Square and then through the surrounding streets.

Some special activities to mark the celebrations take place in Docklands too.

Chinatown Chinese Association.
0171 437 5256

The Chinese Association of Tower Hamlets.
0171 515 5598

CHRISTMAS STREET LIGHTS   WC2/W1
November

Regent Street, Oxford Street and Bond Street all have special Christmas light displays and the tradition of inviting a celebrity to 'switch on the lights' is now an annual event. Regent Street, in recent years, has been voted the best.

Trafalgar Square and Covent Garden have specially decorated Christmas trees, which are also honoured with a lighting up ceremony mid-November.

Covent Garden, WC2.	0171 836 9136
Oxford St, W1.	0171 629 1234
Regent St & Bond St, W1.	0171 629 1682

CITY OF LONDON FESTIVAL   EC4
July

Featuring mainly classical music, the City of London Festival uses some of the most beautiful buildings in the square mile as venues during its 3-week run.

St Paul's Cathedral is the setting for several choral and orchestral music concerts and the halls of the livery companies – Stationers, Drapers and Fishmongers among them – play host to artists such as the Britten String Quartet and international artists like the Moscow soloists.

There are also several concerts in the Tower of London, featuring the ceremony of the Keys, and open air events in Broadgate Arena.

St Paul's Cathedral, St Paul's Churchyard, EC4.
0171 248 2705

City of London Festival.
0171 377 0540

THE COVENT GARDEN FESTIVAL WC2
May

The Covent Garden Festival for Opera and the Musical Arts was founded in 1993 with the intention of providing a platform for young talent and to make opera more accessible. Specially commissioned works and world premières make up a large portion of the festival, and performers have included Music Theatre London, young talent from the Metropolitan Opera in New York, Ulster Music Theatre and The Scottish Early Music Consort, as well as an Impro Musical at the Donmar Warehouse.

The Festival also aims to make use of the huge variety of potential venues in the Covent Garden area, from the actor's church St Paul's, to Bow Street magistrates' court, where a special production of Gilbert and Sullivan's *Trial By Jury* was staged.

One of the most popular events, weather permitting, is the relaying of opera performances from the Royal Opera House to crowds in the piazza, via a giant video screen and sound system.

There are also many free opera and entertainment events taking place on the Festival stage in the Piazza, plus workshops and celebrity interviews at various venues.

Covent Garden Festival, Covent Garden, WC2.
0171 240 0560

COVENT GARDEN MARKET FESTIVAL OF STREET THEATRE WC2
September

It doesn't really matter what time of year you visit Covent Garden inasmuch as the lunchtime performances attract some of our finest street performers who regularly draw large and admiring crowds.

The Festival of Street Theatre can best be described as a celebration of street performance. Stilt-walkers, puppeteers, living statues, slack-rope acrobats and aerial artists are just some of the additional attractions that are booked to supplement the more regular street performers over this 2-week festival.

Performances take place between 12noon and 2pm daily in the Piazza.

Covent Garden Piazza, Covent Garden, WC2.
0171 240 0560

THE DAILY MAIL IDEAL HOME EXHIBITION   SW5
March

The first Ideal Home Exhibition took place in 1908 and since then the homes jamboree has continued to expand year by year, now attracting over half a million visitors each March.

The main attractions of the exhibition have always been the show houses, designed and furnished by some of the 500 exhibitors at the show to inspire similar creations at home.

There is also a huge range of demonstrations on cookery, DIY, gardening and all matters domestic, as well as those infamous gadgets.

Open Mon–Fri 11am–9.30pm Sat–Sun 10am–7pm.

Earls Court Exhibition Centre, Warwick Rd, SW5.
0171 385 1200

The Daily Mail Ideal Home Exhibition.
0895 677677

DANCE UMBRELLA
October/November

One of the most popular and prestigious of London's annual arts festivals, Dance Umbrella showcases a vast range of dance talent and endeavours to promote London as one of the dance capitals of the world.

The first festival took place in 1978 and since then a number of major dance companies have become closely associated with the festival, including DV8, the Siobhan Davies Dance Company and the breathtaking Momix. More than 20 companies take part each year over the month-long run of the festival and the venues include Sadlers Wells, The Place in WC1, the ICA in The Mall and Riverside Studios in Hammersmith, where a range of exhibitions and workshops accompany the dance performances.

Artistic director, Val Bourne, commissions a number of new works for the festival each year and has also increasingly featured the work of foreign dance companies, including performers from Israel, Japan, America, Spain, Holland, Belgium and France.

For those who know about dance or for anyone looking for a vibrant, moving, compelling and memorable piece of visual entertainment, Dance Umbrella fits the bill.

Dance Umbrella.
0181 740 4141

DOGGETT'S COAT AND BADGE RACE
July

Thomas Doggett was a famous Irish comedian who, when he died in 1715, left a legacy for the Doggett's Coat and Badge Race! This involves a maximum of 6 Thames watermen battling it out in their single sculls between London Bridge and Chelsea Bridge. It starts at 11.15am and usually lasts about half an hour! The winner's award – a splendid red uniform with a silver badge!

Doggett's Coat and Badge Race Information.
0171 626 3531

ELECTION OF THE LORD MAYOR OF LONDON EC2
Michaelmas Day, September

Members of the public used to be allowed to attend the election of the Lord Mayor of London and the Election of the Sheriffs of the City of London but as the Livery Men have first call and seats are limited, that's no longer possible.

If you want to see the aldermen, masters of the livery companies and high officers of the City in full dress, there is a short procession of all the dignitaries (usually about 140) from the church of St Lawrence Jewry to the Guildhall.

Guildhall, Gresham St, EC2.
0171 606 3030

THE FA CUP FINAL
May

The biggest sporting event of the year needs no further explanation! The Cup Final will take place at Wembley on 20th May this year.

Wembley Box Office   0181 900 1234
Wembley Information   0181 902 8833

FESTIVAL FOR MIND, BODY AND SPIRIT SW1
May

A major festival, which promotes alternative lifestyles, natural health, healing, personal growth, physical fitness, human potential, spiritual awareness and green issues together as unified theme. Now in its nineteenth year it is always held at the Royal Horticultural Hall and the 1995 dates will be the 20th–29th May.

The huge range of stalls in the exhibition hall are complemented by an excellent programme of workshops, demonstrations, lectures and performances providing information, education and entertainment.

This is the perfect way to see and find out about all the different therapies available.

New Life Promotion
c/o Royal Horticultural Hall, Greycoat Street, SW1.
0171 938 3788 (information)

(see also pages 49–60)

THE FLEADH N4
June

The first Fleadh (the Gaelic word for a festival of music – pronounced 'flah') took place in Finsbury Park in 1989 and the day-long festival of Irish rock and folk has now become an annual highlight both for the London Irish and lovers of the lyrics of Van Morrison, Christy Moore and the Pogues.

The Fleadh, Finsbury Park, N4.
0171 284 4111

FOUNDERS DAY   SW3
June

The Royal Hospital is a 1682 Wren building founded by
Charles II for veteran soldiers.

The resident Chelsea Pensioners have celebrated their
Founder's Day since 1952 by parading outside the Royal
Hospital and then presenting themselves for inspection by a
member of the Royal family.

Royal Hospital, Chelsea, SW3.
0171 730 0161

GREAT BRITISH BEER FESTIVAL   W14
August

This is the biggest Beer Festival in the country, organized by
the Campaign for Real Ale and held at Olympia's Grand Hall.
This is where you can taste over 400 different real ales and
interesting foreign beers alongside traditional cider!

The festival runs from 1st to 5th August with a lunch
(11am–3pm) and evening (5pm–10pm) session daily. Brass
bands, steel bands, folk bands and classical quartets are
amongst the live music on offer and there's lots of hot and
cold food available to help soak up the beer!

Campaign for Real Ale   01727 867201
Earls Court & Olympia   0171 385 1200

GREAT SPITALFIELDS PANCAKE RACE   E1
Shrove Tuesday, March

This used to be the Soho Pancake Day Race but a couple of years ago
the organizers, Alternative Arts, moved it to Spitalfields in the City.
Teams of 4 are made up of local people, businesses, associations, etc.,
and compete with each other by running with frying pans and tossing
their pancakes as they go! It starts at 12noon and is usually supported
by a well known charity who provides teams of celebrities to join in
the fun.

If you want to enter the race you will need to apply to the organizers
in advance.

Spitalfields Market, Brushfield St, EI.
0171 247 6590
0171 375 0441 (information)

GREENWICH FESTIVAL   SE10
June

This annual riverside arts festival has been taking place in the first 2
weeks of June since 1970. It tries to incorporate various areas of the
borough into the festival, and in 1994 events took place in recently
reprieved Oxleas Wood, on the river, and in a series of Kenwood-style
open air classical and jazz concerts were introduced in Greenwich
Park.

Each year it opens with free music and entertainment in Cutty Sark

Gardens on the first day, climaxing in a fireworks display over the Thames

Over its 2-week run the festival features a mixture of music, theatre, dance and comedy with such artists as Stephane Grapelli, Fascinating Aida and Felicity Lott taking part.

Greenwich Festival, Greenwich, SE10.
0181 317 1085

THE GROSVENOR HOUSE ART and ANTIQUES FAIR   W
June

The Grosvenor House Fair has a reputation for high-quality antiques with prices ranging from £100 up to £1 million.

The Fair is held in the Great Room of the Grosvenor House Hotel (the largest hotel room in Europe) and runs for 10 days. Every item in the fair is vetted for quality and authenticity, and the exhibits include furniture, ceramics, silver, jewellery, Oriental and other works of art.

Although primarily aimed at the serious collector (and with admission at £12 you need to be serious), the Grosvenor House Fair offers the chance to see quality antiques in a beautiful setting.

The Grosvenor House Art and Antiques Fair,
Grosvenor House, Park Lane, W1.
0171 495 8743/0171 499 6363

GUY FAWKES NIGHT
November

There are always lots of private and public firework displays throughout London to celebrate the anniversary of the Gunpowder Plot of 1605 and details are extremely easy to come by, either through newspapers and listings or by calling your local borough.

Highbury Fields, Islington is generally felt to have one of the most impressive displays but other large ones are usually to be found at Primrose Hill, Ravenscourt Park, Alexandra Palace, Battersea Park and St John's Church, Hyde Park.

• Captain Fantastic is the fireworks fanatic's treasure trove.
Fantastic Fireworks Limited, Rocket Park, Pepperstock, Beds LUI 4LL.
01582 485555

HAMPTON COURT PALACE FLOWER SHOW
July

The younger sister of the Chelsea Flower Show, the Hampton Court Show made its debut in 1990, and was taken over by the Royal Horticultural Society in 1993.

The 25-acre site, in parkland at Hampton Court, is much larger than the space available in the grounds at Chelsea, allowing for 24 full-size show gardens and a display of over 20,000 roses by the British Rose festival. There is also an Amateur National Rose Show.

Plants are on sale throughout the 4 days of the show which, although it lacks the tradition of Chelsea, can in fact be a lot more fun.

Hampton Court Palace, East Molesey, Surrey.
Royal Horticultural Society.
0171 630 1979

HER MAJESTY'S JUDGES AND QUEEN'S COUNSELS ANNUAL BREAKFAST   SW1
October

Each year, on the first Monday of October, a special service is held at Westminster Abbey to mark the opening of the law term. The service is attended by nearly all the judiciary, in full regalia, who then form a procession and walk to the House of Lords for their 'Annual Breakfast'! The service starts at 11.30am so the procession takes place about 12.15pm.

Westminster Abbey, Deans Yard, SW1.
0171 222 5152

HORSEMAN'S SUNDAY   W2
September

This service of 'the blessing of the horses' takes place at 12noon on the 3rd Sunday in September. It's been going for about 26 years and like the London Harness Horse Parade, was apparently started in order to draw attention to the plight of horses, specifically those stabled in Hyde Park!
    The vicar of St John's and many of the congregation attend on horseback. The service takes place in the forecourt of St John's and afterwards, the blessed animals wend their way to Kensington Paddock (north of Kensington Gardens) for the afternoon horse show which includes show jumping and other horse-related activities.

St John's Church, Hyde Park Crescent, W2.
0171 262 1732

HORSE OF THE YEAR SHOW   Wembley
October

The showcase of the British Showjumping Association. A chance to see the top British and foreign horses and riders competing in this major international event. There are 12 different showing classes, including hunters, hacks and cobs competing in different competitive categories – dressage, mounted games, driving and showjumping.

Horse of the Year Show information.
01203 693088

Wembley Arena, Empire Way, Wembley.
0181 900 1919

THE INTERNATIONAL BOAT SHOW   SW5
January

The world of boating comes spectacularly to life every January at the Earls Court Exhibition Centre. With 650 exhibitors and 800 craft based round a central pool, where watersport displays include waterskiing and windsurfing, every aspect of boating, large and small, inland and on the high seas is covered.
The International Boat Show information   01784 473377.
Earls Court Box office information and tickets   0171 373 8141.

THE INTERNATIONAL PERFORMANCE MOTOR SHOW   W14
February

This is the newly renamed *Evening Standard* Motor Racing Show. It is a 3-day event specifically geared to performance-modified and racing cars, with over 715 exhibiting companies in the Grand Hall at Olympia.

   Fun extras include a kart track, comedy evening, simulators and lazer quest!

The International Performance Motor Show information.
0181 892 9252

KENWOOD LAKESIDE OPEN AIR CONCERTS   NW3
July/August

Run by English Heritage, the concerts take place on Saturday and Sunday evenings throughout June, July and August. The music performed includes classical favourites from orchestras such as the Royal Philharmonic and the London Mozart Players, and in recent years jazz and opera have been introduced. The orchestras are housed in a covered podium across the lake from the audience, protecting them from the inevitable showers or downpours.

   The grounds seat 8,400, with 1,600 on deckchairs. However, most people prefer the blanket-on-the-ground option, gathering together a few friends, food and wine for a picnic before the concert – indeed half the fun is observing what other people have brought to eat.

   Most popular are the annual fireworks concerts, which have increased in number to keep pace with the demand and always sell out first. 1992 also saw the introduction of laser concerts to the programme.

   Kenwood is miles from the tube and parking is a nightmare, so get there early and consume your wine at leisure.

   Ticket prices from £7.00.

Kenwood Park, Hampstead Lane, NW3.
0181 348 1286
0171 413 1443 (tickets and information)

• English National Heritage also run a similar series of concerts at Marble Hill House in Twickenham 0171 973 3426.

• Other summer evening open air concerts take place at Crystal Palace Bowl, SE26, on Sunday afternoons (0181 778 9496) and the Holland Park Theatre, W11 (0171 603 1123).

THE LONDON CHRISTMAS PARADE   W1
November

New York has, for years, been celebrating the lead-up to Christmas with their world-famous Macy's Thanksgiving Parade which takes place on Broadway annually.

   1994 saw London following suit with the first Grand Christmas Parade in London's West End 'to celebrate Father Christmas's official arrival in London'! In truth it ensured that the first day of Sunday Christmas shopping in the West End was heralded by an enormous parade with specially themed floats, cartoon characters, dancers, actors, marching bands, clowns, jugglers and stilt-walkers.

The parade starts at 11am outside the Royal Academy of Art on Piccadilly and proceeds via Piccadilly Circus along Regent Street and Oxford Street, ending up at Marble Arch about an hour and a half later. If 1994 is anything to go by all details relating to the parade will be heavily advertized.

THE LONDON CLASSIC MOTOR SHOW   N22
March

If your passion is cars pre-dating 1979 then the London Classic Motor Show is a must.

This is a weekend devoted entirely to everything and anyone who works with or on classic cars. There are hundreds of wonderful old cars on display, an auction of classic cars and memorabilia, an autojumble which, apparently, means a spare parts sale(!) as well as all the usual trade stands associated with large-scale events.

The London Classic Motor Show.
012 966 31181

Alexandra Palace, Alexandra Park, N22.
0181 365 2121

THE LONDON CONTEMPORARY ART FAIR   N1
January

After 6 years, the London Contemporary Art Fair (also known by the rather snappier title of Art '91/2/3/4) is establishing itself as a major event in the art calendar.

The art fair, held at the Business Design Centre in Islington, gives art novices and experts alike a chance to look at and buy the work of both new and established modern artists.

It does look a little like an art supermarket, with works from over 65 galleries on display, but the range of galleries and dealers represented is impressive, including, in recent years, Annely Juda, Flowers East, Anthony d'Offay and Karsten Schubert. The works on sale range in price from under £50 to over £2,000.

Among the artists whose work has been featured are Bruce McLean, Ken Kiff, Paula Rego and Richard Hamilton – but don't expect to find any of them at the lower end of the price scale. There is now also a photography section, introduced in 1994 and run by the Photographers Gallery.

One of the main attractions of the show is the chance to see work that is normally only displayed in the kind of Bond Street gallery most of us feel too intimidated to walk into.

Business Design Centre, Islington, N1.
0171 359 3535

LONDON FASHION WEEK
March/October

Despite the fact that our fashion designers consistently remain a worldwide inspiration, London has always struggled to compete with the other international capitals when it comes to the twice-yearly catwalk fashion shows in March and October.

Now, however, things finally seem to be settling down, with the younger designers showing in Harvey Nichols and the major names putting on their catwalk shows in the British Fashion Council Tent, which seems to have taken up near-permanent residence outside the Natural History Museum.

Unless you're one of the 4,000 international journalists and buyers who are invited to Fashion Week, gaining entry to any of the fashion shows is difficult; however, it is sometimes possible to get into the shows of the newer, younger designers. Also, watch out for any tie-in fashion events, which will be listed in the *Evening Standard* or the fashion press. Often a promotions company will sponsor a special public catwalk show to launch a new product around the time of Fashion Week.

Other more accessible events and a chance to catch the top designers of the future are:

• Graduate Fashion Week in June at the Business Design Centre, where fashion students from 13 colleges display their graduate collections in exhibitions and shows.

• The London Festival of Fashion in November at Battersea Park, a series of seminars and 17 individual fashion shows depicting London fashion and the top designers' stores.

London Fashion Week	0171 581 2931
Graduate Fashion Week	0171 499 5047
The London Festival of Fashion	0171 351 5233

Business Design Centre, Islington, N1.
0171 359 3535

LONDON FILM FESTIVAL
November

When the first festival took place in 1956, it featured 15 films; now it shows over 200 films in its 3-week run. The main aim of the London Film Festival is to broaden the range of films cinema-going Londoners are offered and to bring the best of any year's cinema from all over the world. New British films shown usually number about 20, and there are sections for US independent movies, French films and selections from Asia, the Far East, Latin America and Africa.

Part of the festival's policy includes giving a platform to small-budget films for whom success at the festival can help win a coveted distribution deal.

The *Evening Standard* 'Film on the Square' section offers the chance to see some of the big American movies months before their scheduled release date. These screenings are among the most popular and you need to book early.

The glitziest occasion of the festival, for which the public can also buy tickets, is the opening gala, screening the year's biggest British movie. It is a black-tie affair at the Odeon Leicester Square and many of the big stars attend.

The programme for the festival is published in October each year. Tickets for all the screenings can be booked in advance by post or telephone, or bought at the special ticket booth in Leicester Square.

London Film Festival   0171 928 2695
National Film Theatre Box Office   0171 928 3232

• Other annual London film festivals include the Lesbian and Gay Film Festival, the Jewish Film Festival and the Latin American Film Festival. Details from the National Film Theatre.

LONDON HARNESS HORSE PARADE   SW11
Easter Monday

This parade first took place in 1885 and, as with Horseman's Sunday, its objective was to improve animal welfare and draw attention to the plight of working horses.

The display of horses, drays, carts, brewer's vans, etc., is very impressive. Judging of the horses usually starts about 9am and finishes a couple of hours later.

Traditionally this has always been held at Regents Park but this year the venue moves to Battersea Park and there are now plans to develop the Harness Horse Parade into a day of events.

Battersea Park, Queenstown Road, SW11.
0181 871 7530

London Harness Horse Parade. Information
01733 234451

LONDON INTERNATIONAL FESTIVAL OF THEATRE
June/July (biennial)

Since the first festival in 1981, LIFT has concentrated on bringing to London the best of contemporary theatre from all over the world.

Among the 20 productions in the 7th festival, held in 1993, were the first-ever Vietnamese theatre company to visit Britain, a history of the Notting Hill Carnival, Latin American music on Clapham Common, the Peking Opera and a lament for Sarajevo.

Nearly 100,000 people saw one of the 175 performances which made up the festival. The 8th festival (1995) promises to be just as exciting.

Another feature of the festival is its use of London's outdoor spaces: canal basins, derelict sites, parks, the river, the boating lake at Regent's Park, zoos, farms and power stations have all been LIFT venues over the years.

There are also numerous discussions and workshops centred around festival events.

London International Festival of Theatre.
0171 490 3965

LONDON INTERNATIONAL MIME FESTIVAL
January

The London International Mime Festival is now the world's largest and longest-running festival of visual theatre. In recent years it has featured companies from Japan and Russia as well as major home-grown talent like Ra Ra Zoo, Mime Theatre Project and Theatre de Complicite.

The first festival took place in 1977 at the Cockpit Theatre and since then, as the festival has evolved, so too has the concept of mime. The most recent festival involved 23 companies in 9 venues over 18 days and encompassed every form of physical and visual theatre, the only prerequisite being – no text. Subjects for the shows ranged from 1950s cinema to TV stardom and *Neighbours*. Comedy plays a major part.

Over 18,000 people attend the festival each year and the organizers are glad to offer guidance and help.

London International Mime Festival.
0171 637 5661

LONDON INTERNATIONAL BOOK FAIR   W14
March

The annual bookfair at Olympia is primarily a trade event, attracting booksellers, publishers, agents and rights representatives from all over the world. Deals are struck, new titles announced, books bought and book trade gossip exchanged among the 800-plus exhibitors.

The Bookfair also opens to the public after 2.30pm each day and all day on the final day, offering an insight into how the world of publishing works.

Some bookstores, like Dillons, run special events to coincide with the Bookfair, such as seminars on writing a bestseller. Look out for leaflets at bookshop counters in the weeks preceding the fair.

London International Bookfair.
0181 948 9899

Olympia Exhibition Centre, Kensington, W14.
0171 603 3344

LONDON JAZZ FESTIVAL
May

1993 saw the first London Jazz Festival, which grew out of the original Camden Jazz Week, and is the result of a collaboration between Serious Speakout and the boroughs of Camden, Islington and Hackney.

The Festival provides a 10-day mixture of events, concerts and workshops at a range of venues from The Forum in Kentish Town to the Lilian Baylis Theatre at Sadlers Wells and features some of the best of London's emerging jazz talent as well as international names.

Despite its youth, the The London Jazz Festival has already managed to put together some dynamic programmes, attracting such artists as Andy Sheppard and Stan Tracey.

London Jazz Festival.
0171 911 1652

THE LONDON MARATHON
April

With over 25,000 runners, the Marathon is London's biggest sporting success story and has now become the world's largest road race.

The first Marathon took place in 1981, organized by Chris Brasher, who had been inspired by the atmosphere at the New York Marathon. Since then, over a quarter of a million people have completed the distance of 26 miles, 385 yards. The as yet unbeaten record of 2 hours, 8 minutes and 16 seconds was set by Britain's Steve Jones in 1985.

The Marathon is really split into 2 parts: the international competition and the club runners, amateurs, joggers and fancy-dress charity fun runners who are the bulk of the field.

The best place to watch is Greenwich, where the race starts; you can then use the foot tunnel to catch up with the runners, or go straight to the finish at Westminster Bridge.

The London Marathon.
0171 620 4117

LONDON STROLLATHON
July

A fun family event which has been organized by the One Small Step Charitable Foundation for the last 5 years.

Basically a sponsored walk which covers 10 miles of London, with all funds raised being given to children's charities such as the Bobath Centre, Whizz Kidz and Save the Children. Live music bands are dotted along the route and everyone ends up at the Events Centre based in one of the big London parks where family fun, food and frolics can be enjoyed by everyone. Cadbury's sponsor the event and donate a large amount of free chocolate bars!

Strollathon London.
0171 232 2255 (hotline)

LONDON TO BRIGHTON VETERAN CAR RUN
November

The rally was first held in 1896 to celebrate the abolition of the Act that forced cars running at 2mph to be heralded by a walker waving a red flag, also known as Emancipation Day.

Only cars built before 1905 can enter and they start gathering in the Serpentine Road from 5.30 am. The first cars are waved off at 7am, with the final ones usually starting to wend their way from Hyde Park, across Westminster Bridge, and down to Brighton via the A23 at about 9am.

The cars look truly magnificent and a lot of the drivers and passengers dress to suit their vehicle's vintage, so there is always a great sense of occasion. Crowds tend to line the route most of the way, and with an average speed of 20mph, cars start arriving in Brighton round 11am.

The rally is always held on the first Sunday of November.

Serpentine Road, Hyde Park, W2.
0753 681736 (RAC Rally Office)

LONDON TO BRIGHTON BICYCLE RIDE
June

27,000 cyclists take part in the London to Brighton bicycle ride and the event, organized by the British Heart Foundation, is so popular that it is usually fully booked by the end of March.

Starting time is 6am at Clapham Common but the bikes have scheduled departures over 3 or 4 hours. The 58 miles are covered in about 3 hours by the experts and British Rail lay on special facilities for bringing bikes back to London. To take part you must register with the British Heart Foundation.

British Heart Foundation, 14 Fitzhardinge Street, W1.
0171 935 0185

THE LORD MAYOR'S PROCESSION AND SHOW
November (usually second Saturday)

Every year thousands of spectators line the streets of the City to welcome the new Lord Mayor into office and to participate in the City's most spectacular event in its ceremonial calendar. The ceremony dates back to the thirteenth century and it's an opportunity to see the gilded State Coach (built in 1756) which carries the new Lord Mayor from Guildhall to the Law Courts to be received by the Lord Chief Justice. 140 colourful floats representing businesses, livery companies and charities ride alongside the armed services, the City police and representatives of the Corporation of London in a blaze of colour and pageantry.

The procession starts at 11am from the Guildhall, via St Paul's Churchyard to arrive at the Royal Courts of Justice in The Strand at 11.50am. It then returns via Temple Place and Victoria Embankment to Queen Victoria Street and the Guildhall.

A traditional English fair is held in Paternoster Square from 12 noon until early evening and at 5pm there is a display of fireworks from a barge on the Thames. The best views are from Waterloo or Blackfriars bridges and Victoria Embankment.

The Lord Mayor's Procession and Show.
0171 332 1456 (information and route maps)

MAY FAYRE AND PUPPET FESTIVAL   WC2
May

The first reported viewing of a Punch and Judy show was by London diarist, Samuel Pepys, in 1662.

The May Fayre and Puppet Festival has been celebrating this fact for the last 20 years by holding a day of events in St Paul's Church Garden in Covent Garden. The fun starts at about 10.30 and runs through till 5.30. There are lots of street performers, workshops for children and, of course, puppets!

St Paul's Church Garden, Covent Garden, WC2.
May Fayre and Puppet Festival.
0171 375 0441

NEW YEAR'S EVE CELEBRATIONS

December

Trafalgar Square is the traditional London New Year's Eve venue, but not for anyone with a dislike of crowds, rowdiness and general drunken mayhem.

The New Year is welcomed in with choruses of *Auld Lang Syne*, dancing in the fountains and the possibility of being kissed by someone you've never met before!

The best part is that London tube travel is normally sponsored by a drinks manufacturer, so you get a free trip home.

NEW YEAR'S DAY CELEBRATIONS

January

For the past 8 years New Year's Day has been celebrated by the Lord Mayor of Westminster's Parade with marching bands, floats, veteran cars and cheerleaders. In January of this year it was renamed the 1995 London Parade although the Lord Mayor of Westminster was still allowed to join in!

It is the largest parade in Europe and the procession usually includes over 30 international bands and lots of different street entertainers. The parade's route is just over 2 miles long and starts on the south side of Westminster Bridge at about 12.30pm, wendings its way from Parliament Square through Whitehall, Trafalgar Square, Pall Mall and Regent Street, ending up at Berkeley Square, with crowds lining the route and cheering them on their way.

It's a great spectacle and one way of getting rid of the New Year blues – as long as you don't have a hangover!

London Parade.
0181 566 8586 and/or 0171 332 1456

NOTTING HILL CARNIVAL

August Bank Holiday Sunday and Monday

There are several different versions of the history of the Notting Hill Carnival, but in essence it started about 30 years ago, a small spontaneous echo of the carnivals which Trinidadian immigrants to the area remembered from home.

Since then, it has grown to become the world's third largest carnival, after Mardi Gras and Rio. Approximately 2 million people throng the small maze of streets each year to enjoy the mas (masquerade), music, costumes, spectacle and atmosphere.

Although the carnival attracts visitors from all over Europe, it remains at heart a London event. Suggestions have occasionally been raised to move it from Notting Hill – perhaps to Hyde Park, where there would be more space and policing would be easier – but organizers resist this, wanting the carnival to remain where its history lies.

Sunday is children's day, and the main procession takes place on the Monday. Getting to and from carnival is always the worst part, so leave the car at home and use the buses and tubes.

Notting Hill Carnival.
0181 964 0544

PEARLY KINGS AND QUEENS HARVEST FESTIVAL WC2
October

Although the Pearly Kings and Queens of London are often seen as
part of big London ceremonies and pageants, this occasion is purely
for them and is based in their own church, the beautiful St Martin-in-
the-Fields which overlooks Trafalgar Square.

With all the members of the Pearly Kings and Queens Association
attending the Harvest Festival it is a highly colourful occasion and
always takes place on the first Sunday in October at 3.30pm.

St Martin-in-the-Fields, 5 Martin Place, WC2.
0171 930 0089

THE PROMS SW7
July/August/September

The Proms are held every year from the third week of July through to
the middle of September at the Royal Albert Hall, and, for many, the
Last Night of the Proms is the highlight of London's musical season.

The programming is extremely diverse; it is played predominantly by
the BBC Symphony Orchestra but includes guest players and
orchestras as well. Tickets go on sale in May and range from a
minimum of £2.00(standing) or £3.50(seated) to £42. The entire
season can be purchased for as little as £70 – an opportunity worth
considering as it has the advantage of guaranteeing admission to the
Last Night. The purchase of 5 or more seats entitles you to apply for a
Last Night ticket! The BBC booklet detailing the programme is
generally available in May (£3) in all major bookstores.

Several concerts are preceded by talks starting at 6.15pm.

Tickets: by post from Proms Concerts, Royal Albert Hall, SW7;
by phone on 0171 823 9998

QUIT-RENT CEREMONY WC2
October

This tradition has been followed for the last 700 years.

The Queen's Remembrancer receives the Quit-rent of a bill-hook, a
hatchet, 6 horseshoes and 61 nails as token rent for land or property
given long ago. An annual cremony since 1234. Proceedings start at 3.30.

Free tickets can be obtained by writing to The Chief Clerk to the
Queen's Remembrancer, Room 118, Royal Courts of Justice, Strand,
WC2.

Quit Rent Ceremony Information.
0171 936 6131

REGENT'S PARK OPEN AIR THEATRE NW1
May to September

The Open Air Theatre has seen the thespian debuts of such theatrical
luminaries as Vivien Leigh, Deborah Kerr, Greer Garson and Jessica
Tandy since it first opened in 1932. More recently, such rising young
stars as Ralph Fiennes have given their first public performances at
the theatre.

Although Shakespeare continues to be the mainstay, the programme has widened under the excellent direction of Artistic Director, Ian Talbot and several of the recent productions have either won or been nominated for Olivier awards. There is also an afternoon programme for children and some Sunday evening events with performers like the Comedy Store Players.

Combined with supper and a glass of mulled wine a visit to the Open Air Theatre is still a great way to pass a summer's night in London – but don't forget to take some warm clothing!

Ticket prices range from around £7 to £16.50.

Open Air Theatre, Regent's Park. NW1.
0171 486 2431

REMEMBRANCE SUNDAY
November

The Remembrance Day service takes place on the Sunday closest to Armistice Day (11th November). This is a memorial day for those in all 3 Services and Allied Forces who gave their lives in the two World Wars and other conflicts.

A march from Birdcage Walk via Great George Steet and Parliament Street arrives at the Cenotaph (designed by Sir Edwin Lutyens in 1920) at 10.35am.   A 2-minute silence at 11am is heralded and ended by a gun fired from Horse Guards Parade, after which the Last Post is sounded by Buglers of the Royal Marines.

The Queen then lays a wreath at the Cenotaph, and is followed by members of the Royal Family, representatives of the Government, Commonwealth Governments and the Services. The Bishop of London conducts a short service of Remembrance.

Remembrance Sunday Information.
0171 930 4466

RICHMOND FESTIVAL
July

A 10-day festival of performing and visual arts which highlights the work of local professional performers, artists and musicians who live in the Borough. They also include work of people who have been closely associated with Richmond.

One of the highlights is the Music Village which takes place at the weekend. The Music Village is a festival of non-European traditional arts and culture. The 1994 programme featured Morocco and included folk music, story telling and crafts. In 1995 they will focus on Pakistan.

Venues include Richmond Theatre, Orange Tree Theatre, Richmond Green and, of course, the Thames.

Richmond Festival Information.
0181 332 0534

ROYAL ACADEMY SUMMER EXHIBITION W1
June

The Royal Academy Summer Exhibition, founded in 1769, represents a rare chance to see the work of completely amateur artists exhibited alongside the likes of David Hockney.

Around 12,000 paintings are entered for the exhibition each year and every one, whether amateur or professional, is judged in the same way – passed down a line in front of the team of Royal Academicians who whittle down the entries to the final 1,800 selected paintings. Those that are immediately rejected receive a chalked 'x' on the back, while those selected receive a 'd' for doubtful (this is as positive as it gets) and are then sent forward for potential hanging. As well as art there is also a sculpture room and an architectural room.

Each year there is controversy among art critics as to whether the standard of the works is higher or lower than the year before. For the gallery-goer though, the enjoyment lies in the fun of deciding what you 'like' and 'hate' without feeling the need to be influenced by who the artist might have been, and preferring a painting by a retired headmaster from Prestatyn to that of someone regarded as an art establishment figure.

Almost all the works on display are for sale and prices range from £50 to tens of thousands of pounds.

Royal Academy, Burlington House, W1.
0171 439 4996

THE ROYAL TOURNAMENT SW5
July

The Royal Tournament takes place from the 18th to the 29th July against a pageantry of massed bands from all 3 armed forces. This is an annual occasion when the Army, Navy and Royal Air Force work together to provide spectacular musical and physical displays in a 2$3/4$ hour show.

1995 is the turn of the Royal Air Force to lead the tournament and events include the Field Gun competition, Services Dog Display, Musical Drive of the Kings Troops, RAF Motorsports display, the Household Cavalry and a visit from the French Foreign Legion. There are also plans to include a Street Party for the first time.

Earls Court Exhibition Centre, Warwick Road, SW5.
Royal Tournament Box Office 0171 373 8141

RUGBY LEAGUE CUP FINAL
April/May

The other major sporting event of the year! The Rugby League matches are always held at Wembley and this year the Cup Final is booked to take place on 29 April 1995 (see p.85).

Wembley Box Office.
0181 900 1234

Wembley Information.
0181 902 8833

SOHO JAZZ FESTIVAL
September/October

With the opening of Ronnie Scott's club in Frith Street over 30 years ago, jazz became a permanent Soho fixture. Many jazz clubs have come and gone in that time, though the best, like Scott's and the 100 Club (100 Oxford Street), remain.

The Soho Jazz Festival was founded 9 years ago by jazz fan Peter Boizot, owner of Kettners (Romilly St) and Pizza on the Park (Knightsbridge) where live jazz is on the menu each night.

Artists who have been involved in the festival since then include the Charlie Watt's Quintet and Strings. The festival has expanded over the years and now features daytime and evening events as well as poetry and photography, all taking place in Soho settings made for the music.

Soho Jazz Festival Information.
0171 434 3995

SPITALFIELDS FESTIVAL   E1
June

Now in its seventeenth year, the Spitalfields Festival takes place each June in Nicholas Hawksmoor's architecturally splendid Christ Church, which is regarded as one of Europe's most important baroque buildings.

Originally built between 1714 and 1729, the church fell into disrepair and stood empty for a number of years in the mid-Seventies, with only the crypt in use, as a residential rehabilitation centre for homeless alcoholics.

A restoration programme was begun in 1976, and is continuing slowly. For the past 6 years services have been held in the church once again.

The Spitalfields Festival's classical baroque and modern music programme includes new works commissioned specially for the festival from composers such as John Taverner. There is a strong emphasis on choral music to take full advantage of the Church's acoustics. Concerts are predominantly in the evenings but there are also lunchtime recitals. Guided walks around the Spitalfields area and talks on Georgian street life, the Jewish East End and tours of Dennis Severs house (see p.206) are all organized to co-incide with the festival. Some of the concerts are also relayed to Spitalfields market and there is a programme of exhibitions and educational events.

Spitalfields Festival, Christ Church, Commercial Street, E1.
0171 377 0287

SUMMER IN THE CITY   EC2
August

Summer in the City can best be described as a week-long fun but educational festival aimed at children between 2 and 10 years old.

Organized and held at the Barbican Centre there are entertainers, magic shows, puppets, clowns, children's theatre, music, dance, games, story telling and a series of workshops.

There is a special picnic area and catering geared to childrens' taste is available. Crèche and changing facilities are provided.

It's usually held during the first week of August and runs from 9am–8pm daily. The entrance fee is £2.00 adults/£4.00 children.

Barbican Centre, Silk St, Barbican, EC2.
0171 638 4141
0171 638 8891 (box office)

TEDDY BEARS' PICNIC   SW11
August

Another event geared to children up to the age of 8, though there is no age limit. The Teddy Bears' Picnic is from 1pm to 4.30pm at Battersea Park – there is lots of entertainment laid on, lots of teddy bears about and it is really just a fun family outing.

Battersea Park, Queenstown Road, SW11.
0181 871 6349

TOWER OF LONDON CHURCH PARADE   EC3
April, June and December

The Tower of London Church Parade takes place 3 times a year – Easter Sunday, Whit Sunday and the Sunday before Christmas.

The Resident Governor of the Tower of London inspects the yeomen warders in state dress both before and after the morning service on each occasion. They march up from the Queens House to the Church in the Tower of London 15 minutes before the 11am service.

Tower of London, Tower Hill, EC3.
0171 709 0765

TROOPING OF THE COLOUR   SW1
June

This annual ceremony takes place on the Saturday closest to 11th June, the Queen's official birthday.

The colours are the standards of various regiments, one of which is selected for 'trooping' each year. The practice began in the eighteenth century, when soldiers would raise their colours to locate a rallying point. It became a formal ceremony during the reign of George III.

To get tickets for the ceremony you should write, before the end of the previous February, to the Brigade Major (Trooping the Colour), Headquarters, Household Division, Chelsea Barracks, SW1 8RS. The tickets (£12.50 each) are allocated by ballot and limited to 2 per application. Tickets are also available for the rehearsals.

If you don't have tickets you should arrive early and find a vantage spot somewhere along The Mall. The timetable is as follows: 10.40am Queen leaves Buckingham Palace. 11am arrives Horse Guards Parade for the gun salute and to inspect the troops before leaving at 12.30pm to return to Buckingham Palace for a 1pm appearance on the balcony, and a flypast by the RAF, coinciding with another gun salute at the Tower of London.

Horse Guards Parade, Horse Guards Avenue, SW1.
Trooping the Colour.
0171 930 4466

WATCHNIGHT SERVICE   EC4
New Year's Eve

If you don't feel like battling it out among the crowds in Trafalgar Square you can go to the other extreme and attend the Watchnight Service. This is a rather lovely New Year's Eve service which takes place at St Paul's Cathedral starting at 11.30 pm. Although St Paul's seats 2,400, this service is very well attended.

St Paul's Cathedral, Ludgate Hill, EC4.
0171 248 2705

WIMBLEDON LAWN TENNIS CHAMPIONSHIPS
June/July

Wimbledon remains the world's favourite tennis tournament, managing to retain a strawberries-and-cream Englishness, despite the increasing pressures of big business sport.

The ticket allocation system for Wimbledon continues to vex and baffle, though determined attempts have been made in recent years to cut down on the number of tickets that end up in the hands of touts.

The majority of public tickets are issued through an annual ballot. You should write for an application form to The All England Lawn Tennis Club, PO Box 98, Wimbledon, SW19 5AE, between 1st September and 31st December of the preceding year. If your luck is in you could end up with the ultimate prize – a pair of men's finals day tickets.

The other way in is to join the queues for the tickets held back for daily sale (however, all Centre Court tickets for the last 4 days are allocated in advance).

One of the best days for this is the middle Saturday, when 2,000 Centre Court tickets are sold to the public at reduced prices. The earlier you start queuing, in either Church Road or Somerset Road, the better. The atmosphere is good humoured, but be prepared for a long wait.

Alternatively, if you go along in the late afternoon there is usually a much smaller queue and you should still be able to see around 3 hours of tennis.

The All England Lawn Tennis Club.
0181 944 1066
0181 944 2244 (recorded information)

• Another way for keen tennis fans to get close to the action is to apply for a job connected to the championships. The tournament advertises each year for experienced car drivers, aged over 21, to drive officials and tennis stars at the championships. The advert appears in the Monday 'Creative and Media' section of the *Guardian* in either January or February.

• Catering companies also need extra staff for a variety of jobs through the Wimbledon fortnight. Contact Town and Country Catering, event recruitment, on 0181 998 8880 in October or November of the preceding year.

CONFERENCE AND EXHIBITION CENTRES

ALEXANDRA PALACE AND PARK   N22

Known universally as 'Ally Pally', Alexandra Palace once housed the
BBC's first television studio.

It is currently run as a multi-entertainments centre with a vast
range of events including trade shows and sponsored concerts by radio
stations such as Capital and Kiss FM. Trade shows are suitably diverse
and range from The Road Racing and Superbike Show to the London
Bridal Fair.

Alexandra Palace, Wood Green, N22.
0181 365 2121

BUSINESS DESIGN CENTRE   N1

The former Royal Agricultural Hall in Islington, N1, was restored and
reopened as the Business Design Centre in 1986.

The BDC now also holds a wide range of annual exhibitions, many in
the areas of art, crafts and design and can supply a full list of events.

Business Design Centre, 52 Upper Street, Islington Green. N1.
0171 359 3535

CHELSEA OLD TOWN HALL   SW3

A venue for The Chelsea Spring and Autumn Antiques Fair, Chelsea
Old Town Hall's calendar of events includes jumble sales, bazaars,
fashion shows and antique sales.

Chelsea Old Town Hall, Kings Road, SW3.
0171 352 3619

EARLS COURT   SW5

The Earls Court international exhibition centre plays host to a wide
range of consumer events including The Royal Tournament, the
annual *Daily Mail* Ideal Home Exhibition and the London
International Boat Show as well as many of the major trade fairs such
as the International Food Exhibition and the British Toy and Hobby
Fair. The inclusion of a second hall, which came into effect in 1994,
does create enormous opportunities within the centre for dramatic
displays – the Boat Show definitely benefits!

A full calendar of all the events is available.

Earls Court Exhibition Centre, Warwick Road, SW5.
0171 370 8144 (current event information and list of events)
0171 373 8141 (box office/tickets)

OLYMPIA CONFERENCE CENTRE　　　　　W14

The main events take place in the tiered 450-seat theatre auditorium with the back-up of 2 conference rooms and banqueting facilities. Events encompass product launches, exhibitions (London Wine Trade Fair, London Book Fair and Autumn Needlecraft Fair) and fashion shows.

Olympia Conference Centre, Hammersmith Road, W14.
0171 370 8337

WEMBLEY ARENA (see p.85)

• Some others:

Barbican Centre, Silk Street, EC2.
0171 628 2295

Commonwealth Institute, Kensington High Street, W8.
0171 603 4535

Guildhall, Gresham Street, EC2.
0171 606 3030

Kensington Town Hall, Hornton Street, W8.
0171 937 5464

Queen Elizabeth 11 Conference Centre, Westminster.
0171 222 5000

Royal Horticultural Society's Halls, Greycoat Street and Vincent Square, SW1.
0171 828 4125

HELPLINES

GENERAL HELPLINES

When you have a problem or face a crisis there is usually someone somewhere who can help, but first you need to know where to start. We found all the support and advice agencies extremely helpful. Don't be put off by telephone answering machines – a lot of the helplines are staffed by volunteers who will get back to you.

AGE CONCERN

An advisory service for anyone of pensionable age plus. They also run day-care centres, drop-in centres, befriending and good neighbour schemes and a legal service. Mon–Fri 10am–6pm.
Age Concern.
0181 665 0357

ALCOHOLICS ANONYMOUS

Confidential helpline for those who feel they may have a drink problem or who are concerned about the drinking habits of someone close to them. Can put you in touch with one of the 500 AA groups across London. 10am–10pm daily.

Alcholics Anonymous.
0171 352 3001

AL ANON

24-hour helpline offering support and help to relatives and friends of those with drink problems. Also run Al-Ateen especially for teenagers coping with alcoholic parents.

Al Anon.
0171 403 0888

ALONE IN LONDON

24-hour phoneline offering advice and counselling for under-21s who are homeless or alone in London.

Alone in London.
0171 278 4224

THE AMARANT TRUST

The trust was set up to promote a better understanding of the menopause and greater awareness of the benefits of Hormone Replacement Therapy (HRT). They publish written information and also have recorded telephone information lines.

The Amarant Trust.
0171 490 1644

• Help is also available from the pioneering Menopause Clinic at King's College Hospital (0171 346 3336).

ARTSLINE

This service gives information and advice service to disabled people about arts events in London and access to venues. It produces a monthly publication. Mon–Fri 9.30–5.30.

Artsline.
0171 388 2227

BACUP

Service staffed by nurses offering advice, information and support to cancer sufferers. Mon–Thur 10am–7pm Fri 10am–5.30pm. Their counselling service on 0171 696 9000 can make appointments for free one-to-one, group or couples counselling. Mon–Fri 9.30am–5pm and until 8pm on Tuesday and Wednesday evenings.

Bacup.
0171 613 2121

BISEXUAL HELPLINE

Helpline run by the London Bisexual Group which can offer help and advice and gives details of their meetings in London. Can also give details of the London Women's Bisexual Group. Fri–Wed 7.30pm–9.30pm.

Bisexual Helpline
0181 569 7500

BODY POSITIVE HELPLINE

Support by and for people who are HIV Positive. Mon–Fri 7pm–10pm Sat–Sun 4pm–10pm.

Body Positive Helpline.
0171 373 9124

CAPITAL RADIO HELPLINE

General helpline which will try to answer queries on any subject or refer callers to other services who may be able to help. Mon–Wed and Fri 9.30am–5.30pm Thur 9.30am–9pm.

Capital Radio Helpline.
0171 388 7575

CHOICES

Support service for black people with alcohol problems and their family and friends. Organizes individual and group counselling sessions. Mon–Fri 10am–5pm.

Choices.
0171 737 3363

CITIZENS ADVICE BUREAU

The head office for the greater London area, which will be able to give y
the address, number and opening times of your nearest Citizens' Advice
Bureau, offering free advice on legal, financial and personal problems.

Citizens' Advice Bureau.
0171 251 2000

CITY CENTRE

This information project for office workers specializes in offering advic
and guidance to VDU users and information concerning RSI (repetitive
strain injury). They publish a VDU factpack (£6) and the *Office Worker
Guide to Repetitive Strain Injury* (£4) and offer advice on health and
safety matters and equal opportunities. Mon–Fri 10am–4pm.

City Centre.
0171 608 1338

COMMISSION FOR RACIAL EQUALITY

Advice on any matter connected with racial discrimination.

Commission for Racial Equality.
0171 828 7022

CRUSE

Counselling service for the bereaved.
   Mon–Fri 9.30am–1pm and 2pm–5pm.

Cruse.
0181 940 4818

FAMILIES NEED FATHERS

This support organization for fathers separated from their children ha
number of groups across London. Mon–Fri 9am–5pm.

Families Need Fathers.
0171 613 5060

GINGERBREAD

A self-help association for one-parent families and their children,
Gingerbread has around 25 groups in the London area offering
friendship and support. Mon–Fri 9am–5pm.

Gingerbread.
0171 240 0953

LAW CENTRES FEDERATION

Will put you in touch with your nearest law centre. There are 26
branches offering free legal advice in the London area. Mon–Fri
10am–6pm.

Law Centres Federation.
0171 387 8570

LONDON FRIEND

Advice and counselling for gay men and lesbians. Daily 7.30pm–10pm.
A women-only service is available on Sun, Mon, Tues 7.30pm–10pm on 0171 837 2782.

London Friend.
0171 837 3337

LONDON LESBIAN AND GAY SWITCHBOARD

24-hour advice and information service.

London Lesbian and Gay Switchboard.
0171 837 7324

LONDON LIGHTHOUSE

The Lighthouse, Britain's first major residential and support centre for men and women affected by HIV and AIDS, opened in November 1988. A drop-in centre is open from 9am to 9pm 7 days a week and provides an informal meeting place, as well as providing support and information services and legal advice to those living with HIV, their family and friends.

London Lighthouse.
0171 792 1200

LONDON RAPE CRISIS

24-hour counselling helpline providing advice, support and help for women who have been raped or assaulted.

London Rape Crisis Centre.
0171 837 1600

LONDON WOMEN'S AID

In London 100,000 women each year seek help for violent injuries received in the home. London Women's Aid offers referral to women's refuges for women at risk from physical or verbal abuse from their partner. Telephone staffed Mon–Fri 10am–4.45pm. Answerphone message at other times gives duty numbers.

London Women's Aid.
0171 251 6537

LONDON WOMEN'S CENTRE

The LWC, a resource centre for women, is home to a large number of women's organizations, including the National Childcare Campaign, Women's Training Link and the Women's Sports Foundation.
There are several different-sized conference rooms available for hire and the centre also has a video-editing suite, a computer-training centre and a gym. A wide range of courses take place and there is also a cafe. Mon–Fri 8am–10pm Sat 8.30am–10pm.

London Women's Centre, 4 Wild Court, Kingsway, WC2.
0171 831 6946

MEDICAL ADVISORY SERVICE

A medical helpline staffed by nurses. Mon–Fri 5pm–10pm.

Medical Advisory Service.
0181 994 9874

MEET A MUM ASSOCIATION

Estimates indicate that between 10 and 15 per cent of new mothers go to see their doctors suffering from postnatal depression and many more suffer in silence. Meet a Mum aims to offer a support service, providing help, information and reassurance. Mon–Fri after 3.30pm. Sat–Sun 11am–8pm.

Meet A Mum Association.
0181 656 7318

MISSING PERSONS HELPLINE

The National Helpline deals with over 30,000 calls for help every year. The 24-hour service runs a register of missing persons and advises on how best to direct efforts to find them. They will also put you in touch with other organizations that specialize in a particular situation.

Missing Persons Helpline.
0181 392 2000

NARCOTICS ANONYMOUS

A helpline for anyone with a drug problem, Narcotics Anonymous operates in a similar way to Alcoholics Anonymous and holds meetings all over London. Call 0171 281 9933 for a list of their meetings. Mon–Sun 10am–8pm.

Narcotics Anonymous.
0171 498 9005

NATIONAL ASTHMA CAMPAIGN

Funds research and provides information and literature about all aspects of living with asthma. Mon–Fri 9am–5pm.

National Asthma Campaign.
0171 226 2260

NATIONAL COUNCIL FOR ONE-PARENT FAMILIES

Around 25 per cent of children in inner London are living in one-parent families. The National Council provides free information for lone parents and acts as their national voice. Mon–Fri 9.15am–5.15pm.

National Council for One Parent Families.
0171 267 1361

NATIONAL STEPFAMILIES ASSOCIATION

This service provides advice and support to anyone living in a stepfamily, and also runs the Stepfamilies telephone counselling service on 0171 372 0846. An answering machine message will give details of the counsellor on duty. The service operates Mon–Fri 2pm–5pm and 7pm–10pm.

National Stepfamilies Association.
0171 372 0844

PARENTS ANONYMOUS

Helpline for parents who feel they cannot cope and need support. An answerphone message will refer you to the volunteer on duty.

Parents Anonymous.
0171 263 8918

PARENTS AT WORK

Parents at Work recently changed its name from The Working Mothers Association, and aims to help all working parents and encourage 'family friendly' working practices among employers. It publishes various books, including *The Working Parents Handbook, Balancing Work and Home*, and a comprehensive Maternity Pack. An information hotline operates on Tuesdays, Thursdays and Fridays from 9am to 1pm and 2pm to 4pm and they also organize local groups.

Parents at Work.
0171 700 5771

PARENT NETWORK

Helpline for parents who are having problems relating to or dealing with their children. Discussion groups form part of the counselling. Mon–Fri 9am–5pm.

Parent Network.
0171 485 8535

POSITIVELY WOMEN

An organization for women who are HIV positive, they also operate a helpline on 0171 490 2327 Mon–Fri 12noon–2pm. (see also p.272).

Positively Women.
0171 490 5515

RELEASE

24-hour confidential drugs counselling and referral helpline. Specializes in offering help with criminal and legal matters related to drugs.

Release.
0171 603 8654

RIGHTS OF WOMEN

Telephone legal advice helpline for women. Tue–Thur 12noon–2pm and 7pm–9pm, Wed 3pm–5pm and 7pm–9pm, Fri 12noon–2pm.

Rights of Women.
0171 251 6577

SAMARITANS

Confidential 24-hour phone line for anyone in distress or despair or wh◖ may be contemplating suicide.

Samaritans.
0171 734 2800

SANELINE

Helpline for sufferers of mental illness and their friends and families. Daily 2pm–midnight.

Saneline.
0171 724 8000

SHAC, LONDON HOUSING AID CENTRE

Works on behalf of the homeless and those living in bad housing. Mon–Fri 9am–1pm.

SHAC, London Housing Aid Centre.
0171 404 7447

SUZY LAMPLUGH TRUST

Set up by Diana Lamplugh, mother of missing estate agent Suzy, the Trust offers advice on safety for women, and has a number of free publications on the subject. They also sell personal alarms. For details, send a self-addressed envelope to the Suzy Lamplugh Trust, 14 East Sheen Avenue, SW14 8AS. Mon–Fri 9am–5.30pm.

Suzy Lamplugh Trust.
0181 392 1839

TERENCE HIGGINS TRUST

Advice, information and practical support for anyone with, or concernec about, AIDS and HIV infection. The Trust also operates an AIDS/HIV Positive Hotline on 0171 242 1010 which is open daily from 12noon to 10pm and a Legal Line on 0171 405 2381, open Monday and Wednesday between 7pm and 10pm (see also p.272).

Terence Higgins Trust.
0171 831 0330

NATIONAL ASSOCIATION OF VICTIM SUPPORT SCHEMES

This scheme was set up to offer help and support to victims of crime. Mon–Fri 9am–5pm. Answerphone to take messages outside office hours

National Association of Victim Support Schemes.
0171 735 9166

WOMEN'S HEALTH

Health enquiry service on all aspects of Women's Health. Also has a resource centre, runs talks and workshops and can supply a publications list. For details of these call 0171 251 6333. Mon and Wed–Fri 11am–5pm.

Women's Health.
0171 251 6580

WOMEN'S LINK

Confidential service for women offering advice on housing and other issues. Mon–Fri 10am–4pm.

Women's Link.
0171 248 1200

EMOTIONAL AND RELATIONSHIP PROBLEMS

Seeing a trained counsellor or therapist can give you the opportunity to talk through a situation or problem in the strictest confidence with someone outside your circle of family and friends. A good counsellor will remain non-judgemental, whilst enabling you to explore your thoughts and feelings to achieve a clearer insight into yourself and your situation.

Sessions are usually weekly and last an hour, but this depends on each individual's particular situation, as will the total number of sessions needed.

Your GP may be able to refer you for counselling, but you could have to wait several months for an appointment. Alternatively a GP should be able to provide a list of private counsellors and their specialities. Family planning clinics may also be able to advise you and private counsellors usually accept self-referrals. Many complementary health centres offer counselling and psychotherapy (see p.49–56), or you can contact a professional body for details of qualified counsellors or therapists working in your area. Fees for private counselling are usually around £30 per session, but can vary according to ability to pay.

THE ALBANY TRUST   SW12

The Albany Trust offers counselling for emotional, sexual or relationship problems which are causing psychological distress.

The Trust is a charitable foundation, set up in 1958. They also specialize in psychosexual counselling, including confusion over sexual identity and counselling for sexual abuse, sexual dysfunction and issues concerning HIV and AIDS.

The standard fee is £30 per session for individuals, £40 for couples, but reduced fees can be arranged where appropriate.

The Albany Trust is located within the Sunra Centre which offers a full range of holistic health therapies. The Trust also offers training courses for those interested in becoming professional counsellors.

Albany Trust, Sunra Centre,
26 Balham Hill, Clapham South, SW12.
0181 675 6669

BRITISH ASSOCIATION FOR COUNSELLING

The Association can supply a list of qualified counsellors in your area, together with their specialization and an indication of fees. They publish a fact sheet, *Counselling and You*, and can also offer advice to those interested in training as a counsellor.

The British Association for Counselling, 1 Regent Place, Rugby, Warwickshire. CV21 2PJ.
0788 578328

THE INSTITUTE OF PSYCHOSEXUAL MEDICINE

The Institute trains doctors in psychosexual counselling. If you send a self-addressed envelope to the address below, they can supply you with list of qualified members, indicating whether they are NHS or private. Their office is open on Thursdays from 10.30am to 3.30pm; a telephone answering service operates at other times.

The Institute of Psychosexual Medicine, 11 Chandos Street, W1.
0171 580 0631

LONDON MARRIAGE GUIDANCE COUNCIL

The London Marriage Guidance Council sees around 4,500 couples each year, and has 120 counsellors.

The LMGC now operates separately from Relate and the main difference is in the emphasis placed on a high level of training. Director Renate Olins says, 'We have acknowledged that counselling is a career opposed to a purely voluntary occupation and our training, which is fee paying, lasts for 4 years and is externally validated, reflects this.'

The LMGC stresses that it is for all couples or individuals in relationships, not just those who are married (last year 48 per cent of those seen by LMGC were living together). You can see a counsellor alone or with your partner.

There are over 20 centres throughout London, but you should call the head office in the first instance. Fees are £35 per session, but are negotiated on ability to pay, with £1.50 per £1,000 of gross income being the guideline.

A preliminary session can normally be arranged within 2 or 3 weeks, but there may then be a waiting list for the most popular appointment times (usually evenings).

London Marriage Guidance Council, 76a New Cavendish Street, W1.
0171 580 1087

MARIE STOPES

The Marie Stopes Clinic offers relationship counselling and psychosexual counselling to both individuals and couples (see over page).

Marie Stopes House, 108 Whitfield Street, W1.
071 388 0662

WOMEN'S THERAPY LINK

This organization offers one-to-one counselling and therapy by women for women. They can discuss your needs over the phone and then put you in touch with a qualified therapist close to your area, or if necessary refer you on to another organization. Fees are on a sliding scale.

Women's Therapy Link also run occasional workshops.

Women's Therapy Link, 111 Bray Fellows Road, NW3.
0171 916 0123

SEXUAL PROBLEMS

The following London organizations all work in the areas of contraception, pregnancy, abortion and sexual concerns and can offer practical advice and help, without referral from a doctor.

BROOK ADVISORY CENTRES

The Brook Centres specialize in offering advice on contraception, pregnancy and abortion to under-25s.

There are 13 centres across London. Telephone the head office for details of your nearest centre, or call their recorded information line on 0171 617 8000.

Brook Advisory Centres, 153a East Street, SE17.
0171 708 1234

MARGARET PYKE CENTRE   W1

The Margaret Pyke Centre is one of the largest family planning centres in the world offering a free, self-referring contraceptive service for all women.

The centre offers all methods of contraception as well as pregnancy testing. For urgent problems there is an advice sister who can be seen on a walk-in basis from 9.15am to 4pm (Mon–Fri) and a helpline on 0171 734 9351 which operates Mon–Fri between 9.15am–4.30pm.

Other services include fertility counselling and treatment, vasectomy and female sterilization, cervical treatment and a 40+ clinic.

The Margaret Pyke Centre, 15 Bateman Buildings, Soho Square, W.1.
0171 734 9351

MARIE STOPES   W1

Marie Stopes's 1918 book *Married Love* pioneered the idea that women might actually enjoy sex and in 1925 she went on to open Britain's first birth control clinic.

Marie Stopes services include contraception, Well Woman checks, pregnancy testing and abortion, as well as treatment for premenstrual syndrome, gynaecological consultations, cervicography and sterilization.

Some of the services are quite expensive, but clients praise the supportive atmosphere, and the high standards of care.

They also offer Well Man checks, prostate screening and vasectomy.

Marie Stopes House, 108 Whitfield Street, W1.
0171 388 0662

Founded in 1968, the PAS aims to offer help, sympathetic counselling and medical treatment to women with unwanted pregnancy and fertility-related problems. A registered charity, they try to keep their fees as low as possible.

Services include a walk-in pregnancy testing service, abortion (including the abortion pill RU486), morning-after birth control, cervical smears, sterilization and donor insemination advice.

Pregnancy Advisory Service, 11–13 Charlotte Street, W1.
0171 637 8962

AIDS

If you are concerned about the possibility of HIV infection, there are a number of organizations who can help and advise you. The Terence Higgins Trust has a helpline, open from noon to 10pm daily (0171 242 1010) and can also offer face-to-face counselling. Or you can contact the National AIDS helpline free of charge on 0800 567 123. This is a 24-hour service.

If you decide you do wish to be tested, STD clinics and departments of genito-urinary medicine can carry out the test, and have the best safeguards for protecting your confidentiality. However, if you are still worried you can give a false name when you take the test – this is perfectly legal. They will also offer counselling before the test and back-up afterwards, whether the result is positive or negative.

It can take anything from a few hours to a few days for the results to come through, depending where you are tested. These are some of London's clinics:

University College Hospital Special Clinic. Appointment preferred.
Mon–Fri 9am–11.30am and 1pm–5pm. Gower Street, WC1.
0171 388 9625

St Mary's Hospital Special Clinic, Praed Street, W2.
No appointment necessary. Mon, Tues, Thur, Fri 9am–6pm Wed 10am–6pm Sat 10am–12noon.
0171 725 1697

Charing Cross Hospital, Genito-Urinary Clinic.
No appointment necessary. Mon–Fri 9.30am–12.30pm, 2pm–5pm.
Fulham Palace Road, W6.
0181 846 1567

The Lydia Clinic. Walk-in Clinic. Open Mon, Wed, Thur, Fri 9am–6pm Tues 10am–6pm. St Thomas's Hospital, Lambeth Palace Road, SE1.
0171 928 9292

The above clinics can also offer advice and testing regarding sexually transmitted and other genito-urinary infections.

Capital Guide Maps

**LONDON UNDERGROUND
AND BRITISH RAIL ROUTES**
Indicates Travelcard Zones

**BUS ROUTES AND
TOURIST ATTRACTIONS**
Where major routes intersect and Central
London's places of interest

WHERE TO CATCH YOUR BUS
How to find the correct bus stop for your journey
in four key Central London locations

**NIGHT BUS ROUTES IN
CENTRAL LONDON**

POSTAL CODES
London divided according to district
and postal codes

London Underground and British R

Underground stations outside the zones:
Amersham, Chesham, Chalfont & Latimer,
Chorleywood, Rickmansworth, Watford,
Croxley, Moor Park.

Key to Lines

	Station	Interchange Station
Bakerloo		
Central		
Circle		
District		
East London		
Hammersmith & City		
Jubilee		
Metropolitan		
Northern		
Piccadilly		
Victoria		
Waterloo & City		
Docklands Light Railway		
British Rail		

Underground stations outside the zones:
Epping, Theydon Bois, Debden

Explanation of zones

	Station outside the zones
6	Station in Zone 6
5	Station in Zone 3
4	Station in Zone 4
3	Station in Zone 3
2	Stations in both zones
1	Station in Zone 1

Equivalent Bus zones

The rail and bus zones vary at a few locations. Details of bus zones are shown in Local Bus Guides.

* Mornington Crescent closed for rebuilding.

Some stations and lines have restricted opening times. For further information telephone London Transport's Travel Information Service on 0171-223 1234.

Bus Routes and Tourist Attractions

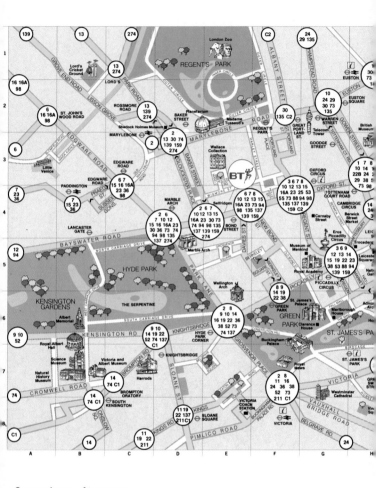

Some places of interest

3L Barbican Centre	5G Eros - Piccadilly Circus	5N Monument	7B Natural History
7I Big Ben	6J Festival Hall	2D Madame Tussauds	Museum
3H British Museum &	7B Geological Museum	5D Marble Arch	3L Old Bailey
Library	7C Harrods	3L Museum of London	3P Petticoat Lane
6F Buckingham Palace	6O HMS Belfast	5G Museum of Mankind	2D Planetarium
6I Cabinet War Rooms	6I Horse Guards Parade	6K Museum of the	7F Queen's Gallery
4G Carnaby Street	7I Houses of Parliament	Moving Image -	5G Royal Academy
5L City Information	7J Lambeth Palace	MOMI	7B Royal Albert Hall
Centre	6N London Dungeon	6K National Film Theatre	6G St James's Palace
5J Cleopatra's Needle	1E London Zoo	5H National Gallery	4L St Paul's Cathedral
6I Downing Street	3A Little Venice	6K National Theatre	7B Science Museum

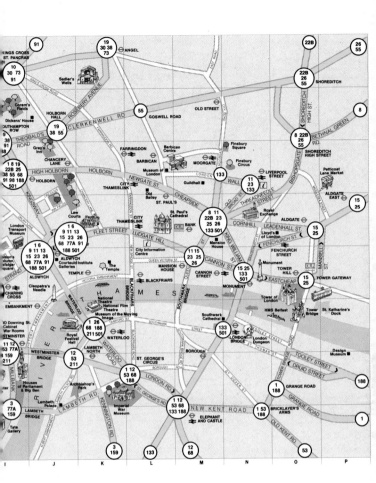

Selfridges

Sherlock Holmes Museum

St Katherine's Dock

Tate Gallery

Telecom Tower

5K The Temple

6O Tower Bridge

5O Tower of London

5I Trafalgar Square &
    Nelson's Column

5H Trocadero at Piccadilly
    Circus

7B Victoria & Albert
    Museum

7I Westminster Abbey

7G Westminster
    Cathedral

Key

 Bus Interchange

Underground Station

British Rail

DLR Docklands Light Railway

London Transport Travel Information Centre

Bus Routes

One Way Only

Riverboat Pier

BT BT Shop
350 Oxford Street
Open Monday to Saturday

Where to catch your Bus

Oxford Circus

Route, Destination and Bus stops

3	Crystal Palace	E L O W
6	Aldwych	P X
	Kensal Rise	B N U
7	Russell Square	HA Z
	East Acton/Kew	KA R U
8	Bow	HA Z
	Victoria	G KB N Q
10	Tufnell Park	HB Z
	Hammersmith	KB N V
12	Dulwich	L O W
	Notting Hill Gate	B M V
13	Aldwych	P X
	Golders Green	A S
15	Canning Town	P X
	Paddington	B R U
16A	Brent Cross	JB R U
23	Liverpool Street	P X
	Westbourne Park	B R U
25	Ilford	HA Z
53	Plumstead	F L O
55	Clapton	HA Z
73	Stoke Newington	HB Z
	Victoria	KB N V
88	Clapham Common	L O W
94	Acton Green	B M V
	Trafalgar Square	L O W
98	Willesden	KA N U
	Holborn	HA X
113	Edgware	JA S
135	Archway	D W
	Marble Arch	F N V
137/A	Streatham/	JC N V
	Crystal Palace	
139	West Hampstead	A S
	Trafalgar Square	L O X
159	Streatham	L O W
	Baker Street	A S

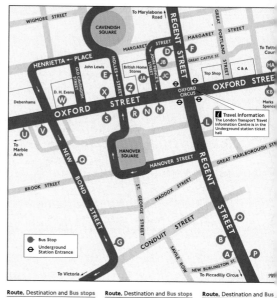

Bus Stop
Underground Station Entrance

Travel Information
The London Transport Travel Information Centre is in the Underground station ticket hall

Route, Destination and Bus stops		**Route**, Destination and Bus stops		**Route**, Destination and Bus	
176	Penge	HA Z	N12	Dulwich	L O W
C2	Parliament Hill	A D		Shepherd's Bush	B M
X53	Thamesmead	E F L O	N13	Potters Bar	A S
Night Buses				Victoria	O X
N3	Chislehurst	L O W	N16	Edgware	B R U
	Victoria	B N U		Victoria	O X
N6	Kensal Rise	B R U	N18	Harrow Weald	B R U
	Trafalgar Square	O Z		Trafalgar Square	O Z
N8	Bow	P X	N23	Ealing	B R U
	Victoria	B N U		Liverpool Street	P X

Route, Destination and Bus	
N73	Walthamstow B
	Victoria K
N79	Hither Green O
N84	Nunhead O
N89	Uxbridge/Ruislip Ka
	London Bridge H
N99	Stanmore B
	Trafalgar Square O
N139	West Hampstead A
	Trafalgar Square O

Trafalgar Square

Route, Destination and Bus stops

3	Crystal Palace	A N
	Oxford Circus	T
6	Aldwych	E
	Kensal Rise	H J
9	Aldwych	E
	Hammersmith	G J
11	Liverpool Street	E
	Fulham	J K P
12	Dulwich	B S
	Notting Hill Gate	T
13	Aldwych	E
	Golders Green	H J
15	Canning Town	E
	Paddington	H J
23	Liverpool Street	E
	Westbourne Park	H J
24	Pimlico	L P
	Hampstead Heath	C
29	Wood Green	C
53	Plumstead	B S
	Oxford Circus	T
77A	Wandsworth	J K P
	Aldwych	F
88	Clapham Common	B P
	Oxford Circus	T
91	Crouch End	F X
94	Acton Green	T
109	Streatham	N V

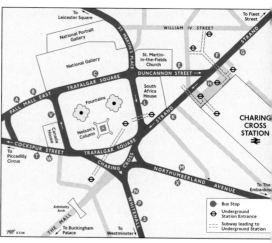

Bus Stop
Underground Station Entrance
Subway leading to Underground Station

Route, Destination and Bus stops		**Route**, Destination and Bus stops		**Night Buses**	
139	West Hampstead	T X	176	Penge	F	North & East London	
159	Streatham	A N		Oxford Circus	C G J	South London	V
	Baker Street	T	X15	Cyprus	F	West London	T
			X53	Thamesmead	B S		

Night bus routes will be subject to changes during 1995, other bus routes may also change from time to time.
For up to date travel information telephone: 0171-222 1234 (24hr).

cadilly
cus

Destination and Bus stops	
rystal Palace	F N
Oxford Circus	C Y
ldwych	G R
ensal Rise	D W
ldwych	B R
Hammersmith	S W
Dulwich	F P
Notting Hill Gate	D Y
ldwych	G R
Golders Green	C W
utney Heath	K S U
ottenham Ct.Rd.	B H
anning Town	G R
addington	D W
attersea	K S U
insbury Park	B H
utney Common	S U
iverpool Street	G R
Westbourne Park	D W
Clapton/Leyton	B H
Victoria	K S U
lumstead	F P
Oxford Circus	C Y
Clapham Common	F N
Oxford Circus	D Y
Acton Green	D Y
Trafalgar Square	F N
West Hampstead	C W
Trafalgar Square	F N
Baker Street	C W
Streatham	F N
Thamesmead	F P
Oxford Circus	C Y

Buses
Crystal Palace	K N
North Finchley	H W
Chislehurst	F N
Oxford Circus	H W
Kensal Rise	D W
Aldwych	B P
Bow	G P
Marble Arch	D W
Kingston	S W
Trafalgar Square	B P

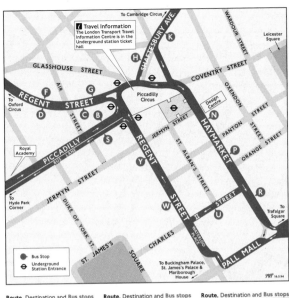

Route, Destination and Bus stops		
N12	Dulwich	F P
	Shepherd's Bush	D W
N13	Potters Bar	C W
	Victoria	G P
N14	Chessington	S W
	Victoria	B N
N16	Edgware	D W
	Victoria	G N
N18	Harrow Weald	D W
	Trafalgar Square	G P
N19	Clapham Junction	S W
	Finsbury Park	B P
N21	Potters Bar	H W
	Trafalgar Square	K P

Route, Destination and Bus stops		
N23	Ealing	D W
	Liverpool Street	G P
N29	Ponders End	H W
	Victoria	K N
N52	Willesden	S W
	Victoria	B N
N73	Walthamstow	D W
	Victoria	G N
N76	Hainault	H W
	Victoria	K P
N79	Hither Green	F N
	Oxford Circus	D W
N84	Nunhead	F N
	Oxford Circus	D W

Route, Destination and Bus stops		
N95	Dagenham	H W
	Victoria	K N
N96	Debden	H W
	Trafalgar Square	K P
N97	Heathrow/Sunbury	S W
	Trafalgar Square	G P
N98	Harold Hill	H W
	Victoria	K P
N99	Stanmore	D W
	Trafalgar Square	G P
N134	North Finchley	H W
	Trafalgar Square	K P
N139	West Hampstead	C W
	Trafalgar Square	G P

ker
eet

Destination and Bus stops	
West Norwood	F M N
Marylebone	S Q
Aldwych	B G
Golders Green	Q U
King's Cross	D N W
Sudbury	E P Z
Turnham Green	E P Z
Camden Town	D N W
Marble Arch	E F
Hackney Wick	D W
Roehampton	A F
Victoria	A F
North Finchley	Q U
Oxford Circus	B G
Edgware	Q U
West Hampstead	Q T
Trafalgar Square	B G
Streatham	B G
Zoo & Camden	Q T
Town	
Marble Arch	A F
Airbus Heathrow	E

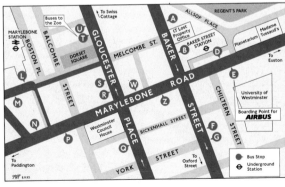

Night Buses
N13	Potters Bar	Q U
	Victoria	B G
N139	West Hampstead	Q T
	Trafalgar Square	B G
Stationlink		L

Night Bus routes in Central London

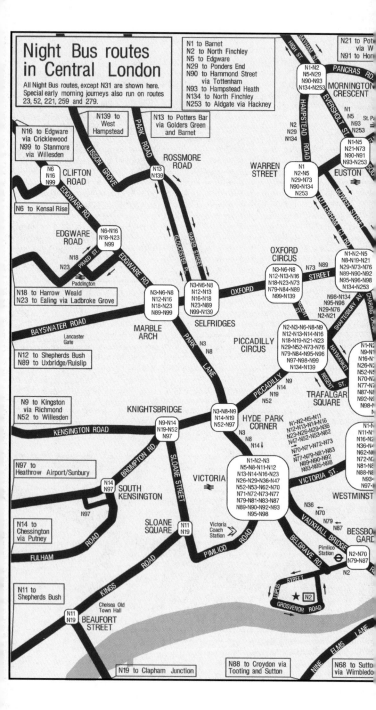

Night Bus routes in Central London

All Night Bus routes, except N31 are shown here. Special early morning journeys also run on routes 23, 52, 221, 259 and 279.

N1 to Barnet
N2 to North Finchley
N5 to Edgware
N29 to Ponders End
N90 to Hammond Street via Tottenham
N93 to Hampstead Heath
N134 to North Finchley
N253 to Aldgate via Hackney

N21 to Pote via W
N91 to Hor

N139 to West Hampstead

N13 to Potters Bar via Golders Green and Barnet

N16 to Edgware via Cricklewood
N99 to Stanmore via Willesden

N6 to Kensal Rise

N18 to Harrow Weald
N23 to Ealing via Ladbroke Grove

N12 to Shepherds Bush
N89 to Uxbridge/Ruislip

N9 to Kingston via Richmond
N52 to Willesden

N97 to Heathrow Airport/Sunbury

N14 to Chessington via Putney

N11 to Shepherds Bush

N88 to Croydon via Tooting and Sutton

N19 to Clapham Junction

N68 to Sutto via Wimbledo

Night bus routes will be subject to changes during 1995, other bus routes may also change from time to time.
For up to date travel information telephone: 0171-222 1234 (24hr).

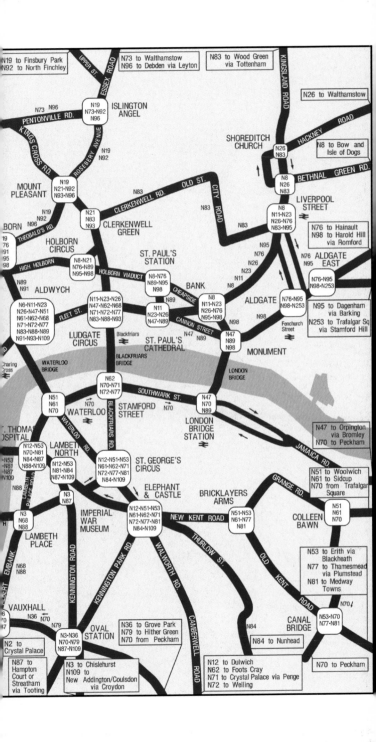

Postal Codes

MINDTRAP

The game that will challenge the way you think!

This mind-bending game contains over 500 teasers and conundrums that will challenge your lateral thinking skills.
See below. . . . for the answer.

Whether in teams or individually MindTrap provides mind-boggling entertainment.

Available from all good Toy and Game Retailers.

Sales Hotline:
081-805 8282

MINDTRAP

A black dog stands in the middle of an intersection in a town painted black. None of the street lights are working due to a power failure caused by a local storm. A car with two broken headlights drives towards the dog but turns in time to avoid hitting him. How could the driver have seen the dog in time?

SPEAR'S GAMES ®

Licensed by
Wind Chimes Limited

© J.W. Spear & Sons PLC, Richard House, Enstone Road, Enfield, Middlesex EN3 7TB Fax: 081-804 2426

A CAMERON MACKINTOSH PRODUCTION

CATS
NEW LONDON THEATRE
0171-405 0072

Miss Saigon
THEATRE ROYAL DRURY LANE
0171-494 5000

Les Misérables
PALACE THEATRE
0171-434 0909

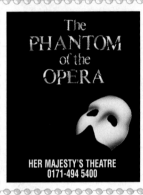

The PHANTOM of the OPERA
HER MAJESTY'S THEATRE
0171-494 5400

Oliver!
LONDON PALLADIUM
0171-494 5020

FIVE GUYS
LYRIC THEATRE
0171-494 5045

FIRST CLASS!
ADD TO YOUR COLLECTION

Early mrning

till late at .

packed

with low p

s.

in

the middle of

London.

TESCO Metro

Every little helps.

311 Oxford St (opp. John Lewis). Bedford St., Covent Garden. Broadway Centre Hammersmith. Portobello Rd, Notting Hill. Cabot Place West, Canary Wharf.

Boots make life a little easier

As well as the usual toiletries and health products you'd except to find, Boots also stock a delicious range of lunch time foods and snacks. We can also normally process most colour print films in just one hour.*

You'll discover there are 62 Boots stores in Central London, most are located within a short walk of the nearest tube station.

*Subject to service availability

Someone Cares

LONDON TRANSPORT
Restaurant
Guide

ANDY HAYLER

★ 150 ★
BEST VALUE RESTAURANTS

'An extremely useful guide for
food lovers at all levels' *Albert Roux*

150 0f the best of London's restaurants, selected for their quality of
cooking, surroundings, service and value for money. Andy Hayler's guide
is packed with accurate, trustworthy and well-organized information on
both restaurants and shops. All you need to know about:

quality of cooking	*standard of service*
lunch and dinner prices	*food shops*
surroundings and décor	*ethnic cuisine*
specialities of the house	*opening hours*
restaurants with private rooms	*buying wine*

Available from your local bookshop at £4.99